Fifteen Jugglers,
Five Believers

THE NEW HISTORICISM: STUDIES IN CULTURAL POETICS
STEPHEN GREENBLATT, GENERAL EDITOR

Fifteen Jugglers, Five Believers

Literary Politics and the
Poetics of American Social Movements

T. V. Reed

UNIVERSITY OF CALIFORNIA PRESS
Berkeley · Los Angeles · Oxford

University of California Press
Berkeley and Los Angeles, California

University of California Press, Ltd.
Oxford, England

© 1992 by
The Regents of the University of California

Bob Dylan, "Obviously Five Believers," © 1966 Dwarf Music.

Portions of chapter 2 originally appeared in *Representations* 24 (Fall 1988).

Library of Congress Cataloging-in-Publication Data

Reed, T. V. (Thomas Vernon)
  Fifteen jugglers, five believers : literary politics and the
poetics of American social movements / T. V. Reed.
     p.   cm. — (The New historicism ; 22)
  Includes bibliographical references and index.
  ISBN 0-520-07521-8 (alk. paper)
  1. American literature—20th century—History and criticism—
Theory, etc.   2. Politics and literature—United States—
History—20th century.   3. Literature and society—United States—
History—20th century.   4. Social movements—United States—
History—20th century.   5. United States—Civilization—20th
century.   6. Social problems in literature.   I. Title.   II. Series.
PS228.P6R44   1992
810.9′358—dc20   91-33396

Printed in the United States of America
9 8 7 6 5 4 3 2 1

The paper used in this publication meets the minimum requirements of
American National Standard for Information Sciences—Permanence of Paper
for Printed Library Materials, ANSI Z39.48-1984. ∞

for Noël and Hart

Fifteen jugglers, fifteen jugglers
Five believers, five believers
—*Bob Dylan,*
"Obviously Five Believers"

Contents

Preface

This book is about changing texts, about the already changed nature of some texts, and about the desirability from a radically democratic standpoint of encouraging these changes. But since texts do not read themselves, this is also a book about changing readers, most particularly about changing those influential readers we call literary critics. The text I am ultimately concerned with is that vast social text we call the world, and my premise is that the putatively other worldly world of literature may tell us some important things about "the real world" of politics, particularly the world of social movements, that we do not learn as readily from other forms of written and spoken language. My aim is to assist the project of convincing literary critics that their work is unavoidably political and needs to become more attuned to radically democratic social movements. Less directly, I hope also to help convince social movement actors (including some, but not enough, critics) that their work needs to become more literary, needs to recognize and utilize some of the complexity, irony, polyphony, and power found in the kind of rhetorical performance labeled literary or aesthetic. Drawing on a metaphor from Bob Dylan, I want to suggest that among those much-needed word and world *jugglers* we call postmodernists, there are and must be some *believers*, believers in political values and practical strategies for social change that move both inside and outside of the postmodern.

I want to interweave questions and strategies emerging from the "new literary theory" (reader response, poststructuralist, new historicist, feminist, neo-Marxist), with questions and the strategies emerging from the "new social movements" (antinuclear, peace, feminist, antiracist, anticolonial, gay, anticorporate, environmental, and so forth). The logic of recent theory leads criticism toward political action, while the logic of contemporary politics leads social movements to questions of representation that can be illuminated by cultural theory. I want to suggest that these two sets of theorized practices, while not reducible to each other, are nevertheless implicated in each other. Many of the best political insights of the new literary theory are in danger of being trapped in a textualist hermeticism; only social movements can realize those insights, not so much by "translating them into action," since language is always already action, but by widening and specifying the field of action sufficiently to offer a serious challenge to the antidemocratic forces of postmodern capitalism. Conversely, while the new social movements are already practicing much of what the new theorists have been theorizing, some of the theoretical insights and rhetorical tricks of literature and cultural criticism can assist these movements in dislodging forms of oppression embedded in oppressive forms.

If literature, politics, and theory existed, this would be a book about their inter-action. But since it is one of my premises that literature, politics, and theory do not exist, at least not as wholly separable practices or fields of discourse, it would be more accurate to say that this is a book about "politerature" as theory. On the one hand, I want to show how certain writing and reading strategies help reveal that the boundaries between literature and politics are themselves fictive and political. On the other hand, I wish to show that theory cannot stand above or around literature and politics but is rather going on amidst and through acts we call literary and political. I do not, however, think that the logics of literature and the logics of politics are the same, and I will have some harsh things to say about certain ways of politicizing aesthetics and aestheticizing politics. Each of my six chapters approaches this inter-action in a slightly different way, but all directly or indirectly address the following questions: What can "literary" strategies tell us about the kinds of political strategies needed by movements today? What can thinking about the strategic needs of social movements do to make literary theory and practice more effective in assisting efforts at radical change? How have literary texts and social movements as (con)texts shaped and been shaped by those conditions labeled "postmodern"? Sometimes these questions are addressed directly, at others times through an extended allegory suggesting that the kind of rhetorical flexibility called forth in performing the "literary" texts I examine is the kind required by political actors in the contemporary world.

Chapter 1 sets these questions in relation to the bodies of theory and practice, political and literary, out of which they emerge. I offer a set of provocations aimed at unsettling certain critical and political orthodoxies (my own included) that inhibit the kind of border crossings I want to examine. I choose the word provocations, rather than argument or position because, though arguments are made, positions taken, I seek less to "nail down" a position than to offer a gentle jeremiad pointing toward spaces where new arguments, new positions are emerging. In Chapter 1 I also introduce the seriously playful term "postmodernist realism" to name certain literary and critical reading/writing strategies that question not only the putative boundary between literature and politics but also the equally fictive, politically fractious boundary between radical humanism and poststructuralism.

Following this initial set of provocations come four chapters in which I perform interpretations of four different kinds of texts: a documentary, a novel, a nonfiction novel/history, and a political demonstration. These readings do not illustrate the general points made in chapter 1 but rather stand in dialogue with them, suggesting that only particular, concrete acts of theorizing (through literature, through movements) can clarify, alter, realize the questions I raise. Placed in chronological order, the texts trace important moments in American radical democratic political culture as it is transformed and transforms itself from the 1930s through to the 1980s, but no attempt is made to give a definitive or comprehensive history. Rather I want to illuminate certain motifs that point up recurring general problematics in the history of "the" left (recognizing that the American left has not been a single coherent entity but rather a cluster of relations cut across by ideological, class, racial, and gender divisions). I have chosen texts that posed important questions about forms and rhetorics of resistance in their own time, but whose prime interest is their resonance for social movements in the present.

Each of my focal texts is viewed as a social matrix, as simultaneously a reflection of and a reflection on both movements and the larger social formation. The texts are treated not as autonomous from the real world nor as simple reflections of it, but rather as reflections on a world in which numerous competing texts, tropes, narratives are already at play. Each text parodies, critiques, or otherwise illuminates the prevailing, normative modes of storytelling in the particular political cultures they re-present and comment on. All the texts also question the boundaries between fact and fiction, pointing up ways in which these putative boundaries have been policed in the interests of dominant political groups.

The first of my readings deals with James Agee and Walker Evans's photographic/prose (anti)documentary, *Let Us Now Praise Famous Men*. Long read as a classic account of the lives of three families of Southern tenant farmers in Depression America, I argue that the text should also and more centrally be read as an interrogation of the politics and ethics entailed by attempts (by artists, critics, political activists) to represent those labeled politically, economically, and/or culturally "underprivileged." I analyze the strategies Agee and Evans use to represent (and refuse to represent) the tenant families as a critique of liberal and Communist representational strategies in the 1930s, and as a model for countering liberal and radical elitisms in the current scene.

Chapter 3 continues this discussion of strategies for representing marginalized social actors through an examination of inter-relations between literary politics and the poetics of black liberation in Ralph Ellison's *Invisible Man*. I begin with an analysis of how as the first novel by an African-American to become securely "integrated" into the American literary canon, the text was inextricably caught in the particular aesthetic politics imposed on black writers during the rise of the New Criticism and the Cold War. Then I turn to examine how what I call the double visionary trickster politics of the novel can illuminate and suggest alternatives to the conflict between integrationist Civil Rights movements and nationalist Black Power movements.

While the first two readings share an interest in the poetics of representing marginalized social actors, the next two chapters take the term actor somewhat more literally and focus on the dramatics of political demonstrations. Chapter 4 reads Norman Mailer's *Armies of the Night*, a nonfiction novel about the 1967 antiwar "siege of the Pentagon," as an analysis of the power and limits of the theatrical politics of the sixties New Left. Chapter 5 analyzes an ecofeminist theatrical demonstration at the Pentagon in the early eighties as an implicit critique of aspects of New Left dramaturgy and as a model for a new, more self-reflexive theatrical politics/political theatrics in keeping with a radically democratic, feminist, new social movement politics.

Each of the four textual analyses is designed to stand on its own as a contestatory contribution to the history of readings of the particular texts I focus on, as well as act as part of a series of reflections on the

interlinked rhetorical practices of literature, criticism, and social movements.

In Chapter 6 I return to the broad theoretical issues outlined in Chapter 1, beginning with some observations about current roles played by
literary intellectuals and about particular theoretical positions that have
kept literary theory and practice from becoming a more effective ally of
contemporary social movements. I conclude by analyzing the politics implied by various theories of "postmodernity" (as general social condition) and "postmodernism" (as aesthetic practice), and by outlining possibilities for bringing various cultural and political forms into some
postmodern populist alliances that could offer more successful challenges to current systems that perpetuate a host of social injustices.

On a more personal level this work is an attempt to bring two parts
of my life closer together: a life lived as an activist in antiracist, feminist,
antimilitarist, union, and ecological movements, and a life lived as a
professional scholar-teacher in the university. At times these two parts of
my life have flowed together smoothly or worked in creative tension, but
at other points the activist and the academic dimensions of my experience have been in debilitating conflict. I do not pretend that there is an
easy resolution of this conflict in what follows, but this book was written
in part out of anger and frustration that I and others like me have not
found better ways to bring the vast intellectual resources of the academy
into the service of wider social change. In this volume I work primarily
on academic turf, on texts produced mostly *outside* social movements,
pushing these texts toward movement (con)texts. In a forthcoming companion volume, *The Arts of Social Change*, I will examine aesthetic
works produced *in* and *for* movements (music, drama, murals, poetry,
and so forth). I want to raise similar questions from another angle, by
bringing movement cultures into contexts of cultural criticism, to explore ways to make them richer and more reflective. In both works the
routes of resistance I chart are presented as some among many possible
ways of bringing cultural criticism and social activism into more fruitful
interaction. The present book, then, is not meant as a call for others to
follow a plan I have already worked out; it is, rather, a call from inside
a set of problems for the assistance of others in exploring new and renewed ways of bridging the distance between criticism and activism.

This book has moved with me through several different environments
but it bears most fully the marks of its first home at the University of

California, Santa Cruz. I owe my biggest debt to the extraordinary intellectual community in and around the History of Consciousness cultural studies program at UCSC. Among the many friends and colleagues who helped this project find its forms I'd like especially to thank Stewart Burns, Kathy Chetkovich, Jim Clifford, Michael Cowan, Ruth Frankenberg, Deborah Gordon, Katie King, Hilary Klein, Donna Haraway, Billie Harris, Deena Hurwitz, Lata Mani, Margit Mayer, Jack Schaar, Barry Schwarz, Zoë Sofia (Sofoulis), and Hayden White. I'd like to offer my deepest thanks and my love to Don Beggs and Elizabeth Bird as the best of friends and the best of colleagues.

Among my newer friends and colleagues at Washington State University, I'd like to thank Fred Schwarzbach and Sue Armitage for helping to provide me with time to work on this book, Alex Hammond for some friendly mentoring that likewise opened up time for the project, and Karen Weathermon for thoughtful proofing and indexing. I am also indebted to Richard Ohmann, Pat Camden, and Jackie Rich of the Wesleyan University Humanities Center for their hospitality and assistance during the final stages of my work. At the University of California Press, I'd like to thank Doris Kretschmer, Mark Pentecost, and Nancy Lerer for patient and professional editorial work.

I owe another deeper, less tangible debt to Bob Dylan for teaching me to juggle beliefs and to Alice and Ted Braun for teaching me to believe in jugglers (and other apostrophic jesters). To my parents, and to Jim, Michelle, and Linda I owe an immense debt for their loving support. Last and most I give my love and thanks to Noël A. Sturgeon—my best and most diligent editor, my favorite "affinite" and political conscience, my most influential intellectual companion, and the person who has brought the most joy (bundled and otherwise) into my life.

                                                                                              T. V. Reed

ONE

Literary Politics and the Poetics of Social Movements

READING THEORY

The last several decades have witnessed numerous revolutions and counterrevolutions in literary, cultural, and social theory. The great up-heavals of the neo-Marxist, feminist, structuralist/poststructuralist, postcolonialist era may not be over, but there is evidence that things are slowing down and that a new period is beginning.[1] These theoretical rev-olutions have left in their wake a greater philosophical self-consciousness and rigor, a rich array of new tools of the trade, and a formidable body of work challenging existing systems of domination. They have also done important work in making it more difficult for conservatives to mask their political interpretations as neutral, commonsensical, transcenden-tal, or purely aesthetic, and in making oppositional voices a part of the curriculum.

But one characteristic of a period of great theoretical energy is a ten-dency to be profligate in the "expenditure" of that energy. Looking back on my work and that of others who share my political concerns, I sense that amidst the excitement of high theorizing we have had a tendency to forget that, as Stuart Hall puts it, the point is not to produce theory but to produce change. There can be no question of being "against theory" or "beyond theory" since even the most putatively "close" reading is thoroughly shaped by theoretical considerations (which have simply been hidden from the critic or which the critic has hidden from the reader), but there are good reasons to move against and beyond a certain fetishizing of Theory for Theory's sake. One characteristic of the new period we are entering is likely to be greater care in understanding what theory can and should do, greater care in choosing which deconstruction and reconstruction projects are of abiding importance.

Reading theory in recent years, I have sometimes been reminded of a story told about surrealist Marcel Duchamp who at one point gave up painting to devote himself to chess. It is said that Duchamp, a superb player, would sometimes lose a match because he chose a "beautiful move" over one that would have been more effective. Such a stance is admirable in the world of games, but in the world of politics the choice of theoretical moves can be a matter of life and death, and I can't help feeling at times that some elegant moves have been purchased at too great a human cost. I sense a growing restlessness in the ranks of academic theorists these days, a growing desire to make the work count for more in the wider world where it is still possible for an American president to improve his job rating by "deploying" orientalist and nationalist tropes to justify deploying 500,000 (disproportionately nonwhite and working class) troops to slaughter 100,000 "others" halfway across the globe. The complacent grins of Reagan and Bush continue to remind us of the relative ineffectuality of our efforts to counter militarism, racism, sexism, colonialism, heterosexism, environmental devastation, economic exploitation, and a host of other injustices.[2]

Even "beautiful theory," theory practiced primarily for its aesthetic pleasure, has its place, but the tendency of theory to autonomize itself, to lead off in directions further and further removed from specific political struggles, is a vexing one for those of us who believe theory should illuminate our attempts to make the world a more just and decent place. At a certain point, however pragmatically grounded it may be initially, the twists of rhetoric lead theory to generate its own questions, its own logics, ones that produce certain pleasures, but that can make it more difficult to "rise to the level of the concrete," to the level of possible wide-scale political interventions.[3] Recent theory has been quite persuasive in showing the ways in which language is power, but we have been less successful in finding those points where such knowledge converges with larger forces of resistance and liberation. In this chapter I want to sketch the political and critical assumptions that inform my work and to explore some emerging lines of inquiry that may help forge stronger links between literary theory and radically democratic "new social movements."

LITERARY-TEXTUAL-CULTURAL STUDIES:
A GENEALOGY

What forces now at work can take the best elements from the theoretical revolutions of the recent past and direct them more effectively toward sites of resistance in and beyond the university? One way to answer this question is to posit a theoretical trajectory over the last several decades that moves from "literary" to "textual/rhetorical" to "cultural" studies. In tracing such a genealogy, however, the task must not be to chart a simple progress but rather to show how even as each of these terms denotes a widening terrain that seems to contain the earlier one, the previous terms act upon, question, disrupt attempts by the latter ones to subsume them. I want to argue, for example, that within the terrain currently labeled "cultural studies" there remains a place for a semi-autonomous "literary" realm and that "culture" itself must constantly be brought under "textual" scrutiny even as the term culture is used to expand theory and method beyond the narrowly textual.

Literary studies started its transformation into textual studies through various efforts in the 1970s to at once dissolve and broaden the category of "literature." These efforts arose from a rebirth of rhetorical analysis that entailed a twofold erasure of boundaries. On the one hand, the great critical "discovery" of the twentieth century, that language uses people more fully than people use language, means that even many scientists and social scientists are being forced to recognize that their discourse is not transparently realistic but constructed by and subject to historical-linguistic determinations and contingencies. This "discovery," which many still resist, has cast the shadow of ficticity over all supposedly factual or objective discourse by arguing that an unavoidably figurative (literary) dimension exists all along the continuum of linguistic expression in whatever domain. Much recent theoretical activity labeled poststructuralist involves the use of variants of rhetorical analysis to uncover a fictive, figural dimension in discourses and disciplines previously based in nonfictive claims (i.e., Derrida shifting the concerns of philosophy from the plane of semantics to that of semiotics, or Foucault shifting the question of history from facts and figures to the figuration of facts via discursive practices). Initially literary studies enabled these new theoretical practices by providing key tools for these rhetorical analyses and by offering up avant-garde literary texts that provided models for the alternative writing practices needed for these theories to achieve distance from the realism they criticized.

But even as this process was at work bringing the natural and the social sciences closer to the interpretive realm of fictional or literary discourse, a related process was "deconstructing" the putative purity of the
aesthetic realm. Indeed, critics as diverse as E. D. Hirsch, Tzvetan Todorov, Terry Eagleton, and Rita Felski have concluded that literature as
such does not exist, that there is no clear boundary between literary and
nonliterary language.[4] This leads to the argument that literary texts
should no longer be fetishized as autonomous art but rather should be
analyzed as part of a rhetorical continuum where different kinds of writing (literary, historical, ethnographic, political, and so forth) are shown
to produce differing kinds of textual/political power.[5]

In place of literature, some critics, following the Russian formalists,
adopted the term "literariness" to describe the quality of works that draw
attention to themselves as language, rather than presenting themselves as
transparent reflections of reality. But since not all works labeled as literature are constructed in this way and some works not thought of as
fiction do draw attention to themselves as language, the quality of literariness spills out into nonfiction realms.[6] (This transgressing or blurring of fact/fiction boundaries is one key element of the texts I examine
below.) In place of the poles objective/subjective or factual/fictional, one
could lay out a continuum of works that acknowledge more or less of
their inventive, fictive, or rhetorical nature. At one pole would be realist
works of fiction and most natural science and empirical social science,
as well as most traditional journalism, while at the other pole one would
place most avant-garde literature, experimental writing in ethnography,
history, sociology, and the "new journalism," as well as, of course, some
forms of literary and cultural criticism.

From this perspective, the almost banished concept "literature" or
"the aesthetic" returns but without its sense of absoluteness, since, as
Eagleton puts it, "Some texts are born literary, some achieve literariness,
and still others have literariness thrust upon them."[7] What is occurring
is a displacement of the aesthetic from an ontological category to a historically contingent epistemological one, a recognition that to view
something aesthetically is to enter into a mode of reading that is often,
though not always, encouraged but never fully determined by the object
being read. That "literature" is a historically variable, unstable category
does not mean that literature or the aesthetic disappears, but only that
it is displaced to a matching of historically specific and changing sets of
conventions between author/text and reader, or, in the case of those texts
that only become literary, to a process or mode of apprehension imposed

on a different set of conventions (i.e., an aesthetic hermeneutic replacing a religious one in reading the Bible as literature).[8]

This means, however, that all attempts simply to reduce or translate the literary into some other mode (i.e., the sociological) are doomed to failure. While aesthetic texts are always serving ideological purposes, it is a mistake to reduce them to other, general ideological processes because this mystifies the specific ideological work they do. Literature is subject to historically contingent but nonetheless real aesthetic laws or logics that have particular effects in the world on particular groups of readers. Even sophisticated versions of the notion of "literature as symbolic action"—a notion that views literary acts as symbolic resolutions of some putatively external social conditions or contradictions (as in Fredric Jameson's system)[9]—are inadequate if they do not attend to the text's specifically literary actions, to attempts by the author/text to elaborate certain formal possibilities or solve certain formal problems that are exorbitant vis-à-vis the text's ideational content but that form part of the reader's experience to the extent that she or he comprehends the text's aesthetic conventions.

These formal elements never exist in total isolation from sociopolitical determinations shaping a given text (and the very notion of "the aesthetic" as a play with forms has historically variable political implications), but in the context of "modern," "Western" literature we can never leap over the play of form in search of some putatively more basic social truth. Against those orthodox radicals who still dismiss literary texts as "bourgeois," as well as against those radical formalists who search for inherently revolutionary texts, I work from the position that the meaning of texts lies primarily in their use, in their appropriation in particular circumstances, rather than in any essential content or form. Most existing "reader-response" and "reception" theories, however, have tended to blunt the political implications of this argument by falling back on the insular, bourgeois individual as reader or by recontaining the community of readers within a narrow realm of experts.[10]

The kind of textual or rhetorical criticism that emerges from this problematic maintains the best insights of various critical formalisms, from the Russian formalists to the American New Critics to deconstruction, while recognizing that since no text can impose fully its mode of reading on a reader, forms exist ultimately as social relations created in specific contexts of reception (indeed, with "reception" better conceived as a kind of [re]production of the text). This kind of rhetorical criticism is always situational, always about the triangulation of author (as social site of initial production), text (as ongoing verbal archive), and reader (as socially situated inheritor/producer of meaning in particular moments of articulation). Form does not exist in texts or in readers but in a social relationship between the two—form is the name we give to the rhetorical relation between the text/world and political readers/actors.

Radical "literary" criticism needs to acknowledge a variety of "aesthetic" ideologies existing historically and in contemporary usage, with varying degrees of closeness to or distance from everyday linguistic practices. This means that no single aesthetic theory can encompass the range of objects called literature. Some forms of literature, or some parts of a given literary text, may be quite close to and thus largely amenable to sociological analysis (both Richard Wright and Saul Bellow, to mention but two examples, are deeply indebted in particular works to specific schools of sociology whose insights they self-consciously fictionalized), while others (Gertrude Stein or Donald Barthelme, for example) may be far more interested in the play of form as form. No literary work is either purely formalist or purely sociopolitical in orientation, but it is reductive and misleading to ignore the fact that varying degrees of interest in questions of form animate various works labeled literature because those degrees often mark specific political possibilities and limits.

Moreover, no political hierarchy should be presumed to exist across this range. Each kind of aesthetic can be politically conservative or progressive depending on specific reading formations surrounding it at a given moment. The most extreme form of defamiliarization, for example, is neither inherently liberatory (as the Frankfurt school believed) nor inherently reactionary (as proponents of one or another form of social realism propose). Rather it is a specific, historically contingent achievement of distance from everyday communicative practice that produces specific pleasures but ambiguous meanings. Whether that pleasure is turned toward "escape" or toward re-evaluation of everyday ideological practices will depend on those with the power to shape reception at a given moment.

The task of radical criticism should not be to condemn as mere play the pleasures of form (after all, critics indulge in them more than most, and the attraction of theory itself is in part its formal pleasures), but neither can it be to work from a naive belief that pleasure is always subversive (as some postmodern theories seem to suggest). Pleasure is never neutral, but it also is never wholly contained by a given ideology. We need to play through this contradiction, neither condemning nor embracing the pleasures of consumerist capitalism but contesting for them by attempting to attach politically progressive meanings to (some of) these pleasures.

Gregory Jay offers this ambitious outline of the general concerns rhetorical criticism needs to address in analyzing these various layers and moments in a given text:

> Rhetorical analysis needs to describe: (1) the set of discursive possibilities offered to the writer by the cultural archive [i.e., prevailing genres, conventions, and styles, intertextual possibilities and so on]; (2) the assumption within the text of a contemporary audience whose knowledge must both be used and resisted; (3) the projections within the text of a future audience constituted by its decipherment of the text; (4) the social and institutional sites of the text's production and reception; (5) the figurations of subjectivity offered or deployed in the text; (6) the effects of self-reflexivity inscribed in the text; (7) and the possible contradictions between the text's cognitive, performative, didactic, aesthetic, psychological, and economic projects.[11]

Obviously every act of criticism cannot attend to every one of these factors, but Jay's list gives an indication of the complexity of the task and the way in which such criticism becomes necessarily social and historical.

Both the strength and the weakness of this rhetorical methodology reside in its positing of the notion of the "social text." The textualization of the whole social world, the transformation of all social objects into text, was a theoretical gesture of immense importance initially in dislodging politically conservative versions of empiricism. But it is a gesture that these days often provides more blindness than insight by obscuring the way in which different social domains construct their differing objects through very different logics.

A kind of literary imperialism has covered the social world with an illusory patina of playful textual fluidity that institutional inertia, among other things, belies. A model based on the relatively open, thinly institutionalized practice of interpreting "literary" texts is not so easily transferred to domains whose "texts" are created and maintained by far more rigidly inscribed, institutionalized practices. With regard to what I will call the "poetics" of social movements, for example, it is clear that aesthetic models can take us only so far. At a certain point, other "*sociologics*" must be acknowledged and other tools of analysis must be applied. If it is theoretically possible (and to the literary imagination feasible) to articulate (link) any text or discourse to any other, for example, only sociological or ethnographic work on certain thickly layered "texts" ("traditions," "institutions") can tell you in a given historical situation whether certain linkages have been or are likely to be resisted and certain others successfully made. This knowledge is not simply empirical but it works at a level of specificity in which rhetorical figures take on historico-cultural dimensions, reveal themselves as embedded in those cultural rhetorical (con)texts Aristotle designated by the term *phronesis*, and which might be loosely translated into contemporary terms as local knowledges. Similarly, current trends to resituate various high and popular cultural texts that had previously been analyzed in isolation back into the socio-logic of everyday life implicitly acknowledge the limit of certain kinds of textualist gestures.

The critical force best positioned to overcome the limitations of textualism, while maintaining its theoretical insights, is that rapidly expanding body of work labeled "cultural studies." This term, like any complex, useful notion, has been subject to a variety of interpretations, but I use it here to designate the intersection of a set of theoretical tools (including but not limited to rhetorical analysis) with a commitment to practical political engagement.

In one version of the story, the name derives initially from the Birmingham Centre for Contemporary Cultural Studies in Britain, but the concept is larger than the name and it would be a mistake to see it as a British import or as a new instance of American Anglophilia. Cultural studies is emerging at this time in the United States for specific political and theoretical reasons, and it has the potential to be a serious challenge to virtually all existing structures of knowledge/power. The British version of cultural studies was conceived not as another discipline but as a political intervention aimed at making intellectual work more effective in political battles inside and outside the university. And it is this political commitment, along with certain sociological and ethnographic methodological tools developed by cultural studies practitioners to implement this political desire, that can now be usefully grafted onto indigenous cultural studies efforts in this country.

I use the term "cultural studies" to designate a movement at the level of the production and exchange of knowledge (primarily, but not exclusively, in the university) that seeks to consolidate and advance the radically democratic politics that became institutionalized in programs like Women's Studies, and Chicano, Native American, Asian American, and African American studies programs in the wake of the social movements of the 1960s and early 1970s.

The fact that the label "cultural studies" has achieved a certain fashionableness recently suggests that the project it represents has reached a crucial stage. Cultural studies can either become merely a glossier mirror of existing professionalized policings of inequity, perhaps even assisting in the imperial conquest of fields like ethnic and women's studies, or cultural studies practitioners can use its current prestige to reassert a more powerful position for democratic agendas that are currently under attack from the right.

To accomplish the latter, cultural studies must be conceived not as a new academic discipline or interdiscipline, but as a critique of existing disciplines designed to reveal their complicity with social injustice, and as a space in which to produce work aimed to assist as directly as possible current struggles for social transformation. It is emerging at a time when various dispersed, sometimes even warring, marginalized groups inside and outside the academy are realizing that new modes of alliance will be needed to resist conservative assaults on democracy and to advance democratic opportunities further.

Much of the important work of cultural studies has been and should continue to be in the area of mass or popular culture where much wide-scale public knowledge is contested. But there is also a role to be played by those of us whose preferred object of cultural study is that which tradition has defined as the "literary" text. The role of literary theory and criticism in cultural studies will be at once more modest and more bold than it has been in recent years. The new literary studies will be more modest by resisting the kind of textualist and professional imperialisms I alluded to above. But it will be more bold in that once certain facile versions of textualism have been displaced, criticism will be able to pursue more actively those points where it can reach out effectively into broader "texts" of the social.

A number of kinds of critical practice have arisen to relocate the literary within cultural studies. One mode might be called the history of popular reception, and aims to recreate the collective subject(s) of the text by reconstructing modes, styles, conventions, and formulas of reading in a given audience in a particular historical moment. This approach has been especially useful in dealing with "popular" literature, but it can also be used to examine widely read (or widely taught) "elite" works as well.[12]

A second mode of criticism, the kind of criticism I employ in this book, entails politically specific interventions into the history of professional reception. It focuses on more specialized or virtuoso readings by literary critics who represent and mediate literature for a primarily academic audience. It too is concerned with understanding how others have read the text under consideration, but its main purpose is to produce new readings of use in particular current pedogogical-political contexts. These two kinds of rhetorical criticism obviously cross paths at various points, since professional critics too are embedded in wider, popular conventions of reading, and since they in turn shape those wider community conventions, especially as the expansion of higher education has exposed more and more citizens to professional modes of reading. But it is useful to distinguish between the two because it allows us to think more carefully about the political efficacy of texts, to think more carefully about the forces that keep our readings insulated from, or allow them to be diffused into, the wider social formation.

Both of these kinds of reading involve complex layerings of dialogue and argument in which the critic must interrogate her or his own reading conventions while trying to discover those peculiar to a given group or critic under study. These dialogues always take place on treacherous epistemological ground, moving between the Scylla of positivist claims to reveal the text "in itself" (that either remove a work from history altogether or lock it in its moment of birth) and the Charybdis of subjectivist claims that there is no text there at all (that rob a given text of the specificity that makes it worth examining in the first place).

The text exists only in the history of its readings or "articulations," but those readings themselves are always generated intersubjectively through culturally located, ideologically shaped interpretive communities (professional and otherwise).[13] In this way, the history of popular reception, by asking "what *has* been made of this text?" can act as a check on the tendency of virtuoso readings to ask only "what *can* be made of this text?" What one might call the legitimation crisis of criticism resulting from the vast proliferation of incommensurable interpretations and interpretive schemata has destabilized the claim of virtuosos of earlier times to have offered the definitive interpretation of a given text. In turn this is forcing critics to confront more directly the grounds and the consequences of their interpretations, to confront more fully the historical and political choices embedded in their rhetorical actions.

The kind of rhetorical criticism that emerges from this crisis uses the term rhetoric in two related senses. It argues that all discourse (including the aesthetic and the critical) is to one degree or another persuasive discourse, that all language is concerned with or implicated in contestations for social and political power. And it assumes also that the means of persuasion are dependent on rhetoric in a second sense, the sense of the underlying, enabling figures (metaphors and other tropes) that make communication (im)possible.

Stated in this way, however, it is clear that there is nothing inherently politically radical about rhetorical criticism (although many still see the assertion that literature is political at all as a radical claim). As I have been suggesting, I think many of us have exaggerated the radical potential of uncovering rhetorical effects without dismantling the institutional "texts" that perpetuate them. The prime difference between a conservative or liberal and a radical position on textual criticism is that while liberals believe the conditions for open political dialogue, for the free contestation of rhetorics, have been (more or less) achieved, radical rhetorical analysis assumes that one of its prime functions is to show how unequal conditions for the exercise of power have been partially (but only partially) constituted by, and maintained through, ideological uses of language. Ideology here means those forms through which unequal power relations are made to appear "natural," "normal," or "inevitable," or are made to disappear, are made "invisible." The claim is that domination is constructed in part through rhetorical acts of omission and commission that continually reproduce unequal access to power (economic, political, rhetorical power) based on racism, sexism, heterosexism, and economic exploitation. Where liberalism believes rhetorical pluralism exists, a left textual criticism needs to relentlessly argue that rhetorical pluralism does not yet exist and will only be achieved by substantial transfers of political and economic, as well as representational power.

In addition to this liberal-radical dialogue, however, left rhetorical criticism must also contend with a putatively more radical claim about the indeterminacy of rhetoric. This latter dimension as articulated by post-Nietzschean rhetoricians (most notably in the United States by Paul de Man) poses new problems in that it claims that all discourse necessarily disguises the underlying contingency that enables it to appear rational on the surface (rhetoric as the unconscious of logic), while producing the illusion that a speaker/author can know fully the intention and/or the effect of his or her language. The question this raises is, can a left rhetoric at once acknowledge this contingency and indeterminacy and still make claims to intervene politically on behalf of radical positions?

The problem is that rhetorical criticism seeks to understand and/or unmask the workings of rhetoric but has only more rhetoric with which to do so. This perspective has given rise to a number of essentially (and I choose that adverb carefully) nihilist, radically anti-interpretive positions. But it is equally amenable to a variety of constructivist positions grounded in notions of radically democratic hermeneutics. I, for example, do not presume that there are any uncontestable ontological or historical or epistemological grounds underlying my readings here. My grounds are political, based on assertions about what is politically desirable and directed as a call to rearrange our common lives, a call based not in my individual will but in contestatory groups and structured languages that give me voice. I assume that under current social conditions there is no neutral ground or language of arbitration outside power, but I also assume that radical democratic politics is about creating the material conditions for the most open and equitable exercise of persuasive power. I believe all teleological, metaphysical, ontological, or otherwise absolute claims upon the real to be inimical to such an effort (including nihilist metaphysical claims for what one might call contingency as ontology). People, of course, bring various more or less absolute and foundational beliefs with them into politics, but such beliefs must be translated into collectively contestable terms to become part of a specifically democratic political realm.

Absolute knowledge is not only not necessary for democratic political action, but it is inimical to such action. For democratic politics is preeminently an arena of contingent judgments, of judgments made in the context of uncertain, collective contestation about meaning and value.[14] From this perspective, the arena of democratic politics is the space where truths and values should be allowed to contest without hope of final resolution, but in search of sufficient (if often temporary) consensus to maintain optimum social diversity, freedom, and justice (all themselves contestable grounding concepts to be negotiated and renegotiated by the polity). Politics rests on a degree of ontological contingency and epistemological uncertainty, but unlike the hyper-avant-gardist literary or critical text, it cannot pretend to live there alone; democratic politics must acknowledge enabling sociohistorical constraints even as it seeks (relatively) uncoerced, free, and open rhetorical contestation.

The kind of rhetorical criticism I advocate is aimed at helping to constitute a more democratic political realm by pointing out the hidden contingency of dominant claims on the real while acknowledging the necessarily contingent nature of alternative and oppositional claims. This is a relativistic position, but it does not mean that all claims on the real are equally valid. To argue that all knowledge is produced historically and subject to relative cultural limits does not preclude judgments about the political justness or unjustness of various representations, decisions, or actions within those specific historical conditions or between specific cultures in conflict. As Judith Newton and Deborah Rosenfelt express it, "seeing knowledge as a form of historical practice does not mean we cannot lay claim to degrees of its relative coherency and completeness while maintaining all the while a vision of its inescapable provisionality."[15] "Relative . . . completeness" here to me means challenging the absence of those previously denied access to the means of representation, to the material and symbolic tools needed to exercise knowledge/power.

At present, alas, we have no convincing theory or vision of how to attain such relatively uncoerced communities. Recent high philosophical attempts to theorize such polities have ranged from Jürgen Habermas's suggestive but thus far rationalistically reductive heuristic notion of "universal pragmatics," to his archnemesis Jean-François Lyotard's equally idealist call for the proliferation of mutually untranslatable "language-games." From Lyotard's perspective, Habermas's search for a rational speech community subject to certain universal principles of justice is a repressive one that denies the possibility of multiple rationalities and irrationalities as the bases for various political affinities. From Habermas's perspective, Lyotard's position evades the question of the normative value of such diversity itself, and of the necessity for some minimal principles of rational agreement to maintain these diverse communities free of constraint by other such communities.

Their most recent work suggests that the two are beginning to confront each other's claims, with Habermas opening up toward some notion of multiple rationalities, and Lyotard grappling with the question of minimal conditions for the elaboration of his sublime heterotopias. But neither Habermas nor Lyotard has shown much interest in confronting those collective subjects in contemporary social movements whose theoretical and practical efforts parallel, test, and implicitly criticize their political visions and anti-visions. Were they to do so, I think they would find that meaningful political work at the present time requires that we intensify the encounter between the kind of heteroglossia celebrated by postmodernists like Lyotard and the enabling ethical preconditions for such speech insisted upon by critical humanists like Habermas.[16] Because radical humanist rhetorics continue to be immensely important sources for political mobilization, while poststructuralist rhetorics have just begun to exercise that kind of power, a pure anti-humanism position (if such could exist) would be a political mistake. We need instead a far more nuanced and dialectical approach that brings the rhetorics of radical humanism and the rhetorics of postmodern theory into concrete conflict around questions of effective political practice.[17]

THE POETICS OF SOCIAL MOVEMENTS

Thus far I have been using two terms—"new social movements" and "radical democracy"—that I would like to define more specifically in order to clarify my position. The term "new social movements" refers generally to all those movements emerging since the 1960s that cannot be contained easily within a traditional Marxian paradigm of class struggle or within liberal notions of reform. This includes various anticolonial struggles, feminisms, environmental movements, antiracist struggles, movements on behalf of sexual minorities, nationalist and localist struggles, peace and antinuclear movements, as well as new forms of movement within the working class. These diverse manifestations are far from forming a single, coherent political position (indeed they strategically resist the reduction of one position to another), but many are cross-linked in interesting ways, and, I want to suggest, all are movements to expand the concept and the practice of democracy.

Many of these movements share with contemporary literary theory a distrust of easy binary oppositions: they seek to get beyond static dichotomies like reform/revolution, culture/politics, public/private, symbolic/real, black/white, gay/straight, male/female. Virtually all these struggles are concerned with the redistribution of social and cultural as well as economic capital. Virtually all raise questions about social representation, identity and difference, hierarchy and equality, centralization and decentralization. They suggest the possibility of new movement strategies aimed at creating multiple, semiautonomous, decentralized, nonhierarchical political units, as opposed to ones working to seize or re-form state power, but most also recognize the immense centralizing power of transnational capitalism.[18]

One of the more interesting theorists of these movements, Alberto Melucci, argues that through these movements a

> new public space is designed beyond the traditional distinction between state and "civil society": an intermediate public space, whose function is not to institutionalize the movements nor to transform them into parties, but to make society hear their messages and translate these messages into political decision-making, while the movements maintain their autonomy. . . . [These] movements do not exhaust themselves in representation; collective action survives beyond institutional mediation; it reappears in different areas of the social system and feeds new conflicts.[19]

Contemporary movements tend to see representation of their needs and desires as always incomplete, as always in danger of transformation into a new system of domination, but they also understand the practical, often life and death, need to institutionalize aspects of their agenda-in-process.

The particular American movements I have placed myself in, or which have placed me in their midst, seem to me sites where the tradition of "radical democratic" thought and practice meets the intensified contingencies of postmodernity. I choose the label "radical democratic" to describe these movements both because and despite of the fact that the term has gained a certain currency of late among postmodern theorists. The strength of the term is that it can on the one hand be used to lead postmodernists to realize that there is a long tradition of struggles to extend democracy by people who have been devastatingly marginalized by class, race, ethnicity, gender, or other social difference. And on the other hand, the recent adoption of the term by some postmodernists can force more entrenched representatives of the "tradition" of radical humanism to remember that traditions cannot be taken for granted but exist only as they are actively re-made through specific contemporary representations.

Beyond this I think the term "radical democratic" is the best one under which to organize a counterhegemonic project in the United States for three main reasons. First, I take the category to be the most inclusive, capable of raising, through its central commitment to fully egalitarian social relations, issues of political economy and class (Marxism), gender (feminism), hierarchy (anarchism), power/knowledge (poststructuralism), as well as questions of race, ethnicity, sexuality, and the exploitation of nature. (I am, of course, aware that the radical democratic tradition, to the extent that it can be isolated from other radical currents, has only slowly and unevenly opened itself to an examination of some of these specific oppressions.)

Second, the term "radical" is usefully polysemic: it calls us to "roots" but leaves partly open the question of both where the roots of oppression and the roots of resistance lie. It provides insurance against forgetting that the history of struggles for liberation is replete with examples of one domination replacing another, and of monolithic strategies overwhelming multiple, irreducibly different needs and desires.

Finally, it is imperative for those who wish to bring about radical change to respect the particular, already existing languages of resistance among those whom we would change; in the United States this has meant and continues to mean struggling to expand the meaning of "democracy."[20] Particularly at a time when the left has been placed on the defensive, radical criticism needs to seek out those points where it can speak to and transform existing political and cultural forms. This means in the American (con)text seeking out those points where a faltering liberalism opens itself to more radical possibilities, rather than using forms of rhetoric that distance us from those whom we would persuade.[21] This strategy has been made even more imperative by recent events in the Communist world. The collapse of the Cold War is profoundly reshaping international and domestic political fault lines, creating at once great dangers and great opportunities for the left. While the right has been quick to capitalize (quite literally) on these developments as the end of not only Stalinism but of all socialisms, the lessening of Cold War tensions can also provide space for far more open discussion of what some radically different, democratically shaped political economies might look like in this country. That opportunity will be squandered if the left does not contest seriously for the terrain of "freedom" and "democracy" it has too often ceded to the right.

As I try to illustrate in the various textual analyses I perform below, literary rhetoric can illuminate those border zones where the putative mainstream opens upon more radical possibilities and can illuminate the ways in which particular political strategies have been caught in traps of rhetoric that limited their effectiveness. As I have been suggesting, however, the political effects of such readings are only possibilities whose realization depends on the bridging of literary, academic, and wider political communities. Social movement cultures and the alternative public spheres sustained by those cultures are the alternative forces needed to realize the project of radical literary criticism.[22] In that sense, social movements are the (con)texts toward which these readings move, but with contexts conceived not as stable surrounding webs but as moving sites of intervention and interaction.

But movements are themselves social texts, and my work in this book is in part a series of speculations on the "poetics" of social movements, on the underlying rhetorical figures that shape them, and on movements themselves as forms of cultural and political expression. As Michael Ryan puts it, in the new movements a "new political rhetoric emerges to the extent that metaphoric political forms, which stressed the subsumption of diverse subordinate movements to semantically more significant, higher-order ideals of unity and identity, give way to metonymic forms that stress the greater variety of contingent connections, contiguous links that are not in the order of subordination but instead of coordination in an equal and diverse field of possibilities."[23] As Ryan goes on to suggest, this need not and should not entail the attempt posited by some postmodernists to ban or deconstruct all metanarratives (an impossible, utopian task, as well as a politically misguided one so long as hegemonic metanarratives continue to be efficacious). Rather the political task should be to coordinate (while maintaining some indissoluble tensions between) differing metanarratives of resistance (class solidarity, feminism, postcolonialism, etc.), each of which will have within it certain similar tensions between micro- and metanarrative structures (i.e., differing regional inflections within postcolonial discourse).

Movements are complex, elusive phenomena whose nature is much debated and whose parameters are constantly in flux these days. Thus when I claim to direct my critical efforts ultimately toward "new social movements" it is as much to raise questions as to offer political answers. I am not pointing to static, empirical objects whose boundaries are fixed, but I am pointing toward thousands of actual individuals forged into collective subjects fighting various kinds and layers of oppression, including resisting various metatheoretical attempts to objectify them in ways that ignore their capacities for representing and for theorizing their own actions.

Movements are also complex messages, the most powerful oppositional messages we have. Like all messages, however, they must be interpreted (even by their authors), and those of us who have as our job the creation of contexts of decoding have a role to play in creating strong readers in/of contemporary movements. How we play that role will depend on the model of criticism we bring out into the world, for interpretive acts are political in themselves and they are also models of larger political relations. One of the prime arguments made by a number of recent social movements is that the internal organization of the movement must mirror the values one is seeking to create in the larger social realm. I believe that this analysis needs to be carried over into the realm of critical practice where our models and acts of interpretation need to be consistent with the political values we hold.

Janice Radway has suggested one model for this kind of critical practice, arguing that as a critic and theorist she has a political responsibility to engage in dialogue with readers of the texts she analyzes, not because they alone hold the empirical truth about their experience, but because the process of dialogically negotiating the truth (for the theorist and her/his subjects) necessarily brings the theorist closer to the (con)text in which any theory can prove politically efficacious. Radway, in other words, challenges us to investigate the political assumptions of the theoretical enterprise itself, suggesting that it is too often an allegory of elitism rather than an allegory of democratic dialogue.[24]

← very profound, nice to see some
interest in the crisis of lit 49.

Since most critics usually do not have the kind of access to readers Radway's work on contemporary popular texts allows, I think for most of us following her logic would include scrutiny of our pedagogical practices as well as developing a model of criticism that grants texts a certain degree of autonomy as sites of resistance to interpretive strategies, one that views all meaning as a negotiated social process. This would mean viewing professional interpretation as a threefold dialogic process by which critics engage (1) previous critics, (2) the otherness of the text, and (3) the projected audience(s) for their work. Such a process could be viewed as a series of concentric hermeneutic circles, each marking a community of inquiry rather than stressing putatively individual virtuosity in writing or reading (with the virtuoso writer or reader viewed à la Bakhtin as a transforming conduit for social languages, as a subject always already created by and in dialogue with his/her society).

The boundaries of social movements cross those of the academy, but I use the term here primarily to indicate not only extra-governmental but extra-academic forces. Social movements, seen as extra-institutional sites of dissonance, can provide empirical sources of challenge to the aesthetic temptations of theory. By this I mean that the totalizing tendencies of (all) theory can be resisted best not by the production of written textual heterogeneity (as some radical formalisms might have it) but by exposure to the actual diversity ("heteroglossia") of living political subjects.

THE FICTION OF POSTMODERNIST REALISM

I call the writing that emerges from these political and critical positions, "postmodernist realism." This names at once a mode of writing and a mode of reading, one that features self-reflexive, realism-disrupting techniques but places those techniques in tension with "real" cognitive claims and with "realistic," radically pragmatic political needs. To the extent that I use the term below to characterize a "literary" genre, it is, like all generic classifications, a fiction, a rubric to denote a certain interaction between a horizon of critical expectations and a set of textual practices.

Postmodernist realism is not simply postmodern realism, a return in our time to some unproblematic realist position (though literary realism was never as naive as modernists pretended it was); rather it is a particular kind of postmodernist strategy. Postmodernist realism incorporates the avant-garde critique of "realism" as a form implicated in hegemonic processes but is critical of the excessively formalist and overly general character of that critique.[25] It insists on trying to trace the "play of signifiers" backward and forward to specific social sites, sites conceived not as static "referents" but as contested zones with particular historical layerings of meaning. While modernist techniques were probably never as liberatory as the Frankfurt school and others believed, they no doubt did, especially in such actively avant-gardist moments as Dada and surrealism, have some power to disrupt bourgeois norms. But in recent years a proliferation of avant-garde, self-reflexive techniques have been used to sell all manner of consumer goods, consumerist images, and patriarchal/capitalist ideological positions. These once avant-garde techniques have not lost all their disruptive power but they have become useful to capitalism as elements of a "repressive desublimation," to use Marcuse's term, in which a disorienting pseudopolyphony of discourses rather than a single, realist one is a prime agency of hegemony. If one element of our postmodern condition is that such formal play has become in some situations not merely neutralized, but positively useful to hegemonic processes, useful because of the market's need for the "new" (Pound's call to "make it new" resounds in advertising agencies across the land), then resistance will require some rhetorical strategies that are new with a difference. Thus postmodernist realism, while recognizing that self-reflexive, ironic, avant-gardist techniques can still play a role in breaking up hegemonic "realist" readings (which maintain sectoral but not universal importance), suggests that such radical forms are not sufficient and cannot take the place of critiques that illuminate material conditions of cultural production and reception.

Postmodern theorists are correct in seeing that hegemony is often served by rhetorically bridging the aporias between "reality" and "representation," by effacing one's own contingencies under a claim to transparent "realism." But deconstructing such bridges, exposing such aporias, does not leave us floating in midair as if in some Roadrunner cartoon; by the law of political gravity, we must come down somewhere, and postmodernist realism comes down amidst attempts to overcome social relationships of inequality that ground unequal access to "cultural capital" (including, often, unequal access to the cultural capital needed to make "critical" analyses).[26]

Where much postmodernist art opens itself to contingency and formal eclecticism in the name of a new (anti)aesthetic, postmodernist realism breaks the illusion of aesthetic integrity for a different reason—to point out the political logic through which even oppositional art has been turned into a commodity under late capitalism. In the face of such incorporative power, only an explicitly political analysis of the ideological

stakes of this formal play can make form effective in challenging entrenched power. My work hypothesizes that politically effective texts today need both the self-conscious play of "literary" forms that open up
new ways of seeing and being, and an analytic framework that explicitly
articulates the social, political, and economic forces that play through
and around texts, including those forces that seek to incorporate and appropriate even oppositional writings/readings.

When this political-analytic dimension is not present, it is the critic's
task to provide it, and when, as in the texts I examine here, there are
partial gestures toward such analysis, the task is to draw them out further, to encourage the development of this mode. Radical artists and critics have overestimated the power of "articulateness" in the sense of eloquence of style, and underestimated the need for "articulation" in the
sense of active reading of "texts" into political (con)texts of meaning-
making.[27]

Behind the oxymoron postmodernist realism, there is also a challenge
to all monolithic conceptions of the postmodern. As I argue in more detail below (chap. 6), I think the concept of the "postmodern" is best seen
as a hypothesis that must be tested in each particular text or (con)text in
which it is claimed to be operative. The social scene is far more complexly and contradictorily nuanced than the assertion of a uniform postmodern condition can encompass. Realist discourses, for example, continue to be immensely influential amidst as well as against postmodernist
ones. I would insist, therefore, that oppositional movements need to de-
ploy traditional, realist forms in certain strategic contexts: to challenge
empiricism on its own terms so long as it remains one sectorally dominant ideological stance, and in other contexts as a "residual" element (to
use Raymond Williams's term) that can be used against the emerging normative reflexivity of postmodernism. At the same time, as a number of
critics have shown, there are forms of postmodernist aesthetic discourse
that clearly seek to dislodge other ideological forms of postmodernism,
to go through postmodernism to some other place.[28] Because the texts of
domination play across the whole range from realism to postmodernism,
oppositional texts too must necessarily move across this range.

In this book I concentrate on texts that attempt to encounter and work
through (in both senses of the term) the problematics of postmodernism
rather than positing the postmodern as itself the real and the true. On
one level, as Fredric Jameson ironically points out, postmodernism may
well be the realism of late capitalism, may embody the reality of the commodification and de-realization of culture (at least in some sectors of
some social formations). Indeed, anyone who posits postmodernism as

a discourse about a world in which the "real" can no longer be found must deal with the irony that to do so is to posit this "reallessness" as our real state of affairs.[29]

On the other hand, it is precisely this putative realism of postmodernists (i.e., acceptance of an allegedly irresistible status quo) that postmodernist realism wants to challenge as ideological, as a mode that leaves unchallenged the unequal distribution of cultural capital that emerges dialectically with the unequal distribution of economic capital by class and social capital by race, gender, nationality, and other factors. Such a position must, realistically speaking, posit some outside to postmodernism even as it acknowledges that all of us are, to one degree or another, constituted as subjects within it. And that outside, I have been suggesting, is constituted by postmodernist realism not as an already known empirical reality but as a set of questions directed toward real (con)texts of production and reception, real struggles over the making of meanings about which it is argued that certain voices continue to be privileged over others ("voices" of men over women, Westerners over non-Westerners, heterosexuals over homosexuals, and so forth).

Postmodernist realism is a mode of writing that cuts across traditional genres and forms, since it has as one of its premises that narration (or narrativity) and other formal elements inform both fictive and factual, literary and nonliterary writing.[30] Following conventional usage, I have called the kind of power mobilized by the texts I examine "literary," but one major function of the type of writing these texts employ is to challenge and dislodge such stable categories as "literary," "critical," "historical," and "political," both as descriptions of kinds of writing and as kinds of knowledge. Postmodernist realism is a form that attempts at once to recoup the power of fiction for historiography and political writing, and to persuade fiction to take history and politics more seriously. But in the name of realistically radical politics, it also resists exaggerating the extent to which certain postmodern textual strategies can simply be transferred into wider arenas of action. My readings of the various kinds of texts presented are meant, then, as examples of strategies for writing with and against the grain to create politically useful interventions. The force of my underlying argument has been put pointedly by Gayatri Chakravorty Spivak: "The world actually writes itself with the many-leveled, unfixable intricacy and openness of the work of literature."[31] The world is not as easily shaped and reshaped as is a literary text, but if Spivak's observation is true, as I think it is, then literary studies need not be other worldly, but can provide us with one important mode of access to the play of power and resistance in the current scene.

Aesthetics and the Overprivileged

The Politics and Ethics of Representation in
Let Us Now Praise Famous Men

You are farmers; I am a farmer myself.
—*Franklin Delano Roosevelt*

They cannot represent themselves; they must be represented.
—*Edward Said, representing Marx*

The best political tendency is wrong if it does not
demonstrate the attitude with which it is to be followed. And
this attitude [writers] can only demonstrate in [their]
particular activity; that is, in writing.
—*Walter Benjamin*

ALLEGORIES

Let Us Now Praise Famous Men, a book of photographs by Walker Evans and prose by James Agee, is one of the strangest texts in American letters. Critics have seldom known quite what to make of this generically unclassifiable work.[1] Because it deals with the actual lives of three families of tenant farmers in thirties America, *Praise*, as I will henceforth call the text, is often categorized as social documentary. But the striking beauty of the photographs and the richness of the prose have led other critics to treat the work primarily as an aesthetic object. It is the text's dual status as an "aesthetic" and as a "political" document that interests me. In this chapter, I use *Praise* to clarify what I have called "postmodernist realism," and I read it as an allegory that outlines a politics and an ethics of inquiry into the act of representing the "underprivileged." My allegorical reading means to parallel three kinds or levels of representers: artists, critics, and political organizers, suggesting that in some sense these three are one to the degree that they share certain representational conventions and problems. That is, I believe Agee and Evans, in implicitly and explicitly criticizing what one might call Leninist and liberal democratic modes of representation, embody a radically democratic aesthetic-political stance that points toward a decentered, processual dialogic model of co-representation that applies equally to acts of representation by artists in relation to human subjects, critics in relation to texts, and activists in relation to constituencies.

The last two decades of theoretical upheaval in cultural studies have made it clear that there is no simple way out of the aesthetic and political bind of "representation"—that representation is impossible to achieve, and impossible to avoid (I take this paradox to be, in capsule, one of the major lessons of Derrida's work, one not always heeded by some of his putatively "anti-representational" disciples).[2] But, as my reading of *Praise* will show, this paradox cannot be an invitation to avoid or play away the political effects of texts. Political responsibility cannot be disseminated through formal means alone, but only by actively attempting to shape the dialogical (con)text of reception. There are numerous textual-political strategies through which to articulate aesthetically rich, politically effective representations that acknowledge the partial (in both senses of the word) nature of all such acts of representation. I hope to illuminate several of those strategies here by showing how *Praise* anticipates certain elements of literary postmodernism (and of the reflective, textual turn in ethnography), and how in doing so it embodies an emerging movement practice that (ref)uses representation in new ways.

THEMES AND VARIATIONS

In using but ultimately rejecting the two major aesthetic modes proffered by their time, modernism and realism/naturalism, Agee and Evans created a form that both challenged the political style and aesthetic forms of the 1930s, and pointed toward new aesthetic-political possibilities still being worked out in our time. The work implicitly criticizes both the putatively radical genres of reportage and proletarian literature, and the aestheticism of high modernism. *Praise* is postmodernist, to begin with, in a simple chronological sense: Agee and Evans follow in time, incorporate, and interrogate the literary and photographic techniques of the "high modernist" era (Joyce, the surrealists, etc.). The text is realist in the basic sense that it seeks to tell more of the truth than have previous chroniclers in the interests of a serious intervention into the aesthetic-political representation of a highly charged subject, tenant farmers. *Praise* assaults the normative representational practices of both New Deal liberalism and the Communist party, the two main political forces attempting in the thirties to appropriate the "sharecropper" issue, forces that had by the time of the Popular Front in the late thirties become at points virtually indistinguishable rhetorically.[3]

The collapse of the capitalist economy in 1929 ushered in the most intense period of documentation, the most exhaustive effort to represent the "real" in American history. The economic crash seems to have brought down systems of representation with it. Almost overnight, the rich modernism of the twenties seemed to give way to a new realism. In an emblematic gesture, critic Edmund Wilson moved from *Axel's Castle*, his study of the symbolists, to a "Study in the Writing and Acting of History," *To the Finland Station*. In many cases this shift led to a naive and crude naturalism, but the authors of *Let Us Now Praise Famous Men*, like Wilson himself, brought the culture of modernism with them into their search for the real. Written near the end of the thirties when the vast mound of documentation seemed to have buried reality rather than clarified it, *Praise* embodies the proposition that representational systems are always inadequate, always miss the real, but that this inevitable inadequacy calls for greater aesthetic-political reflexivity and commitment rather than abandonment of the attempt to imagine the real. The text's aesthetic sophistication stands in critique of simple realism, while its political concerns (as embodied in the tenants) critique the normative self-referentiality of (post)modernism.

The word "representation" has a dialogue between politics and art embedded in the very history of its usage, and Agee and Evans obliquely allude to that history in the opening passage of the prose portion of the text.[4] What the authors refer to as the "themes" of *Let Us Now Praise Famous Men* are conveyed through two quotations that appear facing each other near the beginning of the text. First:

> Poor naked wretches, whereso'er you are,
> That bide the pelting of this pitiless storm,
> How shall your houseless heads and unfed sides,
> Your loop'd and window'd raggedness, defend you
> From seasons such as these?
> O! I have ta'en
> Too little care of this! Take physick, pomp;
> Expose thyself to feel what wretches feel,
> That thou may'st shake the superflux to them,
> And show the heavens more just.

The second:

> Workers of the world, unite and fight.
> You have nothing to lose but your chains,
> and a world to win.[5]

The first quotation is from *King Lear* (3.4). But since there are no kings in the world of *Praise*, I assume the theme stated is a more general one—the proper relations between privileged and "wretched" members of a community. And the recommendation regarding that relationship seems fairly clear: the privileged must learn to feel what it means to live a life of deprivation, learn it deeply until they are moved to share the fruits of privilege and "show the heavens more just." But if this statement of the theme seems straightforward, we might bear in mind that it is a realization that comes to Lear in the middle of a long, tragic ordeal. And it comes to a human being, not a king (note the "I" not the royal "we"), to a man who has himself become truly wretched. Moreover, it is a realization experienced, not an idea brought to him from elsewhere. So important, indeed, is this existential component, that I would argue that in a sense the whole of *Praise* is offered as experiential testimony to the difficulty, if not the impossibility, of the privileged learning to "feel what wretches feel," at least through anything as simple as reading a book.

The second quotation, a paraphrase of the closing words of *The Communist Manifesto*, evokes the other side of the political-economic class line. It too seems straightforward in telling the "wretches" to liberate themselves through struggle against those who have enchained them. But in a footnote the reader is warned against a dogmatic, sectarian, or otherwise preconceived interpretation of the words that "mean, not what the reader may care to think they mean, but what they say." Agee is trying to ward off those who would dismiss the slogan as "unamerican," "propaganda," and so forth, by asking readers to reflect on their preconceptions, and by so doing to draw them into closer reading. This presages one of the key strategies of the text—the attempt to create in the reader reflexivity in the place of mere reflex. Agee is at pains to make clear in the footnote that the Communist party owns neither him nor the ideas expressed in the slogan because he wishes to bring the ideas (and with them, hopefully, the party) into fresh contexts where such words can be the beginning, rather than the end, of analysis.

In addition, the authors add a crucial qualification to the slogan's relevance to the text at hand: "[The ideas in the slogan] are not dealt with directly in this volume; but it is essential that they be used here, for in the pattern of the work as a whole, they are, in the sonata form, the second theme; the [Lear excerpt] facing is the first" (xix).

The "work as a whole" refers to "Three Tenant Families," a proposed multivolume work on Southern tenant farmers of which *Praise* was to be the first volume (though no others appeared). The second theme is not "dealt with directly" in *Praise*, largely because Evans and Agee are among the privileged and do not presume that they have learned "to feel what wretches feel." This reticence to deal directly with the theme of class struggle also stems from the text's desire to free radicalism from ossified categories; the subject of the second quotation (removed from its sectarian context) is ambiguous, evoking a not-yet-formed collective subject, rather than some already-existing revolutionary class. We are being told that if larger, collective political relationships are to a large extent "bracketed" (in the phenomenological sense of *epoché*) in this text, this is done for political reasons, and the larger relationships are nonetheless "essential" to keep in mind as we read.

The absence of direct confrontation with this second theme, the efforts of the oppressed to liberate themselves, means that in one sense *Praise* is prepolitical. And as any reader of the text is likely to have noticed, the text is prepolitical in the sense that it seems to have precious little to say, directly at least, about the general, structural sources of, or remedies for, the "plight of the sharecropper." But prepolitical is not the same as nonpolitical, and the text does deal at length and complexly with certain essential, ethical preconditions for meaningful, liberating political discourse and action. Ultimately *Praise* is prepolitical only given certain preconceived boundaries to the sphere of politics, boundaries that the text itself challenges and tries to reconceive. The text challenges certain representational conventions that help keep the tenants from becoming fully political beings.

Praise enacts its critique of aesthetic-political representation on a number of different levels and in a variety of ways, but most basically through an extended effort to "defamiliarize" its human subject matter, to slash through the reader's preconceptions through attacks on perceptual, conceptual, and expressive conventions.

THE SUBJECT OF DISCIPLINES

Agee's own outline of his intention to offer a critique of representation through *Praise* appears as part of a proposal for a Guggenheim fellowship to finance the writing of the text. He writes that his "Alabama Record" (the working title) "will likely make use of traditional forms but it is anti-artistic, anti-scientific, and anti-journalistic. Though every effort will be made to give experience, emotion and thought as directly as possible, and as nearly as may be toward their full detail and complexity (it would have at different times, in other words, many of the qualities of a novel, a report, poetry), the job is chiefly a skeptical study of the nature of reality and of the false nature of re-creation and of communication."[6] This account gives no sense of the polemical passion that is *Praise* in its final form, but this is partly because it was self-evident to the authors that their "skepticism" was to have a polemical and political purpose. In another context Agee lamented the "lack of self-skepticism of all organized reformers and revolutionaries."[7] And it is clear from various assaults on self-satisfied New Dealers and Communists (among the latter he would include himself—skepticism/self-skepticism) within *Praise* that he intends his skepticism as an intervention in a political scene where conventionalized perceptions and representations are stifling political thought and action. More than this, the text suggests that aesthetic representation of the tenants was precisely used to avoid serious political representation and political struggle. The vast effort of documenting America's oppressed was not serving to draw attention to their plight but instead to give an aesthetic illusion that that plight was being addressed.

More specifically, the work is in part a response to a pervasive thirties genre, the documentary book that claimed to give its readers "real" access to other worlds, particularly the worlds of the underprivileged.[8] *Praise* is fueled by fury against this genre and the condescension (whether liberal or radical)[9] endemic to its products. In the "Preamble" Agee acidly parodies this attitude:

> This is a book about "sharecroppers" and is written for all those who have a soft place in their hearts for the laughter and tears inherent in poverty viewed at a distance, and especially for those who can afford the retail price; in the hope that the reader will be edified, and may feel kindly disposed toward any well-thought-out liberal efforts to rectify the unpleasant situation down South . . . ; and in the hope, too, that he will recommend this little book to really sympathetic friends, in order that our publishers may at least cover their investments and that (just the merest perhaps) some kindly thought may be turned our way, and a little of your money fall to us.
>
> (14–15)

Here the aesthetic complicity of those offering "poverty viewed at a distance" is placed in the otherwise effaced commercial context of the publishing industry. For the same reasons, the authors draw attention to the gap between the kind of expectation and quality of relation they sought to bring to their subject as compared to that expected by their employers. Both prefaces ("Preface" and "Preamble") explicitly draw attention to the institutional setting of the work at hand. They attempt to locate their book in the context of institutionalized publishing. They discuss their difficulties in finding a publisher for their work, and the history of their conflict with *Fortune* magazine editors whose appropriative and condescending attitude toward the tenants they mock and reject. (They had been commissioned by *Fortune* to do a photo-prose essay on Southern sharecroppers in the style of a condescending series called "Life and Circumstances." The piece they produced shattered the mold of the journal and was rejected after severe editing failed to make it conform.)[10]

Numerous passages, in the early prose portion of *Praise* especially, are aimed at shaking readers loose from their prepositioned relation to the subject matter, in effect directing toward the "well intentioned" reader some of the representational violence Agee felt he had been asked to direct at tenant farmers.[11] But since the "skeptical" Agee and Evans are clearly not claiming unmediated presentation of the truth, their only way past reader preconceptions must be to use preconceptions and traditional forms, but use them against themselves (hence, "anti-artistic, anti-scientific, and anti-journalistic"). Agee and Evans both at times situate the reader in certain realist assumptions in order to play against those assumptions toward a redefinition of realism and of the real itself. (Indeed, their use of realist tropes is pervasive enough that some critics have mistaken the prose and/or the photographs as naively realist rather than as an interrogation of realist conventions.)

Agee is quite aware that the very terms used to label his putative subjects, "sharecroppers," "tenant farmers," and so on, are not simple, realistic descriptions, but rather politically loaded inscriptions of his subjects. *Praise* fights against, tries to decenter, these preinscriptions throughout, and in an appendix Agee directly critiques the generic use of distinct terms like "tenant" and "sharecropper." This kind of resistance extends to the level of raising questions as to whether the subject of the book is tenant farmers at all (indeed, later I will argue that the tenants are not what the book is about). On several levels the subject or subjects of *Praise* prove difficult to pin down. In their preface, for example, the authors double (or triple) their subject:

> The nominal subject is North American cotton tenantry as examined in the daily living of three representative white tenant families.
> Actually, the effort is to recognize the stature of a portion of unimagined

existence, and to contrive techniques proper to its recording, communication, analysis, and defense. More essentially, this is an independent inquiry into certain normal predicaments of human divinity.

The immediate instruments are two: the motionless camera, and the printed word. The governing instrument—which is also one of the centers of the subject—is individual, anti-authoritative human consciousness.

Ultimately, it is intended that this record and analysis be exhaustive, with no detail, however trivial it may seem, left untouched, no relevancy avoided, which lies within the power of remembrance to maintain, of the intelligence to perceive, and of the spirit to persist in.

Of this ultimate intention the present volume is merely a fragment, experiment, dissonant prologue. Since it is intended, among other things, as a swindle, an insult, and a corrective, the reader will be wise to bear the nominal subject, and his expectation of its proper treatment, steadily in mind. For that is the subject with which the authors are dealing, throughout.

(xlvi–xlvii)

This "nominal" subject shapes and is shaped by the "actual" subject in a number of different ways. Agee's statement of the "subject" enacts the appearance ("nominal subject"), disappearance ("actual subject"), and ambiguous reappearance ("that is the subject . . . throughout") of the tenant families. This dialectical dance is central to the text, grounded in awareness of the "anti-authoritative" (not merely unauthoritative), "contrived" nature of its "immediate" and "governing instruments," and is designed to open passionately ambiguous new political possibilities by dissolving "expectations" of the subject's "proper treatment."

In thirties America, the presence of the nominal subject of tenantry was bound to place the text in the middle of intense political controversy. For the "sharecropper question" was very much on the nation's political agenda on a number of different levels, from the New Dealers who sought to reform their conditions, to the Communists who sought to organize them into unions, to the Dixiecrats who sought ways to get them off the agenda. Thus the nominal subject sets a political tone and weaves through a political motive that significantly alters the stakes, the focus, and finally the nature of the inquiry. The particular "portion of unimagined existence" Agee and Evans sought to "record, communicate, analyze, and defend," in other words, tends to foreground the ideological nature of an inquiry that might otherwise appear to be purely empirical or purely aesthetic (and in this context the two are in a certain sense the same in that each mode would claim a certain distance from the impure, from ideology or the nonscientific).

There are a number of other important elements to this initial statement of the subject that we will have to return to, and one that must be noted now.[12] Notice that there is a certain incommensurability in the four terms used to characterize the project—record, analyze, communicate, defend. The fourth term seems out of place. In a manner that is rather typical of Agee's general style, a clearly polemical notion, "defending," is inserted in what might otherwise seem a neutral, empirical project description. What I hope to show is that "defend" here means primarily defend the subjects of the text against glib representation, against easy appropriation, including easy appropriation by the authors of *Praise* themselves.

BEGINNING TO END THE BOOK

Where then does the critique of representation in the text begin? One answer is that it begins through a questioning of the very notion of beginnings, by making the reader a bit unsure as to just where the text itself begins: with the photographs? with the verbal portion of the text? with the "Preface" that occurs between them (and directs the "serious" reader to skip over it to the "book-proper")? By the time readers get to the "Table of Contents," they discover that they have already read "Book One," Evans's photographs. A similar difficulty confronts the reader trying to find the end of the book. Following one endlike moment and an "amen," a new section begins with the words, "The last words of this book have been spoken and these that follow are not words; they are only descriptions of two images." This is followed by the two descriptions, followed by the title "poem," followed by some (rather bizarre) "Notes and Appendices," followed by a third installment of the divided chapter called "(On the Porch" [*sic*], which "ends" with a promise to begin.

Taken together these gestures form part of the text's attempt to challenge the notion of a "book-proper" as demarcating a representational sphere somehow not coextensive with the world "outside" the text. In the preface the reader is told that *Praise* is "a 'book' only by necessity. More seriously, it is an effort in human actuality, in which the reader is no less centrally involved than the authors and those of whom they tell" (xlviii). There is a tactical effort here to break down the barrier that the very idea and convention of "the book" raises between the reader and the world. The bound book exists as an emblem of this split so long as it is thought somehow to be about the world, but not of the world. The book or bookness frames the discourse, turns it into a monologue that serves to reinforce notions of authority flowing in one direction and diminishing the reader's responsibility for the representation.

Related to this question of the reader's relation to the book is her or his relation to the authors and subjects. In this vein, the authors include in their assault on the book a request that readers send responses to *Praise*, to transform it more fully into a collective effort in proposed future editions and future volumes: "Those who wish to actively participate in the subject, in whatever degree of understanding, friendship, or hostility, are invited to address the authors in care of the publishers" (xlviii). These further volumes did not appear (at least not in book form), and within the logic of the text's argument, the gesture toward other voices can be read as more rhetorical than literal in that it already serves to set in motion a sense of the text as an unfinishable process in which the readers "no less than" the authors and subjects are engaged. By so doing Agee and Evans hope to show that the locus of the representation of the tenants is not in the book, but in the relationships set up between the authors, the readers, and the tenants, relationships which the book mediates but which are not strictly confined to or by it. (In fact Agee maintained a lifelong correspondence with the tenants and sent presents to members of the families he and Evans visited. His sincerity in wishing the book to be seen as a process is suggested by his reaction upon being told that his idea to have *Praise* printed on the cheapest possible paper would mean that it would disintegrate in a fairly short time: the idea delighted him.)[13]

The authors are trying to draw attention to the fact that the web of language that structures experience crosses the edges of the "book" in two directions: we bring interpretive schemata engendered by other encounters with language as embedded in social practices (and by the historically changing structure of the language itself) to the book, and those structures are reinforced or somewhat displaced by the verbal structures of the book. Thus no stable boundary exists to separate the world from the text, or the text of everyday life from the written text.[14]

Praise at once attempts to bleed the book into reality and to transfigure reality into text (that is, into a self-conscious "aesthetic" construct). To enact this dialectic the text aims in two directions: on the one hand, it makes its presentations in typo- and photo-graphic form as intimate and "immediate" as possible (Agee at one point wishes he could put bits of wood, fabric, and excrement on the page [13]), while on the other hand, it injects doubt about any text's ability to achieve immediacy by drawing attention to conventions (including conventions of immediacy) active in the text/world.

For example, in conventional terms, reading a book from front cover to back, the text begins suddenly with Evans's photographs, uncaptioned

and unintroduced. (These photos even manage to precede that mark of
the legal apparatus on the text, the copyright.) Indeed, in the 1960 version of the text the first three photos are of people staring rather suspi-
ciously at the reader as if to ask by what right he or she enters this text,
this world. The placement of the photos before any written signs appear
is a gesture toward immediacy, toward a directness of confrontation, that
is both sanctioned and undermined as the text proceeds. Any initial ease
in appropriating the photos and their subject matter gives way on closer
viewing to a sense of enigma, a sense of having been fooled by their apparent simplicity. The photos eventually raise as many questions as they
answer about their "immediate" subject.

Initially the photos, because of the putative realism of the medium,
serve better to throw the reader/viewer directly into (un)familiar terrain.
But in the larger strategy of the text, the photographs are not ultimately
to be read as truer or more immediate than the prose. The classic, lean,
seemingly straightforward (mostly posed, full-frontal, sharply lighted)
photographs cross-illumine and are illumined by the more baroque,
darkly turning prose in such a way that the capacities and limitations of
each medium may begin to be seen. Through this process mediation itself
becomes a subject of the text.

FICT OR FACTION?

Agee's most direct assault on conventions of immediacy comes through
a refusal of the categories of fact and fiction. As Raymond Williams and
others have made clear, the neat separation of the factual and the fictional, the real and the imaginative, is a relatively recent (post-
eighteenth-century) phenomenon. The word "novel," for example, was
originally used in English to describe both fictional and factual events.
But as "imaginative" discourse became increasingly critical of industrial
capitalist society, it became useful for bourgeois intellectuals to draw
strict distinctions between fictional and factual forms. These distinctions
served and continue to serve to obscure the creative, constitutive (and
therefore political) element in factual discourse, while at the same time
obscuring the social, ideological forces shaping putatively individual,
creative expression in fictive forms.[15] Throughout, *Praise* is an attack on
this ideologically loaded distinction between "factual" and "fictional"
discourse. For Agee, this attack is both direct (i.e., theorized) and indirect. His most sustained direct reflections on the problem of realism that
mediates these questions occur in the middle of *Praise*, in a chapter en-

titled "(On the Porch: 2" [*sic*]. The tortuous twists of his ruminations on the "reality" problem, against which philosophers have stubbed their toes and heads for centuries, do not issue in a solution, but they do suggest a good deal about the subtle plays and interplays of the text with reality.

Given the strict convention of separating fictional discourse from what Agee calls "scientific discourse," he makes it clear why his strategy in *Praise* cannot be to call his work "fiction" or "poetry," but rather must be to show that aesthetic techniques ("art devices," he calls them) are necessary to a representation of the everyday world because they inhabit that world as real conventions (i.e., conventionalizations of the real). Agee fears that no work labeled "fiction," however brilliantly and "realistically" executed, could serve a critique of representation as well as a work that claims to confine itself to rigorous examination of the actual.[16] Art, because of its illusion of a self-contained aesthetic universe, is too easily distanced. Or, as Agee writes:

> The momentary suspension of disbelief is perhaps (and perhaps not) all very well for literature and art: but it leaves literature and art, and it leaves an attempt such as [*Praise*] in a bad hole. It seems that anything set forth within an art form, 'true' as it may be in an art form, 'true' as it may be in art terms, is hermetically sealed away from identification with everyday 'reality.' . . . Even at its best it is make believe . . . because it is art. . . . It is simply impossible for anyone, no matter how high he may place it, to do art the simple but total honor of accepting it in the terms in which he accepts and honors breathing, lovemaking, the look of a newspaper, the street he walks through.
> (240)

Against this convention of "sealing" off the fictive from the real, Agee's strategy must include the claim that he will "be trying here to write of nothing whatever which did not in physical actuality or in the mind happen or appear" (242). This allows him to show how representational conventions function in Life as well as in Art, and that life is falsified to the extent that it is lived and represented merely through realist or naturalist conventions (whether employed by scientists, social scientists, or by artists). Agee writes:

> I doubt that the straight 'naturalist' very well understands what music and poetry are about. That would be all right if he understood his materials so intensely that music and poetry seemed less than his intention; but I doubt he does that [either]. That is why his work even at best is never much more than documentary. Not that documentation has not great dignity and value; it has; and as good 'poetry' can be extracted from it as from living itself: but documentation is not itself either poetry or music and it is not, of itself, of any value equivalent to theirs. So that, if you share the naturalist's regard for the

'real' but have this regard for it on a plane which in your mind brings it level
in value with music and poetry, which in turn you value as highly as anything
on earth, it is important that your representation of 'reality' does not sag into,
or become one with, naturalism; and in so far as it does, you have sinned, that
is, you have fallen short even of the relative truth you have perceived and intended.

(237–38)

In a footnote, he adds, "Failure, indeed, is almost as strongly an obligation as an inevitability, in [this] work: and therein sits the deadliest
trap of the exhausted conscience."

The paradox set up by the inevitability of failure accompanied by an
obligation to proceed even past the exhaustion of conscience, is clarified
somewhat when Agee later in the same chapter speculates about the relation between the documentary and the artistic impulses I've suggested
are at play here: "I think there is at the middle of this sense of the importance and dignity of actuality and the attempt to reproduce and analyze the actual, and at the middle of this antagonism towards art, something of real importance which is by no means my discovery, far less my
private discovery, but which is a sense of 'reality' and 'values' held by
more and more people, and the beginnings of somewhat new forms of,
call it art if you must" (245). In seeking to escape from "art" into "actuality," Agee finds himself driven back to the aesthetic: "call it art if you
must." I am not sure that we "must," and elsewhere in *Praise*, Agee asks
that "above all else" we *not* "think of it as Art." What I think we must
do is see at work a nearly constant attempt to shatter the frame or the
generic cues that normally separate aesthetic from everyday discourse.[17]
In microcosm, this is the movement of *Praise*, a movement in which actuality is used to murder art, "to suspend or destroy imagination," only
in so doing to bring into being "somewhat new forms." Agee both insists
on the reality of the referent, "A chain of truths did actually weave itself
and run through: it is their texture that I want to represent, not betray
nor pretty up into art," and on the inevitable failure of any such representations to capture the real (240).

This breaking of frames also means that the text will respect no disciplinary boundaries in its search for "direct . . . experience, emotion,
and thought." In the preface the authors write: "If complications arise,
that is because we are trying to deal with [our subject] not as journalists,
sociologists, politicians, entertainers, humanitarians, priests, or artists,
but seriously" (xlvii). Why are these practitioners not serious? Because
each of these discursive positions remains trapped in one narrow set of

conventions, thus reducing the complex play of language and world to a single category. So one strategy of the text is to explode these disciplines and this discursive division of labor by using forms drawn from all of these domains to expose their conventional limits through juxtaposition. Thus *Praise* offers a seriously humorous, aesthetically rich, humanely entertaining, sociopolitically sacramental, novel journalism that calls its own representational practices into question.

This list is richer than the triad—report, novel, poetry—Agee suggested in his grant application, and it gives a hint of the range of discourses brought into play in the text. A number of other roles, voices, discourses could be added—autobiographer, philosopher, ethnographer, prophet, pedagogue, and so on—which the text in its seriousness plays against one another and weaves together. In addition, Agee and Evans both offer richly textured pastiches of and allusions to a vast array of "aesthetic" styles—impressionism, expressionism, surrealism, cubism, imagism, naturalism. But these styles never become purely autonomous or self-referential. Or rather, the aesthetic autonomy of *Praise* shapes and is shaped by the political autonomy of those it subjects to representation, subjects who become sites of resistance to aestheticist textualization.

CUBIST SOCIOLOGY

The fictive and the factual are as distinct in *Praise* as the two sides of a Möbius strip. The back cover of one recent edition of the book tells us in bold capital letters that the text is SOCIOLOGY. That may be, but if so *Praise* is surely a novel form of sociology, a form that undermines anything resembling social scientistic certainty by multiplying approaches to its objects of study to create a kind of cubist sociology or a dissociology.

The text does make gestures toward the sociological mode of factual, generalizing discourse, but they are highly skeptical gestures, and they are placed in a context that significantly alters their meaning by merging a sociological voice into a pastiche of aesthetic styles. Agee, for example, invariably places words like "typical" or "normal" or "average" or "representative" in quotation marks to suggest his wariness of their unreflective use (see 100, 262, 264). And while he will occasionally talk about general and typical conditions, he does so against a background of such dense particularity that such generalizations seem impoverished and are thus clearly revealed as constructions, choices made by the observer from a myriad of possibilities shaped in the complex dance of reality and language. At times this even takes the form of parodying the notion of generalization itself. One section introduced with the words "I think I should begin this with a few more general remarks" proves to be a "general" itemization of the variety of odors, "pine lumber . . . heated in the sun," "the odors of sweat in many stages of age and freshness," the "odors of sleep, of bedding and breathing," for example, and a phenomenological reading of the "general" relationships between "bareness and space," in "typical" tenant homes.

This attention to detail is one of the ways in which the text explodes the notion of case study documentation. Where sociological conventions select and shape the "facts" that confirm the theses and premises of the documentor (say, bits of squalor that speak "squalid deprivation"), *Praise* takes the logic of documentation to the point where sense disintegrates or becomes densely ambiguous. A "typical" previous documentor wrote that the typical tenant "made enough to buy two beds, half a dozen chairs, a dresser, a washstand, and a kitchen stove. . . . He does not own anything else, except for a change of clothes and a few odds and ends."[18] Agee, by contrast, expends more than fifty thousand words of *Praise* detailing such furnishings and "odds and ends," including the precise color, taste, and "curl" of the dust that lights upon them, and the number of teeth (27, 3 missing) in a pink celluloid crescent-shaped comb inside a small cardboard box on the Gudger family mantelpiece (158, 172).

Sometimes this intensified documentation takes the form of an extreme geometricism that seems to anticipate some of Alain Robbe-Grillet's experiments in literalism:

> On the left of the hall, two rooms, each an exact square. On the right a square front room and, built later, behind it, using the outward weatherboards for its own front wall, a leanto kitchen half that size. At the exact center of the outward walls of each room, a window. Those of the kitchen are small, taller than wide, and glassed. Those of the other rooms are exactly square and are stopped with wooden shutters. From each room a door gives on the hallway. The doors of the two front rooms are exactly opposite. The two rooms on either side of the hallway are connected inwardly by doors through partition walls.
>
> (138)

This is empiricism with a vengeance, and its hyperliteralism (forerunner perhaps of the super- or hyperrealism of later decades) demonstrates the figurative and motivated nature of most so-called empirical description. To adopt one of Agee's own favored metaphors, we come to see the documentor as a cinematographer setting up a panoramic shot or zooming in on the smallest detail, thus revealing that the camera and its operator are complicit in the seeing, in the creation of the objects seen. An intertwining of real and fictive may also arise from a vague feeling that the description is "really" a set of stage directions for some not yet known play.

When Agee has made his point he can afford to gently parody this exactitude: "Exactly beneath the window of the side wall, a trunk: Exactly across the angle of the side and front walls, and still again, not touching these walls, a sewing machine. Exactly at center behind and beneath the sewing machine, on the floor, a square-based and square-bowled lamp of clear and heavy glass, dusty, and without its chimney, the base broken and the broken piece fitted but not mended into place: Exactly beneath [etc.]" (158–59).

As in Robbe-Grillet's novels, Agee's geometricism sometimes comes to take on a strangely disorienting and poetic quality, but he is not content to rest with it or to claim that it can capture more than a small part of even some literal truth (235). At other times the very reluctance of the "literal" to mean infuses his real text with a sense of untranslatable symbolism reminiscent of Kafka. Frequently precision and wild metaphor are mixed to form a kind of expressionism, as in this passage describing some land in front of one of the tenant's home:

> The forty-foot square land in front of the house, the 'front yard,' is bare of any trees or bushes; there is nothing at all near the house of its own height, or bestowing of any shade. This piece of land is hunched a little on itself in rondure. Through the dry haze of weeds and flowering fennel its dead red yellowness glows quietly, a look of fire in sunlight, and it is visible how intricately it is trenched and seamed with sleavings of rain; as if, the skull lifted off, the brain were exposed, of some aged not intellectual being who had lived a long time patiently and with difficulty.
>
> (139)

Or more wildly, three visionings of a farm:

> These fields are workrooms, or fragrant but mainly sterile workfloors without walls and with a roof of uncontrollable chance, fear, rumination, and propitiative prayer, and are spread and broken petals of a flower whose bisexual center is the house.
>
> Or the farm is also as a water spider whose feet print but do not break the gliding water membrane: it is thus delicately and briefly that, in its fields and structures, it sustains its entity upon the blind breadth and steady heave of nature.
>
> Or it is the wrung breast of one human family's need and of an owner's taking, yielding blood and serum in its thin blue milk, and the house, the con-

centration of living and taking, is the cracked nipple: and of such breasts, the planet is thickly and desperately paved as the enfabled front of a goddess of east india.

(128–29)

This last excerpt in its proliferation of metaphors is also a small example of what might be called the cubist element of the text, its frequent offering of several versions or angles of vision on a given phenomenon. This approach is used in relation not only to objects but to whole narrated scenes as well.

Related to the technique of literalism is the removal of objects from their associated contexts through "mere" itemizations. Beneath the Gudger house, for example, Agee finds (in part): "bent nails, withered and knobbed with rust; a bone button, its two eyes torn into one; the pierced back of an alarm clock, greasy to the touch; a torn fragment of pictured print; an emptied and flattened twenty-gauge shot-gun shell, its metal green, lettering still visible; the white tin eyelet of a summer shoe; and thinly scattered, the dessicated and still soft excrement of hens" (148). This list builds into a kind of surreal collage, but it is also revealed as wholly a part of its context. For example, Agee is quick to point out that nothing on this particular list can be "properly considered junk" since, given the economic conditions of the tenants, everything is saved toward eventual use in some form.

This surreal quality is even more pronounced in Agee's detailing of the "collage" (his word) of bits cut out from magazines, advertisements, calendars that adorns the space above a mantelpiece (164; see also Evans's photograph of this mantelpiece). There are also a few decimated news clippings that Agee dutifully records. Here is one of them:

> GHAM NEWS
> hursday afternoon, March 5, 1936
> Price: 3 cents
>   in G
>   (else
> Thousa
> are on d
> througho
> cording its
> for the Birm
>
> (166)

Data or Dada? This seems at once a kind of Dada found poem and possibly significant information (I can imagine it referring, for example, to

"Thousands on the dole" and thus being reassurance to a proud family seeking federal assistance). Perhaps ultimately it is an emblem of the inexhaustible, necessarily fragmented nature of documenting.

Early in the text Agee notes that "if these seem lists and inventories merely, things dead unto themselves . . . and if they sink, lose impetus, meter, intension, then bear in mind at least my wish, and perceive in them what strength you can of yourself: for I must say to you, this is not a work of art or entertainment, nor will I assume the obligations of the artist or entertainer, but it is a human effort which must require human cooperation" (111). Agee means to leave room in his text for active composition by his readers, and by suggesting that "meter" is a quality of the real, he means to shatter the realist notion that the world can be read prosaically.

In his notes for a grant proposal to pursue the project that culminated in *Praise*, Agee writes that "one part of the work, in many ways the crucial part, would be the strict comparison of the photographs and the prose as relative liars and relative reproducers of the same matters."[19] A "strict comparison of the photographs and prose" suggests that the questioning of representational capacities within each of the two media is intensified by comparative cross-mediation. And both the photos and the prose allude to other media that make the question of cross-mediation or multiple mediation an important one that further highlights the reader's involvement in producing the representation.

Alongside dense documentation and endless inventories, Agee is also capable of a deft impressionism, capturing complex webs of relationship in a phrase or two. In one section, for example, he offers a couple of paraphrased, clichéd quotes from the landlords that tell as much about that relationship as whole books might: "Why times when I envy them. No risk, we take all the risk; all the clothes they need to cover them; food coming up right out of their land." "Tell you the honest truth, they owe us a big debt. Now you tell me, if you can, what would all these folks be doing if it wasn't for us?" (80).[20]

Or suddenly an almost haiku-like imagist line will emerge from a description: "At the end of a slim liana of dry path running out of the heart of the house, a small wet flower suspended: the spring" (131).

When dealing with people rather than objects, Agee often employs a precise, sometimes lyrical phenomenology.[21] Here, for example, he describes a family waking and getting up: "Their legs heavy, their eyes quiet and sick . . . in the sharpening room; they will lift; lift—there is no use of it, no help for it—their legs from the bed and their feet to the floor and the height of their bodies above their feet and the load above them, and let it settle upon the spine, and the width of somewhat stooped shoulders, the weight that is not put by" (83–84). Once again the very precision of the details gives it a weight and strangeness, lets us envision what we merely see all the time.

In one extraordinary passage Agee describes in detail the preparation of breakfast, while at the same time treating it in the language of religious ritual as a morning "Mass." The implements used and the finesse of the gestures employed are brought more fully into our awareness by the striking quality of the analogy—our attention to the living details of the scene is heightened. Thus in complement to the itemization technique, phenomenological description animates the scene, reviewing objects so that having been seen once as autonomous objects, they are now seen precisely as objects shaped in complex relation to those who own and use them. At the same time, through the striking quality of metaphors used, we are made aware of the artificiality, the made-ness of the description (89–90).[22] Indeed, sometimes in the text reality and writing seem to transpose themselves, as when Agee describes the texture of wood on a country church wall as appearing "as if it were an earnest description, better than its intended object" (38).

These various dissociological exposures of fact(itious) knowledge are not, however, done in the name of some celebration of pure, unbridled aesthetic play. For, from Agee's point of view, literary discourse is no less bound by, subject to, convention than is putatively factual discourse. And there is no implicit reason for preferring aesthetic conventions to social scientific or journalistic ones.[23] Thus, against his aesthetic play Agee offers self-reflexive, didactic interventions that function "anti-artistically" to reveal his conventionalizing poetic authority. At one point, for example, he notes that:

> If I were going to use these lives of yours for 'Art,' if I were going to dab at them here, in order to make you worthy of The Saturday Review of Literature; I would just now for instance be very careful of Anti-climax which, you must understand, is just not quite nice. It happens in life of course, over and over again, in fact there is no such thing as lack of it, but Art, as all of you would understand [he is here addressing the tenants directly] if you had had my advantages, has nothing to do with Life, or no more to do with it than is thoroughly convenient at a given time, a sort of fair-weather friendship . . . well understood by both parties and by all readers. However, this is just one of the reasons why I don't care for art, and shan't much bother, I'm afraid. There was an anti-climax.
>
> (366)

This passage not only calls attention to the "distorting element" in art vis-à-vis "lived experience" but, lest that imply the possibility of undistorted representation, weaves an aesthetic notion, anti-climax, into "Life," thus drawing attention to the necessarily conventional nature of the "true" story he is (re)telling. And the gap between the telling and the told is further widened when we notice that in the text of *Praise* this particular passage is in fact not an "anti-climax" but a rhetorical climax.

Agee employs two forms of allusion to artistic/expressive styles to similar ends. On the broadest level, he periodically compares the structure of *Praise* to that of one or another medium, most frequently to film, or to music, but also sometimes to drama or religious ceremony (this can be seen, for example, in his opening list of "dramatis personae" and in such chapter headings as "Recessional" and "Introit").[24] By multiplying these somewhat contradictory structural metaphors he implants the notion of the text as open to multiple readings, or multiple performances, depending on the needs, desires, and skills of the "centrally involved" reader. And he builds a sense of reality as a kind of total art form built of a cubist arrangement of media that have been artificially subdivided into a multitude of conventional genres. In preparing to describe the tenants at work, for example, he writes, "I see these among others on the clay in the grave mutations of a dance whose business is the genius of the moving camera, and which it is not my hope ever to record: yet here, perhaps, if not these archaic circulations of the rude clay altar, yet of their shapes of work, I can make a few rude sketches" (324).

On a less grand scale, these allusions to other media directly serve to reinforce the notion of the indwelling of the aesthetic in the real. At one point, for example, Agee writes, "But the music of what is happening is more richly scored than this; and much beyond what I can set down: I can only talk about it: the personality of a room, and of a group of creatures, has undergone a change, as if [seen through] two different techniques or mediums; what began as 'rembrandt,' deeplighted in gold, in each integer colossally heavily planted, has become a photograph, a record in clean, staring, colorless light, almost without shadow" (404). Thus the delicate shift of a mood is registered as a shift in artistic media, even as the unavoidably "distorting" element of black and white photography is suggested. For similar reasons, Agee sometimes makes it clear that he is writing photographically (one source of his literalist efforts), or cinematically: "and on a pallet a baby lies, spread over with a floursack against infringement of flies, and sleeps and here a moving camera might know, on its bareness, the standing of the four iron bed . . . the huge and noble motions of brooms and of knees and of feet" (149). Here he both alludes to one of Evans's photographs (the baby with the floursack) and maintains a sense of "you-are-there" immediacy even while calling attention to media and their respective capacities/lacks through the reference to the moving camera.

A similar use is occasionally made of allusion to particular artists, as when Agee describes George Gudger's overalls as having in them the "blues of Cézanne." Sometimes these allusions are displaced for surprise, or comic effect: "Rowdy, who, though he is most strictly suggestible in his resemblance to André Gide, is nevertheless as intensely of his nation, region, clan as Gudger himself." (Rowdy is Gudger's dog.) And sometimes they are woven deftly and unobtrusively into the text: Agee describes the aged, crumbling Gudger family Bible as having leaves as delicate as snow, an allusion to Hart Crane's poem "My Grandmother's Love Letters," which includes a line describing the letters as "brown and soft / And liable to melt as snow." This intertextual, allusive form is extended to include long passages from the Bible (including the title poem itself from Ecclesiasticus—typically an excerpt from the more marginal Apocrypha) and at the end of one section two pages of aphorisms from Blake's "Marriage of Heaven and Hell" (rearranged by Agee).

Similarly, motifs from *Lear*, set up by the opening quotation, are woven into or allowed to resonate in the text. When, for example, a key scene of discovered relationship between privileged Agee and the tenants takes place amid a raging storm, we may hear echoes of the "pitiless storm" in Shakespeare's text. Neither the brief allusions nor the longer passages are ever acknowledged as to source, suggesting that Agee sees them as transformed into something else in his bible, his (inter)text that is a document in and of the world. And again they are emblematic of the suffusion of the aesthetic into the real, that is, into the real aesthetic of that which exists.

Agee's simplest and most direct technique (but a "contrived technique" nonetheless) for breaking representational illusion is to confess his incapacity to represent, his failure to capture the "real." Generally these lead not to abandoning the subject, but to a new beginning, until in cubist fashion several angles of vision have been constructed. In attempting to describe the Gudger home, for example, he builds four portraits, each in small or large measure differing from the others, punctuated by "Or by another telling," and similar re-beginnings (140–46). Or in a later chapter, he breaks off a scene in the Gudger home with the words, "But from where I say 'The shutters are opened,' I must give this up, and must speak in some other way" (403). These interjections have been objected to by some critics who view them as false modesty or neurotic self-consciousness (both of which they may also be), but these confessions function admirably in the text as a kind of ultimate didactic bottom line lest the reader miss more implicit critiques. Confessions of representational failure occur at fairly regular intervals throughout *Praise*, and their strategic nature is suggested by the fact that they almost invariably occur not after some particularly "bad" piece of writing, but rather after one of Agee's more brilliant displays. Indeed, this is central to their effectiveness, for it is only after we have been drawn deeply into an illusion of representational adequacy, or correlation to the real, that we are prepared to be jolted by the intrusion of one of these confessions of failure. In other words, if Agee were not an extraordinarily gifted writer, we might simply nod and take these confessions at face value. But given the exhaustively (and at times exhaustingly) adequate representations that precede them, the confessions lead us to wonder what "adequate" adequacy could possibly entail in representation in or out of books.

Indeed, so exhaustive are some of Agee's excursions that he is frequently accused of overwriting. And surely from certain aesthetic perspectives ("realist" or "modernist"), this is true enough. But what can it mean to "overwrite" if not somehow to violate some implicit or explicit conventionalization of adequate, sufficient writing? And it is precisely such notions of precision that Agee is trying to explode. "Adequate" representation could only mean a reification of an ongoing signifying practice in which the reader and the subjects of *Praise* are "no less centrally involved." And because his confessions do not imply the possibility of abandoning his "obligation" to the inevitable "failure" that is the text's fate, the building up of scene upon scene, description upon description, deepens the sense that readers have an obligation to intervene actively in these representations.

Strategically, this "overwriting" is linked to what might be called "underwriting." This involves primarily the refusal to entertain (for long) two key elements in traditional narrative—plot and characterization. I think it fair to say that common objects and the natural landscape are more fully narrated than are the human subjects of the text. There is a kind of animism at work in the text that goes beyond the conventional symbolic use of nature to support or elaborate human situations. Wild personifications (remember the landscape skull above) are common, but they most often serve not to humanize the natural world so much as to free it through radical estrangement. Agee goes so far with this idea theoretically that at one point he rails against the "provincialism" that makes humans value consciousness over the supposedly inanimate (226).

By contrast, the bits of human action, dramatic development, scattered throughout the text seem radically incomplete by traditional aesthetic standards (certainly by realist standards, but even by modernist ones in which impressionism still is largely only a more economical form of dramatization or portraiture). Agee's vignettes do not add up to a story about the tenants that pretends to capture the "essence" of their lives or even a portion of their living. He seems to have realized that he cannot not narrate, that narration is too much an essential element of language-consciousness to be eliminated (or perhaps that it can be questioned only by first being [re]presented). Instead his strategy is to play narration against itself: by using multiple narratives (though not as in, say, Faulkner or Joyce, from different characterological points of view, but from a single, self-questioning narrator); by disrupting chronology; and by leaving lines of plot dangling, without resolution. This means, for example, that his "cubism" extends to the level of re-telling whole scenes in such a way that shifts of emphasis reveal the impossibility of a single comprehensive narration of the action.

And the didactic interventions in *Praise* often suggest that something important, even crucial, has been overlooked, or plotted out, while the seemingly infinite repeatability of these didactic interruptions (it becomes clear that he, we, will never get it right) infuses a radically contingent sense of being in the world. Where the logic of plot, say in the stories called "liberal reforming" or "socialist revolution," may suppress the contingency of action and close off dialogue about what is to be done, Agee's skeptical representations of representations of (relatively uneventful) experiences dramatize and keep open a gap between the social text of the tenants' lives and the readers of those lives that is essential to keeping political vision and dialogue alive.

Something more of what is at stake here can be gleaned from the analogous doubts raised by *Praise* vis-à-vis characterization. Critics have often noted that the tenants are unsuccessful characterizations; they do not emerge as "fully rounded" figures. But this too is by design, not accident (or, by the accident of design, as Agee might claim). The illusion of three-dimensionality in these actually existing characters could close off the sense of their existential being-in-process that Agee wants to keep alive. To make George Gudger a "believable character," to "fully represent" him with all the attendant novelistic baggage of personal history, motivation, and so on, would be to rob him of one of his richest possessions—the capacity to represent himself in an ongoing process of self- and world-creation (including creation of the character named "James Agee"). Even dialogue, were more of it included, could not solve this problem, since the selection of "representative" samples and the placement of those bits of dialogue would still be under the authorship and authority of another.[25] (Later I will modify this claim regarding authorial control.)

Agee's representation of "actual" encounters with Gudger and the other "characters" in *Praise*, filled as they are with Jamesian subtlety and complexity, are also suffused with doubt about the author's "reading" of the characters and the characters' readings of him (see, for example, the marvelous encounter between Agee and ten-year-old Louise Gudger [400–401]). Just as the text cannot not narrate, it cannot not characterize the tenants. But it can offer strong caveats to those who would easily appropriate and class(ify) them, by both revealing and commenting on the revelation of the radical inadequacy, the "false nature of" all our attempts to characterize and narrate the lives of others (and, by extension, of ourselves).

Just as any attempt to isolate a sociological or documentary component of *Praise* leads to questions of aesthetic form, any attempt to isolate an aesthetic or poetic element leads ineluctably to political questions. Poetry I take to mean not primarily the few bits of stanzaic verse scattered through the text, but rather something like a "pure" aesthetic apprehension of the world. And for Agee and Evans this has more to do with the development of an aesthetic "way of seeing" than on finding "beautiful" things (and "beauty" for Agee often has something terrible about it that removes it far from such simple connotations). That is to say, there appears to be no object in the authors' purview that cannot be made / found poetic.

This poeticizing consists most often in an effort to prise objects free of their utility and meaning in the everyday world. And this entails a prising of perception free from its conventional focal points (in this sense, the whole project of *Praise* is, on one plane, poetic). But in seeking this space beyond the normal entanglements of human meaning and the noise of human use, Agee has as his tools only meaning-riddled, use-soiled words. Thus the text's poeticizing, like its various other efforts at (re)presentation, must ultimately fail.

But as we have seen, failure is one of the forms of *Praise*, an inevitability that is also an obligation. The text can at least point to a silent space beyond all the twists, versions, and reversions of its rhetoric, and it can enact a collision of codes that abrupts, momentarily opens up, a gap in which something other appears for an instant before the new trope smooths it over. At times Agee writes as though he wanted ultimately to exhaust all the possible words about a subject, an object, in order to make room at the end of language for a utopian space of freedom, or pure being, he can only signify as "silence."[26]

But just as in general the politics of perception and representation in *Praise* is shaped by and shapes the politically charged nominal subject of tenantry, the politics of poetic perception is often foregrounded by the poetic reshaping or re-viewing of numerous objects central to the household and immediate political economy of the families. Perhaps the outstanding verbal example of this process is Agee's tour de force lyric rendering of George Gudger's overalls:

> The bright seams lose their whiteness and are lines and ridges. The whole fabric is shrunken to size, which was bought large. The whole shape, texture, color, finally substance, all are changed. The shape, particularly along the urgent frontage of the thighs, so that the whole structure of the knee and musculature of the thigh is sculpted there; each man's garment wearing the shape and beauty of his induplicable body. The texture and the color change in union, by sweat, sun, laundering, between the steady pressures of its use and age: both, at length, into realms of fine softness and marvel of draping and velvet plays of light which chamois and silk can only suggest, not touch; and into a region and scale of blues, subtle, delicious, and deft beyond what I have ever seen elsewhere approached except in rare skies, the smoky light some days are filmed with, and some of the blues of Cézanne: one could watch and touch even one such garment, study it, with the eyes, the fingers, and the subtlest lips, almost illimitably long, and never fully learn it.
>
> (267)

Amidst this rhapsody we never wholly lose contact with the backbreaking labor these overalls "represent"—it is there in the references to "sweat," "sun," "age," "musculature," and "the pressure of use." But at the same time, the reshaping of the object into a play of light and texture seems to carry with it a promise of liberation made all the more tangible by its play against the background of hard labor. The promise of liberation cannot be spelled out because, as I will argue in a moment, its place is "outside" the book, but the object freed from use suggests through contiguity the liberation of its wearer, liberation not from labor, since Agee has immense respect for the work of the tenants, but from a system that leaves them no choice about how they labor and denies them the fruits of that labor.

Agee's unsentimental respect for the quality and quantity of the tenants' labor is reflected in the (painstakingly exact, labored) chapter entitled "Work."[27] He is careful throughout to distance himself from those whom he notes would "manage to capitalize . . . politically" on the lives of the tenants, whether by playing up the very real exploitation for their own ends, or by playing it down as "the unvanquishable poetry of the oppressed" (215). Agee discusses his own skeptical communism periodically throughout *Praise*, and his refusal to turn the tenants into political capital is rooted not only in the deep respect I have been elaborating, but also in his own sense of the political-economic structures in which they are enmeshed. Because he sees the tenants as caught up in a "whole world-system of which tenantry is one modification" not likely to be dislodged as easily as many radicals in the thirties believed, he saw little immediate hope for change in their circumstances and thus resents superficial attempts to sell them such hopes (207–8).

REAL PHOTOGRAPHS

Evans's photographs express a similar care in moving between, interweaving, and even reversing aesthetic texts and political contexts. There is, for example, a clear allusion to the oddly sensuous shapes of Joan Miró in the final photograph (Fig. 1) and an even more direct allusion to Vincent Van Gogh's painting of peasant shoes, *Les Souliers*, the painting that stimulated Martin Heidegger's reflections on "The Origin of the Work of Art" (Fig. 2). The contrast between Heidegger's and Evans's "readings" of the painting is illuminating. Where Heidegger takes off on a flight of fancy about universal peasantry, Evans's use of Van Gogh's painting has the effect of making it appear more concrete and rooted in a specific life. The indexical nature of the photograph (its undeniable relation to what Agee calls "unimagined existence") when joined to an allusion to an aesthetic construct (Van Gogh's painting) undermines any claims for the purity or universality of either art or documentary. The universalizing qualities latent in Van Gogh's aestheticizing of the shoes and exaggerated by an interpretation like Heidegger's are driven by the photograph (in the context of *Praise*) back onto the very particular body of "George Gudger," whose specific human weight can be felt in these shoes. At the same time the painterly allusion reminds us that our vision is being directed aesthetically by Evans, that there is no simple documentary apprehension of these objects or of the human being who wears them.[28]

Where Agee sometimes went to great lengths to shock or cajole his readers into new perceptions, Evans's more austere aesthetic sensibility led him to attempt to elicit new visionings from ordinary or conventional lines of sight. He generally refused to move any of the objects he photographed from their found context, and for the most part he avoided bizarre or unnatural angles, preferring to shoot from normal height and straightforward angles.[29] Yet the objects in his photographs achieve an uncanny density. They seem autonomous. Indeed, more than one critic has noted that the objects seem to be posing. They are surely composed, but never in such a way that their given setting is lost or severely estranged. We are invited to view the photos as "art," but they do not insist on it. Indeed, in one of Evans's object portraits, a group of everyday items in the corner of the Gudger kitchen is topped by a brilliant white towel on a line that seems to wait there like a movie screen, a canvas, or photo paper, ready for the artist-reader to compose them anew (Fig. 3).

Evans achieves a similar sense of double vision through allusions to various photographic genres and styles. The portrait of Louise Gudger, for example, with its striking woven straw hat, has about it simultaneously the look of both elegant, high fashion photography, and, through the halo effect of the hat's placement, a touch of medieval hagiographic portraiture (Fig. 4). All of these touches undercut any naive realism, without ever undermining the basic documentary quality of the photos. Just as in Agee, indeed more fully given the photographic medium's necessary indexical complicity with the real, Evans's referent is never lost or overwhelmed but rather seems to grow in autonomy and solidity as it is transformed aesthetically.

Like Agee's words, Evans's photographs interweave and even reverse aesthetic texts and political contexts. Perhaps the finest example of these tropings is one of the few portraits of laboring in the text (Fig. 5). Reminiscent of Jean-François Millet or Camille Pissaro, it pictures a young woman stooping amidst a sensuous sea of cotton leaves. Her spine is bent into the shape of a question mark, the elegant straw hat we've seen before now bent nearly to the ground in labor. The beauty of the composition immediately strikes us, draws us into the scene. But then it holds us until we begin to feel that beauty dash up against the aching coil of the girl's spine and the question punctuated by her body becomes a political one.

And lest we miss the point of such interweavings of poetic and sociopolitical meaning in objects, in the section entitled "Beauty," Agee directly addresses the nature and cost of aesthetic apprehension:

> In fact it seems to me necessary to insist that the beauty of a [tenant] house, inextricably shaped as it is in an economic and human abomination, is at least as important a part of the fact as the abomination itself: but that one is qualified to insist on this only in proportion as one faces the brunt of his own 'sin' in so doing and the brunt of the meanings against human beings of the abomination itself.
>
> (203)[30]

Elsewhere in the text Agee makes it clear that aesthetic apprehension of the tenant's world is a luxury, a class privilege, they, as members of another class who must bend nearly the whole of their existence toward brutal toil, can ill afford (314).[31] Thus he and Evans seek to turn even this beauty, this "cruel radiance of what is," against the abomination of tenantry and against the sins of the overprivileged by letting that beauty become further testimony to the injustice of the tenant system itself, making it a palpable part of the promise denied.

The exorbitant proliferation of literary and visual tropes creates a representational richness that exposes the representational poverty of both liberal and leftist portraits of "sharecropper" lives, while the hovering presence of the existential subjects prevents this utopian dimension from becoming the text's only truth. The polyphonic structure is rescued from the empty playfulness of some postmodernism by a scrupulous attention to the very real subjects of the text and the stakes they have in resisting becoming mere objects of aesthetic manipulation. Agee and Evans at once refuse to use their aesthetic wealth to cover up the various poverties (including representational poverty) imposed on the tenants, and refuse to rob the tenants further by ignoring certain beautiful and graceful dimensions of their lives.

READING RELATIONS AND DEMOCRATIC CONVENTIONS

We Americans of today—all of us—we are characters
in the living book of democracy. But we are also its
author. It falls upon us now to say whether the chapters
that are to come will tell a story of retreat or a story of
continued advance.

—*Franklin Delano Roosevelt*

I hope I have given some sense of how the various discourses of *Praise* form a novel texture. I have called the compositional technique "cubist," but a more precise term for it might be "vortextual," for the text seeks to show consciousness less as a variety of perspectives on an object, than as a kind of vortex upon which an inexhaustible stream of information is drawn and transformed by an endless process of poesis. I have also spoken of the text as exploding disciplined discursive boundaries. But in another sense the explosion precedes (and follows) the text, *Praise* itself being a carefully haphazard (re)weaving of bits and pieces of conventional discourse—religious, sociological, aesthetic, philosophical, scientific, and so on—that reveals the arbitrary and reductive nature of such boundaries. Separated from their protective, well-disciplined contexts, these bits of discourse reveal themselves for what they are—more or less well-educated guesses woven as cloaks to cover an unfathomably complex play of event, meaning, and imagination. But to paraphrase Marx, these cloaks are not woven just as we please but under particular conditions of production, and their colors are not neutral but bear the color-coded class marks of those who wear them (the producers, of course, like George Gudger, can seldom afford cloaks).

The disruptive power of Agee and Evans's text has largely been re-contained by critics who have seen it as either a somewhat strange "realist" documentary, or as a somewhat flawed work of literary "modernism." But as I have indicated, something more interesting is at work in *Praise*. Realism and modernism themselves are questioned in the text, turned into subjects and included as elements in a more comprehensive composition. This process is addressed explicitly in one of the most heterogenous of all the text's chapters, "(On the Porch: 2." In that section, Agee protests against the flatness and reductiveness of "realism/naturalism" but also against a certain hermetic quality associated with modernism in the arts. Both, he claims, somehow fail the test of the Real itself, and this I suggest ultimately makes sense only if the Real cannot exist in book form.

In order to talk about what he is doing, his method, Agee resorts to a series of paradoxes, "asymmetrical symmetry," "inevitable chance," for example, that point toward a process he seemed to intuit but did not clearly theorize. At its center is a process of de-authorization, a displacement of the authors that breaks the bounds of "bookness" in the name of truth as dialogical or collective process.[32]

As I have shown above, the authors begin with the assumption that their readers are rooted in perceptual/conceptual structures that have already coded the "sharecroppers" (if liberals, they have coded them as reformable objects; if Communists, as classed objects, etc.). In playing its representations off against the reader's expectations, the text may serve momentarily to loosen, disrupt these preconceptions, but it is in danger of merely recoding them with equally stereotypic and solipsistic results (as those who point out the sometimes sentimental humanism of the text rightly observe). The text may enrich the "objective" picture through refined "realism" and the "subjective" picture through refined "modernism," and still serve only to reify, reobjectify the tenants and leave unchallenged the epistemological basis of the whole fiction/nonfiction dichotomy.

This concern leads Agee and Evans to use the various distancing techniques of metacommentary, cross-mediation, and purposely flawed representation that I have catalogued above. But this merely shifts the level of the problem without solving it; it is still in danger of merely turning the readers into consumers of what we can now identify as fashionably avant-garde, self-reflexive texts. Thus *Praise*, anticipating this reading, is driven one stage beyond the normative reflexivity we associate with postmodernism, driven out toward the political space outside the "book" (yet inside the text).

The text tries to show that it is ultimately structured by the relationships that develop between the authors and the tenants, relationships we as readers also (partly) enter. Agee's way of acknowledging this Other reality is to make frequent gestures (beginning with the attack on beginnings) toward the tenants and their world as an ongoing process beyond the reach of his words. More than this, throughout the text but most fully in the last third of *Praise*, Agee directly addresses the tenants. They become, among other things, representative readers of the text—not abstract reader-responders but really imagined, living critics of Agee's words. The tenants' relationship to the text becomes a model for other readers, and a caution against taking the text any less seriously than they would.

This political-textual strategy explains, for example, why our initial encounter with the tenants occurs out of chronological sequence. The motivation behind the sequencing is the opportunity it provides Agee to demonstrate through the testimony of one of the subjects of the text, Emma, that he has begun a relationship with them, has gained their trust and even their love (62–64). Conversely, the chronologically first encounters occur only at the end of the text, leaving readers at the beginning of a relationship, and thus reminding them that they have at best only begun to know the tenants, have only begun a relationship with them.

The subjects of *Praise* function, through their real existence, rather like those characters in other works of postmodernism who suddenly take up the pen and write their own portraits or talk back to the author. They form a site of dialogue that is at once inside and outside the "booked" space of *Praise*. They are thus the ultimate hedge against the solipsistic authority of the author, and a tacit recognition that readings are political, are struggled over in the world that they inhabit and that inhabits them.

Agee's way of embodying these dialogical twists can be seen in his treatment of George Gudger. Amidst his attempt to explain his aesthetic practice in "(On the Porch: 2," Agee finds himself confronted with the presence of Gudger:

> George Gudger is a human being, a man, not like any other human being so much as he is like himself. I could invent incidents, appearances, additions to his character, background, surroundings, future, which might well point and indicate and clinch things relevant to him which in fact I am sure are true, and important, and which George Gudger unchanged and undecorated would not indicate and perhaps not even suggest. The result, if I were lucky, could be a work of art. But somehow a much more important, and dignified, and true fact about him than I could conceivably invent, though I were an illimitably better artist than I am, is that fact that he is exactly, down to the last inch and instant who, what, where, when, and why he is. He is in those terms living, right now, of flesh and blood and breathing, in an actual part of the world in which also, quite irrelevant to imagination, you and I are living.
>
> (232–33)

Later Agee adds that his representation of Gudger will depend "as fully on who I am as on who he is," and that therefore he "would do as badly" to eliminate himself from the picture as to invent character, places, or atmospheres (239). Thus there is a kind of doubling of author and character to meet the doubling of Gudger into existing human being and character. And it is through four-way dialogues such as these that the political discourse of *Praise* is enacted.

Evans has to establish this sense of relationship without words. He does so primarily in two ways: by allowing his subjects to compose themselves, and through use of the family photo album genre. Evans's portraits are composed in two senses, both of which contribute to a sense of relationship between equals. The subtle but strong aesthetic composition of the photographs adds dignity and strength to his subjects. More important, the subjects themselves are composed, indeed in many cases, guarded, against the assault of the lens. The portraits are enigmatic, not easily appropriable. And to the extent that they do have the easy appropriability provided by the medium, the photos can function ironically to draw the reader into an intimacy he or she later feels shame for assuming (a sense of shame fostered by Agee's relation to his subject [see, for example, his delicate entry into the Gudger house, 136] then redounding back on the photographs). For related reasons there are very few candid shots; Evans does not wish to catch his subjects off their guard. One of the few unposed shots included (though Evans took many more) reveals a subject who is clearly angry at having her picture taken at that moment.

Evans's use of or allusion to the family photo album genre has a similar intent. The photographs are divided into sections by family, and the group portraits suggest homemade pictures, while the more composed individual portraits suggest commercial studio work. Not only do they give a sense of an intimacy that emerges from and stays within the family, but they suggest that the photographer is serving the tenants (and, indeed, the first group portrait of the Gudgers was made at George's request and under his compositional direction [369]). This sense is enhanced by photos of photos on the wall of the Ricketts' home, suggesting a capacity to reappropriate the medium being used to appropriate them.

But the unavoidable, fundamental political fact that Agee and Evans confront in their attempt to establish a relationship with Gudger is their relative privilege, one conveyed by class and its accoutrements of education, leisure, mobility, and inscribed in the "book" as the further privilege of authorship.

By what strategy, then, can authors with radically democratic commitments, authors who wish to shed the cloak of privilege, proceed? Partly through all the devices outlined above, with the addition of becoming characters in their own text. Agee especially makes himself a character in *Praise;* he objectifies himself and exposes his character to all manner of misreading (including, alas, this one). This would seem to bring him to the level of Gudger as a representation, especially since his confessional obsession makes him a less than wholly sympathetic character. Indeed, just before the climactic (anticlimactic) scene in which the long-awaited political question (What is to be done?) is finally asked, the Agee character is at his least attractive—lustful, covetous, arrogant, neurotic, ambitious, reckless, and nearly suicidal (I am thinking of the scene in which he spends time in town and then drives at breakneck speed back to the tenants [375–86]).[33]

Agee's method, however, lies not so much in his general vulnerability to some abstract reader, as in his particular vulnerability (unverifiable in the "book") to those he has represented. Becoming vulnerable in face-to-face encounter with those one would represent, that is the prerequisite for the political act of representation he offers and withdraws.[34]

The acts of political communion represented in the text are manifold and largely undramatic, simple. Two of them can suggest what I mean: Agee's act of helping Gudger and Ricketts prop up a fallen tree (knocked over by a "pitiless storm") (406), and his acceptance of the shelter and food of Gudger and his wife after his car has become mired in the mud near their home late at night (410–14).

Agee has no illusion that these and other moments of shared labor, food, and intimacy with, even, temporarily, dependence on, his "subjects" give him real understanding of their lives (he obliquely and ironically notes at one point that the difference between his visit and their lives is like the difference between visiting a prison and being an inmate [409]). But these moments represent the possibility of understanding, begin a dialogue. There is in them real equality, a shifting panorama of equalities and inequalities that is present in any relationship, and that has little to do with the abstract equalities proffered by liberal democracy.

And thus it is only after nearly five hundred pages of extraordinary effort to give a sense of the living of his subjects, and only after he is (relatively) certain that he has earned (outside the "book") George Gudger's trust, that Agee can finally talk casually to him "about what the tenant farmer could do to help himself out of the hole he is in" (431).

That this care and respectful caution can in no way be construed as political conservatism Agee makes clear in a remark earlier in the text: "The one thing the [tenants] could most surely receive and understand is what a good revolutionist could tell them about their immediate situation and what is to be done about it: certainly one would be a fool, and an insulting one, who tried much else, or who tried much else before that was accomplished" (313). If Agee does not attempt such a project, it is for two reasons: his own (probably correct) assumption that his skills did not lie in that form of revolutionary activity (a job being performed by a number of dedicated, mostly Communist party, organizers who formed the Sharecroppers Union and other forces of resistance); and his sense that his talent lay instead in using his verbal skills to prepare through

Praise a context in which such a dialogue about what is to be done could begin on decent terms. What is at issue is the quality of the relationship, and the way that shapes whatever political ideologies may frame and be re-shaped by the dialogue.

The "what is to be done" question posed to Gudger is thus the beginning of the unbooked "Volume 2," the taking up of the second theme of the tenant sonata. And the reader of the book called *Let Us Now Praise Famous Men* cannot be privy to this conversation because it takes place in another textual space, the reciprocal space of political dialogue. Within the booked space there is no guarantee that the reader may not have "picked up [the tenants'] living as casually as if it were a book" (13). This is why the most intimate portions of the text are reserved for those readers who have shown the care and the patience to persist through hundreds of pages of dense description of the conditions of this living. And even here, in the last section, "Inductions," Agee adds a further precaution: he addresses his words not to the reader, but to those of whom he writes, addressing each directly by name for a portion of the section. The reader is made to feel a sense of eavesdropping, of reading someone else's mail, that makes the danger of violation of the tenants' lives more palpable.

From the political space outside the book, *Praise* is reviewed, rewoven as a force-field of ideologically contested signs. The authors disappear, or become two readers among many, and the tenants are invited into the dialogue (and, indeed, the "real" subjects of *Praise* have been among its readers and critics).[35] The political space that can only be a silence in the "book" as consumable object enters the "text" re-viewed as a series of relationships in the world.[36] *Praise* becomes a political subject, a site of intersubjective contestation over the meaning(s) of its representations.

And that contestation continues. Both the difficulty of the project undertaken by *Praise* in relation to its time of authorship and its wider, ongoing political resonance are suggested by the history of its reception. As a political agent in the late thirties and forties, the text was not terribly successful. Both its strangeness and the untimeliness of its publication (just as World War II began and the direction of the American social formation shifted drastically) meant that it sold poorly, despite excellent reviews by a number of major critics. But its ongoing power was such that upon being rediscovered after the publication of a second edition in 1960, *Praise* began to receive and create the political readership I have suggested it desired. Agee would have taken great ironic delight in the fact that prime among the text's new readers were young Civil Rights activists in the rural South for whom *Praise* became a kind of bible or handbook on political relationships with impoverished black Americans (a class of folks who had little in common with the white tenants except their chains, their "human divinity," and their desire for justice).[37]

This link to the Civil Rights movement reminds us that the second theme, the efforts of the oppressed to liberate themselves through political struggle, cannot ultimately be voiced in *Praise*. Not because there is something truer in the voices of the oppressed themselves: their self-representations are not more real than Agee's (and are necessarily less rich in some respects). The tenants are as deeply scarred, inscribed, by the distortions of the prevailing ideological systems as any other "reader." It is only that they represent the site of the beginning of the democratic community toward which the entire effort of *Praise* strives, because they have been the most fully damaged by the lack of such a community. The process of collectively creating such a community requires the equivalent of face-to-face vulnerability on the part of the privileged in relation to (in relationship with) those insulted by "the thefts of economic privilege" (307). The privileged must be subject to representation by, must become vulnerable to, those they have for so long presumed to represent.

From this moment the overprivileged may see themselves as strangers, sense the distance that makes representation impossible, makes democracy desirable. Democracy becomes desirable not as abstract equality but as a source of radical difference, as a base from which legitimate differences can emerge. Representation fails the moment one ceases to remember its inadequacy. Representation fails the moment one forgets that, in Theodor Adorno's phrase, "It is an essential aspect of truth that one play a part in it as an active subject."

SONATA FOR CLASS STRUGGLE

This hearing and seeing of a complex music . . . "gets"
us perhaps nowhere. One reason it gets us nowhere is
that in a very small degree, yet an absolute one, we are
already there.

                                                    —*James Agee*

At one of the several conclusions of *Praise* (the last one), this distance finds embodiment, is represented. Agee and Evans, alone in the woods at night, compare notes, analyze, begin composing the text of the lives they have been participating in and observing. As they sit they become aware slowly, tentatively, of the sound of two animals, never clearly identified as to species, calling to each other across the darkness and distance. The language is indecipherable to them, though at times it approaches music with iterations and reiterations of complexly pleasing, everchanging patterns. They let their words fall away and listen to the calls. The darkness and silence intensify the music.

When the calling fades away they begin to talk again, but this night they do not pursue for long their interweaving compositions. Agee writes: "Our talk drained rather quickly off into silence and we lay thinking, analyzing, remembering, in the human and artist's sense praying, chiefly over matters of the present and of that immediate past which was a part of the present; and each of these matters had in that time the extreme clearness, and edge, and honor, which I shall now try to give you; until at length we too fell asleep" (471).

Thus ends the book, with the entire five hundred pages of *Praise* gently erased by a promise to begin and a fall into dream.[38] But there begins also the space where political dialogue and struggle can weave another text, another movement, around the second theme to join the text of *Praise* in sonata form.

Figure 1

Figure 2

Figure 3

Figure 4

Figure 5

THREE

Invisible Movements, Black Powers

Double Vision and Trickster Politics in Invisible Man

I agree . . . that protest is an element of all art, though it does not necessarily take the form of speaking for a political or social program. It might appear in a novel as a technical assault against the styles that have gone before.

—*Ralph Ellison*, Shadow and Act

[O]nly in division is there true health.

—*Ralph Ellison*, Invisible Man

In 1965 a survey of more than two hundred prominent American authors voted Ralph Ellison's *Invisible Man* the finest American novel since World War II. Thirteen years later, a similar survey of professors of American literature yielded similar results, with *Invisible Man* judged the most important postwar novel published in the United States.[1] Whatever else such surveys may prove, they add quantitative evidence to a more general impression that Ellison's novel is perhaps the literary work by an African-American that is most securely lodged in the canon of American letters.[2] But if there has long been something approaching consensus on the aesthetic value of *Invisible Man*, political consensus on the value of the novel has been harder to come by. Like *Let Us Now Praise Famous Men*, *Invisible Man* has been attacked on a number of occasions by left-wing critics who find it insufficiently "committed" or "political" in its treatment of black life in America. Some of these attacks have been reductive and self-justifying, others have been serious and thoughtful.[3] Most have tended to extrapolate from Ellison's own allegedly aestheticist or formalist statements about his book or from his often seemingly moderate political statements in order to find grounds for attacking his novel. Although I will offer a more positive political analysis of *Invisible Man*, it is not my intent to refute these other critics, both because Ellison has already answered them himself and because I believe that from their strategic vantage points some of these critics, particularly the "black aesthetic" critics of the 1960s, made a number of valid critiques. But we are now in a different political context, one that requires different literary critical strategies, and new readings of *Invisible Man* are beginning to emerge that better serve the current historical moment.[4] I want here to contribute to this process of making a new text of *Invisible Man* by viewing it through a set of lenses that upsets easy aesthetic/political dichotomies by looking both at the content of the novel's form and at forms of content sometimes overlooked by earlier critics.

Many of Ellison's critical remarks on his text *have* contributed to an undervaluing of some of the political richness in his novel, but even in Ellison the critic we can find at least two important observations that complicate charges of formalism leveled against him, comments that can help point us toward a more useful political reading of the text. First, Ellison has remarked that once written a book belongs to its audience, not its author; and second, he has observed that protest in a novel may take place as much at the level of form as content.[5] When questions of form are woven into questions about the political content of the novel, *Invisible Man* can be shown to offer formidable radically democratic insights into the discursive and extradiscursive conditions of American racism and the movements that fight racism.

One reason that *Invisible Man* has been criticized for being politically conservative is that it seems to provide little overt political guidance to its readers; it does not, for example, end with an unambiguous call to action (although the "hibernating" narrator claims to be preparing for "overt action" and remarks that he believes in "nothing if not action"). But there are some very good political reasons for this ambiguity: the ambiguity of *Invisible Man* can be read as a far more radical rhetorical and political strategy than one that might have pointed more programmatically toward a "solution" to the "Negro question." Indeed, perhaps the most important element of the text's politics lies in the formal arrangements through which it questions such a programmatic approach to black liberation by putting into dialogue virtually the entire panoply of rhetorical strategies available to black liberation struggles. The political position of *Invisible Man* could be termed a call for double vision as the necessary antidote to the double-consciousness imposed on African-Americans.[6] I mean double vision to connote a number of destabilizing rhetorical and theoretical gestures in the text. At its most general level, double vision could be conceived as a struggle between aesthetic and political imperatives, between a desire for expressive celebration (of an individual, of a culture) and a desire for effective resistance (to racism, to invisibility). But at a deeper level, double vision attacks all such easy dualisms, destabilizing them while acknowledging their continuing power. In double vision, visibility or identity (personal or cultural) is at once achieved and deferred, and political positions are at once embraced and challenged.

The term double vision as I intend it should also, however, suggest the difficulty of "having it both ways," that is, while a twofold vision is preferable to single-focused myopia, double vision also connotes a failure of vision, a blurring that is a diminution of visual acuity. The text's politics is thus torn between a shiftiness that may offer aesthetic richness at the cost of political decisiveness, and political decisiveness that may cut itself off from the (cultural) sources of its power. This double sense of doubleness is most succinctly symbolized by the statue on the grounds of invisible man's black college campus. The statue shows the college founder apparently lifting a veil from the eyes of the kneeling slave. But as invisible man notes, it is difficult to tell from the pose if the veil is being lifted or lowered, and further ambiguity is suggested by the kneeling, subservient pose of the slave. Moreover the very frozenness of the statue suggests a reification of enslavement as much as an overcoming of it. Clearly getting out from "behind the veil" is no simple task, and the dialectics of double vision are tricky.

The play of double vision and the search for a political voice with the flexibility of a trickster in *Invisible Man* at once looks back at a long history of black political and cultural resistance, and presciently anticipates the resurgence of that resistance in the fifties and sixties. Indeed, these two moments are in some sense one, since one of the points of the text is that old rhetorics seldom die, they are simply (or complexly) recycled into new historical (con)texts. Those new (con)texts significantly alter the meaning of old rhetorics, but much depends on understanding and redirecting recurring political tropes, forms that again and again become political traps. The text's rhetorical strategies are important to examine in detail because they suggest alternatives to the powerful and limited rhetorical strategies of the Civil Rights and Black Power movements of the 1960s, strategies that remain the primary discourses available to the struggle against American racism today."

In this chapter I examine three of the modes through which *Invisible Man* illuminates these formal constraints on black liberation struggles.

The first two of these modes could be said to begin with literary questions that become ineluctably political, while the third makes clear that political questions can be illuminated by literary, rhetorical analysis. First, I show how the text enacts a critique of the white male literary and critical canon of American letters, a critique that works primarily through allusion, and which by analogy challenges all simple notions of integrating blacks into a putatively white America. Second, I analyze how the text tries to liberate blacks from the ghetto of literary naturalism assigned them by white critics, a process that through analogy undercuts the basis of all ghettoization of African-Americans. Finally, moving from literary politics to political literature, I demonstrate how the text directly juxtaposes a variety of black political rhetorics/strategies, setting them side-by-side in such a way that their relative strengths and weaknesses can be seen as a step toward transcendence of their respective limits.

WHITE CANONS, BLACK MASKS

The first key form of double-visionary critique proffered in *Invisible Man* is enacted through its weaving of a variety of canonical American literary texts into the texture of the novel in such a way as to re-interpret those texts. Recently critics have begun to elaborate the polemical intent in the thick web of allusion in *Invisible Man*, viewing these allusions as a subtext whose function may best be described as revisionist literary criticism.[7] References to other literary works in *Invisible Man* can be seen as extensions of Ellison's critical writings, which have always displayed a keen polemical interest in the history of American literature and criticism. In "Twentieth Century Fiction and the Black Mask of Humanity," written the year he began work on *Invisible Man*, for example, Ellison criticizes American writers since Mark Twain for eviscerating their work by failing to treat one of the key issues at the heart of American national identity: racism.[8] In the same piece, he also criticizes *critics* for failing to recognize this absence at the heart of writers like Ernest Hemingway, and conversely, for failing to recognize race as a central topic in the great American writers of the nineteenth century, especially Twain and Melville. In *Invisible Man* this dialogue is continued at the level of allusion in the form of an elaborate network of references to *Moby-Dick; Huckleberry Finn;* Lewis Mumford's book of criticism, *The Golden Day;* and dozens of other works; a network of allusions that in effect attempts to rewrite the literary/critical canon.

Perhaps the best example of this is the scene between invisible man and young Mr. Emerson (the neurotic rich boy with a copy of *Totem and Taboo* at his side who fancies himself Huck to invisible man's Jim). The scene criticizes at once paternalistic elements in Twain's treatment of Jim, the relative invisibility of Jim in Twain's account and in criticism about Twain's novel, and rewrites Leslie Fiedler's suggestive if reductive homo-erotic reading of Twain's novel (along with a slap at reductive Freudian readings generally). The more immediate social and literary target of this scene is liberal patronizing of the Harlem or Negro Renaissance of the twenties, and the sexual dynamic that often shaped it—the search for sensual and sexual pleasures repressed by genteel culture but released in alleged Negro "primitivism" (Emerson wants to add invisible man to the aviary in his office alongside other exotic creatures). As the surface of the text proffers a homophobic, stereotyped parody of homosexuals, the al-lusive level evokes complex questions of literary and social engender-ment through its references to Walt Whitman in addition to Twain. By attempting to "lure" invisible man to a rendezvous at "Club Calamus," young Emerson is made to embody a decline of Whitmanian critical primitivism through othering, through a projection onto blacks of re-pressed Euro-American desires. The scene dramatizes the way in which African-Americans (and Native Americans) as the political unconscious of the Euro-American literary tradition are used as a source of sexual and textual pleasure while being denied status as full co-creators of such texts. In turn, however, Ellison's reversal of this project is accomplished by a denigrating "feminization" of the "mainstream" tradition (much as later in the text invisible man is denigrated by the Brotherhood by being assigned to lecture on the "woman question").

The allusions to Twain and Whitman further historicize the othering of blacks by white literary figures, whether it be in the comic form of Jim's minstrelsy or the more openly erotic form found in the twenties. It also simultaneously revises Fiedler's insight about the arrested development of American literary males by (re)placing it into the context of black/white sexual and social relations. By exhibiting young Emerson in his barely restrained lust for invisible man, the text points toward the more deeply repressed issue of race in American literary criticism, and by ex-tension, American social discourse and intercourse generally. It is homo-textuality rather than homosexuality that is the key issue here—the in-ability of white "men of letters" to get outside the text of their selves, their inability to create nonwhite (or nonmale) others as anything but projec-tions of some all-inclusive oversoul. My allusion here to Ralph Waldo Emerson is not gratuitous for he too is very much in this scene; indeed it is the figure of Emerson that ties together the themes I've touched on thus far. For Ralph Waldo Ellison, like his character young Mr. Emerson, is heir to a legacy that has no place for his kind. Through the complex fate of a not-so-hidden naming, young Mr. Ellison is challenging the likes of old Mr. Emerson in part in order to find a place for his (black male) kind in the canon of American letters symbolized by that earlier Ralph Waldo.

This allusive revisionism works not only to reinterpret the canonized "great (white) works" in light of the issue of race, but also at the level of attempting to re-open the canon to include different works by weaving Frederick Douglass, W. E. B. Du Bois, Richard Wright, and others into its textual web amidst the white literary "masters." I chose the word "amidst" rather than "alongside" to suggest that this is not an integrationist strategy, but a way of pointing to the always already intertextualized nature of black and white literary relations in America (Douglass in Melville or Thoreau, Melville or Thoreau in Douglass). This strategy, like the metaphor in the novel's title, means showing not only what was there, but also what was not. Ellison writes, "I felt that I would have to make some sort of closer identification with the tradition of American literature, if only by way of finding out why I was not there— or better, by way of finding how I could use that very powerful literary tradition by way of making it my own, and by way of using literature as a means of clarifying the peculiar and particular experience out of which I came."[9] This passage succinctly characterizes the strategic difference between the first stage of canon reformation that we have just passed through and the new stage we are entering. The complex strategy of making "that very powerful literary tradition" a tradition that can be claimed by African-Americans is the next step beyond finding out why blacks and other Others have not been fully present in our literature and criticism. That process entails moving beyond mere integration of "minority" texts or of establishing parallel "ethnic" literary "sub"-traditions, to a total reshaping of the "majority" tradition in terms of and in the light of the other realities posited by critical rereadings, a move from recognizing or representing the margins to a reconceptualization of the putatively mainstream tradition itself.

In this regard, it is important to note that within the African-American "literary tradition" as constituted largely by white and black males, Ellison's novel itself and its criticism have played a hegemonic role, marginalizing until recently the major contributions of black women. The relative invisibility of strong black women in *Invisible Man* parallels the erasure of African-American women writers that canonization of Ellison's novel itself perpetuated.[10]

Viewed in the light of recent attempts to reconceive the mutual construction and reconstruction of whiteness and blackness, *Invisible Man*'s allusive strategy can be seen as more radical, more aimed at the roots of racist literary knowledge/power, than the (historically crucial) moment of the "Black Aesthetic" of the 1960s. While theorists of the Black Aesthetic were often apt in criticizing Ralph Ellison's public pronouncements, it is no longer necessary to give *Invisible Man* up to the interpretations given to it by its author. Yet if *Invisible Man* was "ahead of its time" in pointing toward the radical revisionism of the current moment, we can only get this point in the present, due in large part to the intervening political struggles (including Black Power) that have cleared the field of some of the racist tropes and practices that made it difficult even to conceive of undermining white male cultural and political hegemony. And as I show below with regard to Ellison's literary ambitions, in its own time *Invisible Man* was at points very much caught up in some of these hegemonic webs despite its iconoclastic power on other levels.

Invisible Man's allusive exploration of and symbolic transformation of the Euro-American literary legacy no doubt also had a further, less selfless goal (one that my opening remarks about critical consensus on the novel's aesthetic worth suggests was successful): the goal of adding still another text to the canon—the text of *Invisible Man* itself. This latter goal is to some extent in (double-visionary) tension with the broader revisionary task—*Invisible Man* is torn between a desire to *integrate* itself into the American canon, and the desire to *decenter* that canon through deployment of its black powers. This double desire in *Invisible Man* to enter and to condemn Euro-American literature and society no doubt reflects Ellison's own ambiguous personal ambitions, but its wider importance lies in the fact that it is an analogue for the general strategic question facing the black liberation struggle at the time the novel was written in the late forties and early fifties. That strategic question, centered in the tension between integrationism and black nationalism, exploded in the 1960s and remains central to black politics today.

Invisible Man continues to speak to present concerns in part because it embodies that conflict, and, at its best, refuses the either/or of separatism versus integration, opting instead for a complex both/and strategy that, among other things, recognizes black and white culture in America as always already integrated, already predicated on occasionally cooperative but generally oppressive, unequal, and agonistic interrelations. Indeed, the text suggests that what is most "American" about America, what most contributes to that long effort of America to escape the "old world," are forms of language, music, and cultural style generally that originate in African-American communities. From such a viewpoint, black nationalism actually underestimates, and undervalues, the blackness of America by insisting on a degree of purity in black experience that by implication leaves "white" culture untouched as well.[11] (The most obvious symbol for this in the novel is the drops of black "dope" that are the key ingredient in making "Liberty Paint's" whitest white paint, the paint used to cover "the national monument.")[12]

But the alternative, a premature, liberal celebration of colorlessness, is also inadequate; it too would render invisible the accomplishments of African-Americans by projecting a drab gray cultural fog. Such a move is challenged, for example, in the epilogue, which satirizes blacks becoming whiter by turning gray and suggests that whites are becoming blacker day by day in their flight from blackness. Such critical gestures qualify, undermine, the abstract, existential humanism much in evidence in Ellison's criticism and in the New Critical formalism forged during the early Cold War that shaped his criticism. Attempts in the novel to get to a "common humanity" are dashed again and again against the shoals of racism, and the cultural costs of such a commonness are constantly reckoned: who would want that pale culture represented by Norton's pre-Raphaelite daughter?

Against both integrationism and black and white versions of separatism, *Invisible Man* demonstrates the dialectical, dialogical production of American culture through the struggle between oppressors and oppressed, offering its highest implicit praise for those works of "black" culture that triumph in the face of oppression (the greatness of the blues and folk wisdom, for example), while acknowledging the irony that in some sense white oppression produced or necessitated the production of those cultural forms.

This particular double-visionary tack occurs also in the text in the form of numerous attempts to fuse and refuse certain classic binary oppositions that have structured social and literary discourse in the United States, including most dramatically black/white, but also aesthetic/political, blindness/insight, writer/speaker, individual/community, and tradition/innovation. Fallacious black/white dichotomies are assaulted most directly in this famous oration on the "blackness of blackness" in the prologue where, "In the beginning . . . there was blackness . . . and the sun," where "black is . . . an' black ain't," where "Black will git you

. . . an' black won't." And if black is and black ain't, so too white is and white ain't. In the American context, no social identity comes without a color-coding, and "whiteness" has always been dependent upon "blackness" as a source of its self-definition.[13]

Given as a parody of a classic black literary form, the call-and-response sermon, the crowd's affirmation of paradox, "black is an' black ain't," at once expresses the subversive intent of the text and the difficulty of conveying that subversive message. Here Ellison codes his text's attack on Black Power/integration dichotomy in a classic form that at once roots his discourse in the particulars of African-American culture and undermines the given categories of race. At the same time, however, the seemingly automatic response of the preacher's audience suggests that they are attending only to the form of the sermon, and missing its paradoxical, subversive content. In this way the scene also foreshadows a deeper paradox in the text, the paradox of radical democratic authorship that asks: How do you preach the need to do away with preachers? How do you lead people to stand without leaders?

Just before the preacher begins his sermon we are given, in a perfect mess of cultural allusion, "an old woman singing a spiritual as full of *Weltschmerz* as flamenco"; such an image is emblematic of the complex multicultural interweavings that make up life in the United States (and life in *Invisible Man*). But such a strategy of pointing to such dialectical interweavings is in constant danger of obscuring the social ground of, in this example, the spiritual, of turning it into a kind of universal sign of suffering and enduring, detached from its particular context in the history of American slavery and its aftermath. *Invisible Man*, however, rather than attempting to isolate the purity of origins, attempts to illuminate the diversity of uses to which a cultural or political tradition may be put; rather than insisting on the purity or authenticity of an original context, it seeks to examine the politics of various contexts into which spirituals have been placed (including the context of the novel itself). At times the text offers black popular cultural forms as the root of resistance to racism, as a source of wisdom, survival, and solace; at other times these forms seem a source of political regression to quiescence. This argument is embodied in the novel in many ways, most particularly through the use of black music and folklore as artistic/political forms alongside and intertwined with Afro- and Euro-American "literary" forms. As Larry Neal has suggested, this strategy means that *Invisible Man* can be seen as far more radical in its attempt to understand the "black masses" and their political predicament than many more overtly

black nationalist or revolutionary works. Because it starts from and respects existing forms of black expressive culture rather than trying to cut
a new black aesthetic out of whole cloth, the novel resists the desire to
"paternally guide [the black masses] down the course of righteous blackness."[14] This position conserves, builds upon, existing popular styles, but
also suggests that they can be turned, troped, in new, liberating directions.

Such a position, however, must also acknowledge that often both literary and popular cultural forms can be conserving forces in the negative
sense of providing a false, aesthetic resolution that leaves power relations
unchanged, unchallenged (a trap that seems to have sometimes ensnared
the author of *Invisible Man*, but from which the text can be "saved"). In
Invisible Man this tension exists at the level of form as a conflict between
what Berndt Ostendorf has called the "modernist" and the "anthropo-
logical" dimensions of Ellison's relation to African-American popular
culture.[15] On the one hand the text absorbs and assimilates these cultural
forms into its aesthetic as "fresh" content; on the other hand it seeks to
validate their usage as a cultural heritage at least as rich as if not richer
than the pagan-Judeo-Christian tradition out of which, for example, T. S.
Eliot built "The Waste Land" (a poem Ellison studied assiduously while
at Tuskegee and in which he found numerous jazz influences).

The elitist side of Ellison as author and critic sometimes seems to want
to "raise" folk forms like the blues to the level of "high" (i.e., literate
European) culture,[16] but the text parodies such attitudes when they
emerge in the invisible man (as in his recoiling from Trueblood's vulgar-
ity), and the better side of Ellison has spoken of the blues aesthetic as a
form that keeps the memory of suffering alive "like fingering the jagged
grain" of a scar, a specifically black aesthetic when contextualized as the
form given to the historical suffering of African-Americans. These tensions between aestheticism and historical memory cannot be resolved
fully in the text for they are precisely dependent upon the reception the
text receives, the use made of it by various audiences. But as I have already suggested, and as I will show in more detail below, the text itself
raises this question of audience reception precisely with regard to these
issues of what to make of its "folkloric" elements.[17]

WEARING WHITE FACE

The second level of protest through form carries on a number of the questions raised by the first level, especially questions about canonicity, while

intensifying scrutiny of the question of literary form itself. Critics have long realized that *Invisible Man* (re)presented a break with the protest naturalism of much thirties fiction, and of Richard Wright's work in particular. Ellison's numerous protestations to the effect that an artist's ultimate loyalty is to the craft of writing rather than the social world at large have been one source of the distrust toward his novel shown by some left critics. But these remarks themselves must be read in the political context of Ellison's debates within and against the official socialist realism espoused by the Communist party (to which Wright belonged and in which Ellison was deeply involved). And as Thomas Schaub details, they must be seen as well within and against the context of the rise of the anti-communist, Cold War "new liberalism" of the forties, with its aestheticist analogue, the New Criticism.[18] Ellison's position (as critic, and to a lesser extent as novelist) partakes of the emerging Cold War anti-communism, but it is ineluctably different in that it carries within it a continuing critique of American racism in which the Cold War humanists themselves (and the Southern agrarian New Critics in particular) are implicated.

Ellison saw his friend and mentor Wright suffer under the constraints of Communist party discipline and felt those constraints himself as he began his apprenticeship under Wright. Both authors realized that these formal strictures were analogous to and partly productive of political strictures in the party that closed off vast realms of theory and experience that needed to be explored if politically effective forms of language and action were to be found. In particular, Communist party literary and other doctrines were dictating ways in which African-American experience could be treated in fiction, cutting short important explorations of that experience and thus largely cutting off debate on the left about black perspectives on their own oppression.

As Ellison put it, Wright encountered in the party a form of "intellectual racism . . . couched . . . in the form of insistence upon blind discipline and a constant pressure to follow unthinkingly a political line." Ellison adds that the point was not so much that only an African-American could know and "tell the truth about Afro-American experience, but that you had to at least get down into the mud and live with its basic realities to do so."[19] And the further point is that Wright had not only been down in the mud but was also peculiarly gifted with the intellectual skills and literary talent needed to understand and express those realities, those forms of oppression. But literature was viewed by the party largely as a

tool for expressing already existing party positions, not as an independent tool for sociopolitical exploration.[20]

In a letter to Wright in 1941 as both men were struggling to come to
terms with their relation to the party, Ellison wrote that "all Marx and
Engels, Lenin and Stalin won't help them unless they understand . . . the
theoretical world made flesh" through literature.[21] In general the Wright-
Ellison correspondence makes clear that Ellison in the forties still wanted
very much to be a leader of his people and that he believed the medium
of fiction could serve that political and moral purpose even as he was
developing his critique of what he called "ideological writing." He fash-
ioned himself and Wright as the "conscience" of "American Negroes,"
and *Invisible Man* both embodies and parodies this desire through its
riotous polyphony of voices, forms, and rhetorics that challenge the restricted languages of naturalism and its political equivalents.

As Michel Fabre and others have shown, the evolution of Ellison's political and literary ideas in the late forties and early fifties is very complex.[22] But I think it can be captured succinctly under the rubric of two
"anxieties." A certain "anxiety of influence" vis-à-vis Richard Wright is
intimately tied to what one might call an "anxiety of affluence" vis-à-vis
the white literary canon. For the break with naturalism is at once a protest against the political limitations of its conventions as he associates
them with the party, and part of Ellison's authorial need to distance himself further from his mentor Wright (to do so he engaged in the classic
act of misprision described by Harold Bloom, at times exaggerating the
extent and bleakness of Wright's naturalism and at other times under-
playing that naturalism by concentrating on Wright's more "literary" European ancestors in order to underline Ellison's own preferred genealogy).

At the same time, the turn away from naturalism seems to be part of
the text/author's attempt to enter the canon whose higher reaches at the
time of the novel's composition were largely reserved for the great modernists (to whom Ellison constantly refers in his nonfiction writing: Eliot,
Joyce, Hemingway, Faulkner, and the like). Indeed the emergence of New
Criticism during Ellison's formative period was further entrenching a
narrowly formalist version of the modernist canon. That Ellison's
double-edged strategies were well-targeted is borne out on the one hand
by the fact that he became the first African-American writer (slowly) "integrated" into the canon as writer rather than "black writer," and on the
other hand by a variety of left-wing attacks on *Invisible Man* for its lack

of naturalistic protest, attacks that in effect attempt to draw Ellison back into a literary ghetto.

Ellison perfectly understood that modernist literary critical values were being used to mark the difference between a great writer and a great Negro writer, or worse still the difference between literature and "mere" sociology. Harvey Webster, for example, wrote in the *Saturday Review of Literature:* "Mr. Ellison has achieved [a] difficult transcendence. *Invisible Man* is not a great Negro novel; it is a work of art that any contemporary writer could point to with pride."[23] In other words, as Lawrence Hogue has argued, the normative racist critical discourse could not conceive of a novel being at once "great art" and "Negro."[24] This is the context in which Ellison began claiming that he was a writer first and a "Negro" second. And this is still largely the context in which African-American writers struggle today against patronizing critics who continue to ghettoize their writing. (When is the last time you heard Norman Mailer described as "the important white novelist," or the last time you saw a review of Toni Morrison or Alice Walker that failed to mention their race?)

Such considerations also overdetermined the choice of the novel's ostensible form, autobiography, a form that since the first slave narrative (America's first, if not only, indigenous genre)[25] has been central to African-American literary expression. I say the "ostensible" form of autobiography because the text defamiliarizes the life narrative, a defamiliarization that begins with the title as it dematerializes its subject, and continues through subversive moments of surrealism, picaresque, and black humor that distance the text from the realism of autobiographic form.[26] By working a history of the "race" into invisible man's story, the text both evokes and parodies the "representative man/Negro" form of black autobiography, pointing to the constant underlying question: why must African-Americans continue to prove their humanity, their existence through autobiography? From Phyllis Wheatley to Frederick Douglass and Harriet Jacobs, to Booker T. Washington and W. E. B. Du Bois, to Wright and Ellison, a peculiar burden of self-justification has rested on black (auto)biographies, a burden related to attempts to deny the literariness of African-American writing, to lock it into sociological form.[27] Ellison thus at once uses and critiques the notion of the "representative life," and uses and critiques a genre that has never been given full literary status, that has been another way of disciplining black writing into putatively subliterary forms. African-Americans have had to prove themselves human before they could prove themselves literary, or prove themselves literary only to prove themselves human.

To counteract this continuing process of literary (re)ghettoization, in *Invisible Man* Ellison seems to have set himself the great task of having his novel make its way into the canon on aesthetic terms largely set by Euro-American writers and critics without sacrificing his political intent to combat American racism. His dilemma was to find a way to do this without making blacks "whiter," without eliminating the positive and negative differences between African-American and Euro-American experience. And his way out was instead to try to blacken the face of white America, or rather to reveal the black skin beneath the white mask on the face of much of what passed for (white) "American" culture.

But as I have suggested, this was a fraught solution; the danger of aestheticizing racism seems present on most every page of the novel. For if realism/naturalism had become a trap for black writers, a way of rendering them invisible as writers or subservient to Marxian or liberal dogma, the formalist modernism that was its alternative led to the traps of literary critical tokenism that *Invisible Man* could not avoid (i.e., winning his personal battle but losing the collective war), as well as to aestheticist temptations to smooth over the "jagged grain" of racism with cosmetically beautiful words. Much of the text's power derives from its attempt to move between these twin dangers of dogmatic content and dogmatic formalism. Thus the text exhibits a kind of "anxiety of affluence" with regard to its ambitions toward literary upward mobility, suggesting that on some level Ellison recognized that the inclusion of a novel written by a black man into the canon could function as but one more form of tokenism with the liberal message: see, a black writer can move into our literary neighborhood, we are not racists, Ralph Ellison is a friend of ours.

Indeed, the entire text of *Invisible Man* can be read as a series of anxious reflections on the power and limits of authorship in that the narrator's search for autonomy and authenticity is inextricably tied to his attempt to tell, to narrate his experience. The truth of the invisible character as passive victim is constantly set against the truth of the narrator as active teller and (re)shaper of the character's experience.[28] But contrary to some readings, I would argue that by the end of the story the reader should be asking if this latest incarnation, invisible man as narrator, is any more free, any less subject to the delusions of self-creation than has been the character who has again and again become trapped in

Interesting interpretation of novel's conclusion

someone else's design, plan, blueprint, or vision that he has mistaken as his own. What surely has changed by the end, however, is that the narrator has become aware of how deeply his story has been scarred and shaped by racism, how the particularities of American racism reinflect the more general philosophical and political problem of autonomy, of authorship of one's experience.

An anxiety of affluence manifests itself as well through a number of smaller allegories of authorship presented in the text. One example now can suggest what I mean; I will return to the theme in the next section. The complexities of black authorship in white America are explored through the scene in which a wraithlike young black girl rises from the college choir to sing a spiritual. The scene has been set carefully by Dr. Bledsoe for the white philanthropists to appreciate black musical piety. But the act of ventriloquism is imperfect because meanings other than those intended by Bledsoe are derived by other auditors, including the invisible man. The girl herself is transformed as the music takes her over until she has become an instrument, a "pipe of contained, controlled and sublimated anguish" (115). She is at once an instrument manipulated by Bledsoe and the white fathers, and the true vehicle of a black spiritual heritage larger than she. Her voice is at once a recorder of the history of black anguish at oppression, and an aesthetic sublimation of that anguish. And her authorship of the performance is doubly, dialectically questioned as the meaning of the text is split into the tradition that speaks through her and the audiences that variously interpret her.

Double vision is thus also the text's attempt to overcome, as well as express, the double-consciousness of being a "black" "American" writer. And the central irony of the text is surely that one of the most fully visible black characters in American fiction is an invisible man, that the palpable "presence" of a character is created through repeated efforts to show how he is not seen. This allows for the very emptiness of the character as a sign to be at once richly full of the legacy of black oppression and an open sign of future possibility, future "signifyin(g)" possibilities for African-Americans after the long hibernation is fully over. Like Malcolm's "X," invisible man's invisibility manages both to show the legacy of slavery and racism, and to point toward the possibility of new identities achievable in the future.[29]

But as narrators, neither Ellison nor invisible man are willing simply to wait upon that future. Instead they must at once show forth the full richness of black culture, in music, in folk tales, in language—all forms inextricably entwined with oppression, all scarred with the history of

Malcolm X

American racism—and do so in a way that transcends simplistic black/ white dichotomies. Double vision must constantly play between the universalizing element in literature (as Ellison's existential humanism conceived it) and the local, particular, historical conditions in which it is always rooted. In particular here it must avoid both creating blacks as wholly other (in an ironic, incomplete reversal of the racist othering they receive from whites), and the emptiness, empty mess of abstract humanism (as an escape from the realities of racism by imaginary projection of a universal "brotherhood" or a rationalizing universal tragic condition). Again and again invisible man tries to bring this vision into double focus, only to fall quickly back into a certain blurriness that is the other meaning of double vision. The visionary quality of *Invisible Man*, its attempt to live an aesthetic resolution of the "race problem," always also eventually falls back into the mess of blurred vision, into a history that has rendered "nonwhite" Americans invisible to the dominant race and often even to one another. Two kinds of formal protest, critique of the canon and critique of literary naturalism, unite around the question of the costs of canonicity as it stands for and stands in for the larger question of the place of African-Americans in the culture of the United States.

ELOQUENCE, AUDIENCE, AND RHETORICS OF LIBERATION

Thus far I have concentrated on showing how the formal, "literary" strategies in the novel are inextricably tied to larger social questions of black oppression and liberation. Now I would like to reverse focus and talk about how attempts to isolate specific black liberation strategies advocated in *Invisible Man* return us to questions about formal rhetorical strategies. As a number of critics have pointed out, the plot structure of *Invisible Man* recapitulates the history of the African-American struggle for survival and liberation. Moving from slavery (the Grandfather) to Reconstruction and accommodationism (the "Battle Royal" and invisible man's version of the Atlanta Exposition address) to the migration northward to industrialism (the factory sequence), and so on, each of these historical moments is linked to one or more liberation rhetorics and strategies. This allows the text to make history present as an array of discursive legacies that are also current and future strategic possibilities. The strategies the text interrogates and puts into dialogue include folk tricksterism (as embodied in the Grandfather, Trueblood, and Peter Wheatstraw); Booker T. Washington's accommodationism (as embodied in Bledsoe/Barbee); paternalistic philanthropic humanism (as embodied in Norton); a white-dominated Marxian humanism (as embodied in Jack and the Brotherhood); separatist black nationalism (as embodied in Ras the Exhorter/Destroyer); and a nihilist version of tricksterism (as embodied in Rinehart). Woven through and among these is another textual voice (the invisible narrator's? Ellison's?) that is torn between Cold War liberalism and a black radicalism symbolized by Frederick Douglass and W. E. B. Du Bois.

I want to look more concretely at some key scenes in which these various liberation strategies run up against historical and rhetorical limits, and at suggestions in the text of a double-visionary strategy to escape some of these double binds. The rhetorical strategies through which the novel enacts its double vision of liberation can be seen best by concentrating on scenes in which the text raises questions about audience and interpretation that double back on the reader to raise questions about how to interpret the novel itself. The issue of audience, of rhetorical reception, first raised in the "blackness of blackness" "sermon," can also be seen as continuing our discussion of the text's "anxiety of affluence." In the first chapter of the novel, for example, the young protagonist's attempt to achieve success in the white world on white terms in his speech before the audience of white city "fathers" both figures Ellison's relation to his white critical audience and problematizes more generally the question of political audiences.

In the set-up to this speech in the "battle royal" scene, invisible man observes that he is anxious for the white male audience to hear his speech because "only those men could judge truly my ability" (25). And in the speech itself, invisible man's eloquence seeks to rise above the inarticulate rough and tumble of his fellow "black boys," to whom he feels "superior," in order to please his white auditors/critics (18). But while he is playing Booker T. Washington, the great white fathers read him largely as a minstrel show, giving invisible man the first of several lessons in the precarious relation between speaker (author) and audience. Much of the rest of the text can be read as an attempt to escape a logic by which acceptance by his audience can only come on white terms, on terms that betray his own people (as represented by his Grandfather), if not his own being.

The scene also serves to set up a notion of complex layers of oppression that are worked through, if never fully worked out, in the remainder of the novel. The battle royal is a site of multiple oppressions in which those in power exercise that power both directly and by proxy. Just as invisible man has internalized white standards through which he tries to distinguish himself from his fellows, the resentment of the young black men is directed (with partial justification) against him even as they too are played as tools of the white fathers by brutally fighting one another. And the white stripteaser is at once oppressed herself, in terror of the predatory men, and oppressor, a tool used to excite unachievable desire in the young black men. She, with the flag tattooed on her stomach, is and is not America, is at once the American dream covered with the makeup that hides its true face (just as the glittering gold of the "coins" turns out to be worthless burnished brass), and a victim of that dream as it is built on the exploitation of women. Sexism and racism are linked here but not equated, since the former can be folded into a text that doubly oppresses black men and women. The "black boys" are made an audience to her performance, but unlike the white men they have no power over her, and they are in turn under the amused surveillance of those with the power to animate the object of desire; the white men vicariously use the sexuality of the young men to enhance and displace their own predatory virility. Both this concern with audience and this vicariously predatory sexuality are motifs repeated and developed in the following chapter (Trueblood's tale).

Always poised against this blurred vision induced by multiple oppressions is the possibility of telling the truth plainly. In the battle royal speech, for example, through a subconscious slip of the tongue, invisible man utters the words "social equality" in place of the more cautious "social responsibility." And it is ironically the mocking response of the white male audience of his smoker speech that elicits the taboo word "equality" from invisible man's political unconscious. Their taunting of his use of "big words" (later echoed by Brother Jack in his put-down of invisible man's independent political initiative) at once suggests the limits of black eloquence aimed toward a white racist audience and sets up an ironic pattern of invisible man learning from the in- or miscomprehensions of his audiences.

The Trueblood episode in chapter 2 ironically echoes and reverses the smoker scene. As a story within a story the episode momentarily displaces invisible man as narrator/orator and, in a kind of call-and-response answer to his speech in chapter 1, invisible man joins the great white father, Mr. Norton, as audience. Trueblood eloquently and craftily articulates the position of the inarticulate, which Ellison calls one of the prime, democratic functions of the novel (v–xx). But invisible man cannot yet hear this story on its own terms any more than the white audience at the smoker could hear him. Instead he identifies with, while misunderstanding, the shock of Norton, and later, the disgust of Bledsoe at the crudeness of untutored blacks. The scene seems designed to push to the limits the text's attack on the kind of false gentility embodied in Norton and Bledsoe as proxies for all those critics who would have black writers write only about either purely uplifting characters or purely victimized ones. Trueblood's incest and subsequent blues-borne acceptance of the act confounds both these positions.

Invisible man is blind to the fact that Trueblood's story shocks Norton not with its crudeness but because it calls up the latter's own guilty complicity in incestuous desire. Norton's creation of a "destiny" for himself through aid to the Negro is tied ineluctably to a suppressed incestuous desire for his daughter in whose name he carries out his philanthropy. His desires, like Trueblood's, are incestuously in-turning, a re-creation of himself in the form of "the Negro," a denial of his complicity in the maintenance of racism analogous to his denial of his incestuous desires. But unlike Trueblood, he cannot face this truth about himself as the grounds for a new position. Norton's daughter's paleness and ethereal quality suggest a kind of inbreeding that allegorizes a white America whose search for purity robs it of substance. PURITY—UNATTAINABLE.

But if Trueblood is more honest and less culpable than Norton in his incest, some critics have been too quick to celebrate Trueblood, ignoring an ironic reading of his name and the fact that it is precisely the whites who celebrate and reward him for his incest; if Trueblood is an assertion of true black manhood against racist castration, one stereotype is merely replaced with another—the superstudly, incestuous "natural man."[30] If invisible man is wrong to condemn Trueblood for bringing down the race, ignoring the material conditions that contributed to his actions, there are limits as well to celebrating him as the true blood. Trueblood is lured into his sin through a dream that reverses the stereotype of black male lust for "the" white woman; he dreams of a voracious white woman who virtually rapes him. This image prefigures invisible man's own interracial sexual encounters later in the novel and echoes the battle royal scene, both scenes showing sexuality as a projected trap for black males, a distraction from and contributor to politicoeconomic oppression. Trueblood's blues reconciliation (he sings his way to acceptance of himself despite his incest) makes him more honest than Norton, but the fact that it only serves to reconcile him to incest casts a shadow over the reconciliation and makes clear that it can hardly be a model for social action. As a metaphor for the political, economic, and sexual double binds imposed on black America, its image of self-acceptance is a simple survival technique. But it is at best a holding action. Trueblood does indeed move without really moving. Stripped of its no longer amusing comic elements, the episode becomes a tragic in-turning of aggression, an assertion of a denied manhood that denies independent womanhood to Trueblood's daughter and wife.

Trueblood's blues solution is, as it were, an aesthetic solution that leaves realities unchanged. Indeed the use of a blues song to reconcile a character to incest suggests that the truth of the blues itself can lead to a kind of pseudo-truebloodedness that is incestuously abusive, rather than the kind of "jagged grain" that keeps political struggle alive. If the priggishness of invisible man and the hypocrisy of Norton push the reader toward sympathy with Trueblood, his folk solution to his dilemma is also only a partial solution in the wider rhetorical context since it suggests a separate, black aesthetic resolution that is undermined by other elements in the scene. Trueblood is drawn as the anti-Remus, the black storyteller as trickster who undermines the minstrel show expectations of his auditors in a way that invisible man could not in his first speech. But by letting us see that in telling his story quite cannily with a white and would-be white audience clearly in mind, the narrator behind the narrator undermines any notion of pure folkness in Trueblood or his story, suggesting instead the ineluctable interrelation of black and white American narratives. Trueblood's blues solution to his double bind displaces but does not eliminate the problem; it attempts a purely aesthetic solution to a social problem. It is also made possible only by a silencing of black women; we do not hear the blues songs composed by Trueblood's wife or daughter.

Indications of Trueblood's wariness and canniness and his masterfulness as a storyteller set him up as another ironic embodiment of black authorship, one that ties craftfulness (much vaunted by Ellison) with craftiness (much needed in a black storyteller in racist America). It is clear that Trueblood has been and is in this version shaping his story to meet expectations and rewards of a white audience, a fact that should put the reader on guard as to the veracity of the larger story (invisible man's and *Invisible Man*'s) in which his story is embedded. It suggests that a black storyteller can never tell a story in unguarded fashion to a white or mixed audience, and it suggests that just as the appearance of total honesty of Trueblood's account fools his immediate audience, a similar joke may be being played on the other, wider, whiter audience, too. Indeed the whole level of black folk culture in the text becomes, as a subtext more available to most black readers than whites, an analogue of the folkloric style of "puttin' on the white man."[31]

If Trueblood is seen allegorically as a stand-in for Ellison, his dilemma becomes clearer. Like Trueblood, Ellison as storyteller is in a double bind; in portraying a character like Trueblood he risks all manner of (white) misreadings, all manner of minstrel interpretations. In constantly working on the edge of stereotype in his satiric characterizations, Ellison must have feared just such responses; in trying to use laughter to shatter the minstrel mask from within, he is in danger instead of confirming that mask.[32] Indeed, Ellison's own anxiety about this problem was still palpable thirty years after the publication of his novel when in the introduction to the thirtieth anniversary edition of *Invisible Man* he wrote: "I would have to approach racial stereotypes as a given fact or social process and proceed, while gambling with the reader's capacity for fictional truth, to reveal the human complexity which stereotypes are intended to conceal" (xvii). This dilemma is thematized later in the novel through the minstrel bank and the Sambo doll, which continue to haunt invisible man despite his attempts to be rid of them. More generally, in pursuing through his intensely lyrical modernism and surrealism so resolutely an aesthetic solution to one "Negro problem" (the problem of Negro authorship), Ellison, like Trueblood, is in danger of fashioning an aesthetic resolution that leaves power relations unchanged. An ironic mirror of Trueblood, Ellison's refinement might be rewarded, as is Trueblood's folksy authenticity, through a mode that reinforces existing oppression. From opposite ends, Ellison and Trueblood participate in a no-win game in which the cost of elite acceptance is alienation from the folk, and the cost of folksiness is condescension.

Invisible man's next lesson in the ambiguities of authorship, leadership, and black power in a white world comes from Trueblood's apparent opposite and nemesis, Dr. Bledsoe. The character of Bledsoe, particularly in relation to his mouthpiece, the blind preacher Homer Barbee, reveals a good deal about the complexity of the position of the Civil Rights leader as it would emerge in the years immediately following publication of *Invisible Man*. Bledsoe embodies the degeneration of second generation black leadership, one that claims to be heir to the (ambiguous) legacy of a Booker T. Washington-esque "founder." For Bledsoe, black power has become nothing more than power over blacks and the subtle joys of walking among and manipulating whites. To maintain this power he needs and enlists the rhetorical powers of one who (probably) sincerely believes in that which Bledsoe cynically manipulates.

Homer Barbee is blind to the outdatedness of his message and to his manipulation by Bledsoe. But even after knowing of Bledsoe's treacherous personal philosophy and will-to-power, invisible man is moved by Barbee, not simply because he is naive but also because there is a partial truth in the founding tale he retells (a "barbarian" Homer, his telling of the black odyssey has dignity and can help decenter the story of Western "civilization" putatively begun by his ancient namesake). That truth is embodied not only in the bombastic bard's metaphors run amuck (as Keith Byerman shows, Barbee's speech deconstructs itself, becoming a vehicle of truth even as it manipulates),[33] but also in the eloquent silence of one of his auditors, Miss Susie Gresham, the "gray-haired matron in the final row . . . who'll never be fooled by the mere content of words" (111–12). She hears beneath the flowery phrases of Preacher Barbee the cadences of truth, of possibility beyond the "blaring triumphant sounds empty of triumphs" (111). Susie Gresham, stereotyped mother figure of the race and like most of Ellison's female characters without much voice of her own, yet embodies not only the past but the future of black womanhood and stands for "Jane Pittman," Rosa Parks, Ella Baker, Fannie Lou Hamer, for women who hear beneath the eloquence of kings a deeper, more grounded task, a radically democratic reshaping of the political landscape. Miss Gresham hears the eloquence but unlike Barbee she also sees clearly. Because she truly sees the promised land, she listens for the true music beneath the transient, self-serving sounds and images poured forth by preachers enamored of their own eloquence. Not yet allowed her own words, she nonetheless is the bearer of a tradition of profound resistance; "in that island of shame" she makes certain that invisible man is "not ashamed," offering a legacy signed by the music of her being and sealed without words.

In the next generation, Miss Gresham's eloquent silence will become the voice of Anne Moody who as a young Civil Rights worker (for the Student Nonviolent Coordinating Committee) recognizes that however beautiful it may be to dream, to dream you must be asleep: "By the time we got to Lincoln Memorial, there were already thousands of people there. I sat on the grass and listened to the speakers, to discover that we had 'dreamers' instead of leaders leading us. Just about every one of them stood up there dreaming. Martin Luther King went on and on talking about his dream. I sat there thinking that in Canton we never had time to sleep, much less dream."[34] The same eloquence that allowed King to help mobilize so many served simultaneously as a soporific that put to sleep resources of self-empowerment in many African-Americans. Like

Barbee, King's sincere belief in his (American) dream is unimpeachable; but, to reverse the text's metaphor, his very ability to see (for others) from the mountaintop inadvertently could keep them blind, or at least keep them from seeing for themselves, thus leaving them visionless when he was brutally swept from the scene. And the Bledsoes and Nortons who came after continue to use both King's words and the words of black power countervoices to rise to positions of power over blacks.

Invisible Man's interrogation of black liberation rhetorics is also embodied in a conflict between the written and the spoken word. The narrator implies in the prologue that he was a failed orator who turns now to written storytelling while keeping alive the possibility that he may once again be an orator (14). I want to suggest that one line of development in the novel is that of the invisible narrator learning to bring his speaking rhetoric closer to the rhetoric of his writing, closer to the sensual, dialogical languages that resonate as context to his more monological speeches. In turn, the text's texture can be seen as striving to imitate the richness and multivocality of a jazz ensemble.[35] This begins to become clearer in the next of invisible man's oratorical performances, his speech at the eviction of the old black couple.

Invisible man's speech at the eviction can best be seen as a kind of jazz performance (and he clearly thinks of it as a performance, evaluating and reevaluating its effects almost independent of intention). Like all but his first speech, this one is improvised, and like much jazz improvisation this one takes off from a cliché (like a clichéd melody or musical phrase in jazz). Invisible man first tries out his humility riff, but so far is the idea of a "peaceful and law-abiding slow to anger people" from the truth of his audience that he is forced to ironize the phrase, to turn it around like a jazz trumpeter toying with a musical phrase until it has turned from sweet to harsh. The audience leads the way through their sarcastic response, until he must pretend and then, becoming caught up in the pretense, seems to cease to know himself if he is or was sincere. His speech has the opposite of its original intent by stirring or helping to stir the crowd to action. Here invisible man as character begins to learn the lesson of the ambiguities of rhetorical reception that *Invisible Man* as text has embodied in earlier scenes. And, as in the battle royal speech, something closer to the truth is drawn out of him inadvertently by the audience.

When a representative of the Brotherhood also misconstrues the intent of the speech and recruits him into the group, invisible man is led into his next key speaking assignment. His Brotherhood speech suggests the

complexities of rhetorical recyclings by improvising on the Southern populism of invisible man's youth flavored with the abstract radical humanism he has learned from the "Brothers." Here again a call-and-response
pattern with the audience leads him on, shapes his discourse. "May I confess?" he shouts in a Baptist style that upsets the Brothers behind him but
elicits, "You're batting .500, Brother," from the audience. These moments of contact with the audience, of concrete metaphorical connection,
open up rhetorical possibilities that soon drown in the sea of abstractions
derived from his mentors until he confesses only emptily that he feels
"more human." The context of staring out into the bright lights even
while calling for his audience to join him in taking "back our pillaged
eyes" reflects back to the blind Barbee unwittingly singing someone else's
song, working someone else's intent. And even his abstract confession is
too much for the Brotherhood theoreticians behind him who seem to find
it politically incorrect, "unscientific," in its emotionalism.

While modeled on elements in the Communist party, the Brotherhood
(a hood over the brothers) here stands for all monological, sectarian rhetorics that mistake their blueprints for the world (mocked with foreshad-
owing by the jive-talking Peter Wheatstraw who sells old blueprints or
uses them for the more concrete task of starting fires to keep him warm
on the streets of New York; the blueprint scene is also a coded swipe at
Richard Wright's "A Blueprint for Negro Writing"). Ellison has said that
the Brotherhood cannot simply be equated with the Communist party,
and recent work by Mark Naison makes clear that relations between
Harlem blacks and the Communist party were far more complex and
more positive than the Brotherhood's relation to the residents of Harlem.[36] Rather I think the portrait of the Brotherhood should stand as a
critique of the monovision (as embodied in the one-eyed Jack, antitrick-
ster) and sometimes blindness of all abstract humanist languages, a critique that should be turned ironically back on the abstract (liberal) humanism in much of Ellison's own critical writing.

In this case, the seductive language of "scientific" logic in the Brotherhood ensnares both audience and party leaders alike, but the latter at
least have the illusion that they are leading others while the followers are
taught, as invisible man soon learns, simply to be obedient. Caught in
the web of their own historical dialectics, the leaders dismiss huge chunks
of life, entire forms of being, that don't fit their blueprint. And they can
do so easily because they are not required, in the words of Ellison to
Wright, to make "the theoretical world flesh."[37] First the old couple at the
eviction are dismissed as "outside of history"; soon the whole black

"race" is pushed either outside or (once again) to the margins of the vision.

The problem with the Brotherhood's vision is not that it theorizes a world; all discourses, however putatively concrete, including novelistic ones, do that. Rather the problem is that their vision is so seamlessly totalizing that it allows no room for the emergence of dissonant information that might lead to a practical or tactical shift in the theory. The role of fleshy, messy concreteness is to generate anomalies that require adjustment of the paradigm, or to force recognition that only multiple visions or theories or paradigms can encompass the complex realities of the historical situation. Moreover, the compensatory power of the Brotherhood's grand vision as embedded in its scientific analysis of history gets in the way of the search for real political power by disempowering all those folks who alone could provide the sources for change. At the same time, the hierarchical structure of the group encourages an internalizing of the power struggle within the organization itself. Only slowly does invisible man come to see that it is in the lived forms of daily life in Harlem that the power to survive, and with it the power to change, must lie.

But before invisible man comes to his realization of the need to actually interact and interthink with those whom one would seek to change, he has encounters with two more representative figures, two more dissonant voices within his community: the black nationalist voice of Ras the Exhorter / Destroyer, and the nihilistic multivocality of Rinehart the confidence man.

The portrait of Ras is in many respects the most impressive testimony to the dialogical, polyphonic quality of *Invisible Man* because while it is clear that neither Ellison nor invisible man cares for black separatism, Ras is given some of the most eloquent speeches in the novel. True, portrayed as a combination of Don Quixote, mad African prince, and Ahab (pursuing blackness as resolutely as the captain pursued whiteness), Ras is a comic figure (and invisible man gets the last "word" in the form of a spear, through Ras's cheeks linking Ahab's harpoon to an African spear). But everyone in the novel is a comic figure at one time or another, and the very fact that only an act of violence, as opposed to eloquence, can quell that voice, is evidence of its (black) power.

One of the most moving scenes occurs during the fight between Ras, Clifton, and invisible man. Ras's "black and beautiful" speech catches even invisible man with its eloquence, and in the process Ras correctly predicts the Brotherhood's selling out of the brothers (and sisters) of Harlem (360–68). Yet another example of displaced power struggle, of a bat-

tle royal again aimed at the wrong target, the verbal and physical struggle
sets the ground for Tod Clifton to emerge as an embodied synthesis of
liberation voices, only to have that synthesis destroyed by disillusion, anger, and white police violence. Like the Black Panthers after him, Clifton
commits revolutionary suicide because he is fed up with political trope-
sters who rhyme trigger and nigger.

Once again invisible man is shown not to be the author of his experience. Tod Clifton shows invisible man that he has been manipulated
like a Sambo by the rhetorical moves of the Brothers. Invisible man then
turns instead to the other brothers and sisters, those in whose name he
has presumed to lead but whose names he does not even know. His final
speech is very different in form and content from those that have come
before. It is a kind of abdication speech that is actually the taking on of
deepened commitment. It is concrete, sensual speech, and it turns its
questions to the audience not "rhetorically" but with true dialectic, true
desire to hear answers he no longer has.

Once again his audience reshapes his intent: "'All right, all right,' I
called out, feeling desperate. It wasn't political. Brother Jack probably
wouldn't approve of it at all, but I had to keep going" (446). Again and
again he can only relate the concrete details of Clifton's death, the shot,
the fall, the blood running from his shattered body. Instead of rousing
them with tales of meaningful martyrdom, he tells the audience that Clifton foolishly believed in Brotherhood and died "like a dog" at the hands
of "a cop [who] had an itching finger and an ear for a word that rhymed
with 'trigger.'" "I do not know," he continues, "if all cops are poets, but
I know that all cops carry guns with triggers. And I know too how we
are labeled. So in the name of Brother Clifton beware of the triggers; go
home, keep cool, stay safe away from the sun. Forget him. When he was
alive he was our hope, but why worry over a hope that is dead?" (446–
48). Once again the twists of his irony are such that he seems not sure
himself what he is really telling the crowd. Does he really want them to
"keep cool," or is he trying to shame them into action?

After delivering his last public speech over Clifton's body and routing
Ras (race) the Destroyer, invisible man is presented with his last temp-
tation—Rinehart, the preacher, pimp, lover, hipster, nihilist trickster. Invisible man is driven from Ras's pure black African identity to the iden-
titylessness of Rine the runner. He is momentarily charmed and attracted
by the deconstructive shiftiness of this confidence man. But ultimately he
turns his back on this play of pure form, this slippery signifier, seeing
Rine's position as at best an image of tactical flexibility but not a role

worth emulating in itself: "Then I looked at the polished lenses of [Rinehart's dark] glasses and laughed. I had been trying simply to turn them into a disguise but they had become a political instrument instead" (488). Rinehart suggests the element of political tricksterism he'll need to further his liberation cause, but it will be a tricksterism rooted in the needs of his "audience," one that is more rooted in and respectful of their lives, one dedicated to lessening rather than deepening their dupedom and exploitation.)

Invisible man's attempt to try out this brand of tricksterism, his attempt to dupe the Brotherhood dupesters suggests, however, that the trickster mode cannot be easily or unambiguously deployed. The question of who is tricking whom emerges in the final chapter in the form of invisible man's attempt to fathom the meaning of the riot that erupts in Harlem. He is tortured by his possible role in bringing it about. Has he been duped again by the Brothers into fomenting the riot to give the Brotherhood more martyrs while illustrating the wisdom of their scientific logic that rebellion is premature? Is this battle royal in no significant way different from the first? But he overhears other theories, especially that it was started by Ras, that Ahab was impaled on his own spear. Or is the riot a collective improvisation; who can say, once set in motion, whether the intent of those who began (or think they began) it is relevant. It takes on its own life, its own forms.

These are questions of interpretation that reflect as well on the form(s) of *Invisible Man* itself. In being put in the position of being an interpreter of the riot and of his own role in it, invisible man embodies the ultimate position of the novel's reader: what will we make finally of the riot of form that is *Invisible Man*?

TRICKSTERS, TRAPPERS, AND TROPESTERS

Ellison's invisible man had to remain underground
despite the fact that he possessed the intelligence and
awareness to envision a new discursive formation,
because extratextual discursive formations had not
been produced.
　　　　　　　　　　　　　　　　　—W. *Lawrence Hogue,*
　　　　　　　　　　　　　　　　　Discourse and the Other

Contrary to claims that the novel abdicates political and "social responsibility" through the literal/literary hibernation in which its narrator seems ensconced at the end, *Invisible Man* can be read as offering an important, nuanced radical democratic political analysis. The text shows that there is no rhetorical strategy, no cultural symbol, no political figure or figured politics that cannot abuse or be abused. There is no strategy that can guarantee "eloquence," that formal connection between idea and audience, no form that cannot be misheard or misread. There is no trope that cannot become a trap. Dangers lie at all points in the process, from the speaker-authors who can be and to some extent must be self-deceived, to the text of *Invisible Man* itself which flows from and into a river of language far too vast to be charted, to the receiving audience which often hears only what it wants to hear and seldom stretches to catch the new music or to see the less visible forms beneath the visible surfaces.

Against the struggle of each liberation voice to achieve dominance, the text searches for a kind of political trickster voice, embodied in the varied texture and self-subverting turns of the narrative itself, a voice that shows the necessity of recognizing the provisionality of all liberation discourses, their corruptibility and their divisiveness, even as it acknowledges their respective value as partial truths. This trickster voice enacts a fusion and points to the already fused nature of African-American and Euro-American sources, including black and white literary modernisms (though Ellison initially, for strategic reasons I discussed above, tended to downplay his debt to African-American literary roots) and a variety of ostensibly folk forms including the blues, jazz, the dozens, tall tales, jive talk, zoot suits, spirituals, and preaching.

Invisible Man suggests that "popular" forms of African-American culture have far greater polyphony and flexibility than do the systematic ideologies and rhetorics of black liberation, or than does the self-limiting form of the autobiography (long the major form of African-American self-expression). But neither these folk forms nor literary modernism are uncritically celebrated; the text shows that both modes are in their own differing ways inscribed with the scars of racism and complicity with racism. The text suggests that any liberation movement worth its name will need to address more complexly the range of positioned voices from which black oppression can be resisted, will need to show that these disparate voices are in fact discursive forms implicated in one another, and will need to respect the variety and diversity of these voices. Something like a fusion of folk wisdom, rhetorical self-consciousness, and political analysis will be required to bring such an array of voices together in concerted, irreducibly multiform movement.

The text celebrates the forms of American blackness and the blackness of American forms, but these forms are not presented as pure but rather as hybrids (like jazz with its African syncopations of European martial music) whose purity is better guarded by recognizing their impurity, their cultural constructedness amidst a struggle to overcome white racism.[38]

From this strategic perspective purity is the danger, for claims to purity always open themselves to corruption: indeed the purer one claims one's rhetoric or symbol to be the more in danger it is of being corrupt(ed). The pure blackness of black nationalism, whether political or cultural, led and leads only to greater insularity until only the blackest one of all forms a party of one (two counting the police agent). And a purely assimilationist strategy likewise denies complexity, whitewashes the legacy of racism and resistance. Rhetorics can be defended best when their capacity to be abused is clearly known. There can be no stopping, resting in the pursuit of a rhetoric of liberation because that rhetoric is always becoming available to enemies of liberation. Every vision must be double, must be, for example, both integrationist and nationalist. And every clear double vision will fall into blurred vision before long.

For every faked symbol like the smooth, unbroken link of slave chain abused by the too smooth Bledsoe, there is one like Brother Tarp's—less pure, a broken link, a mere prison chain not an authentic slave relic, it nevertheless more aptly caught the truth about the struggle against bondage. Tarp's open link is ready for the next political articulation, is open to the new political context. The other material symbols of historical and continuing racism, the gape-mouthed bank and the Sambo doll, like Bledsoe and Tarp's links of chain, can also be misread. For a nihilist trickster like Rinehart there are only various kinds of useful misdirections of his "readers." But for the politically savvy trickster these symbols are also reminders that words too are material signifiers with real referents in history. Neither invisible man nor the reader can afford to leave that signifyin(g) chain behind. Its weighty thereness keeps the past palpably present. If we free ourselves by opening up the chain of signifiers, it is only by feeling the link to networks of resistance and exploitation held in place by, among other things, material chains of language. *Invisible Man* makes clear that real metaphors connect the streets to the pulpit to literature and its criticism. Only by following such metaphorical links back to their sources will liberation be possible and literature be more than another veil. After all, in the next generation a zoot-suit riot and "the word" transform the Rinehart-like "Detroit Red" into Malcolm X, just as Miss Susie Gresham finds her words in Miss Ella Baker; together these active keepers of the faith signify the collective power of black women and men that will one day tear off the veils of racism.

Disrupting the Theater of War

Armies of the Night
and the New Left Siege of the Pentagon

In this and the following chapter I want to develop notions of theatricality implicit in my analyses in earlier chapters. I have argued that both *Let Us Now Praise Famous Men* and *Invisible Man* are texts that ask their readers to "perform" them. In that sense, my play with theatrical metaphors in the next two chapters is merely extending my emphasis on act in the act of reading. Novels (and novelistic discourses), because they are frequently addressed to the isolated individual reader and because they have contributed to the creation of the bourgeois individual, have been viewed by many as poor media for portraying or encouraging the kind of collective action so central to social movements.[1] However, the notion of texts as dialogical performances has begun to move us out into the putatively more public and collective realm of theater. Now I want to push us further into this dramatic metaphor by examining a "nonfiction novel" that interacts with a political event such that the two merge into a theater of ideas and acts that can be made to reveal the always already historically embedded nature of novel readers and novelistic discourses, while at the same time pointing out the novelistic nature of historiography.

DOUBLED JEOPARDY

In 1967 the American antiwar movement laid "siege" to the Pentagon in one of the more celebrated confrontations between the New Left and the

powers that were prosecuting the war in Vietnam. The Pentagon march
and siege are well-remembered in large part because of their treatment
by one of America's more (in)famous authors, Norman Mailer, who
made them the center of his "nonfiction novel," *The Armies of the Night:
History as a Novel, The Novel as History.* The events of "Pentagon week-
end" in October 1967 were a watershed in our political history, and I
argue here that the novel history of those events is part of a still little-
understood shift in our epistemological-political landscape.[2] Specifically,
the text marks a moment of political crisis for the left that is inextricably
tied to the aesthetic, cultural, and epistemological crisis marked by the
term "postmodernism."

Mailer's text has been read either as a more or less realistic, journalistic account of the march/siege, or as a kind of postmodernist, anti-
interpretive "novelization" of the real. But the text can more fruitfully be
seen as resisting both readings, can be read through the lens of "postmodernist realism" as a challenge to the complacencies of traditional literary and historiographic realism that offers literary-political action as
an alternative to the hermetic textualism of much recent critical theory.

The realist pole of readings of *Armies* (as I will henceforth refer to the
book) is epitomized by a *Time* magazine review of the text that criticizes
it for its lack of journalistic objectivity. At the other extreme the text has
been seen as thoroughly "irrealist," "absurdist," and "postmodernist" in
readings such as that of critic Mas'ud Zavarzadeh. One key to these varying interpretations has been the way in which critics treat the fact that
even the autobiographical first part of the text is written in the third person, and that throughout the text there is a "narrator" and a "character"
both of whom are in some sense "Norman Mailer."

Realist critics generally view the text as a straightforward representation of the march on the Pentagon, as some species of contemporary
history or journalism that uses literary devices to vivify its account but
that can nevertheless be read as one would read any journalistic or historical account, that is primarily by checking it against the reality it presumably reflects. In this kind of reading there tends to be a collapsing of
the narrator Norman Mailer and the character Norman Mailer whose
personal ideas, opinions, and beliefs about the march are supported and/
or contested by the critic. The realists like to isolate various of the character Mailer's ideas or beliefs that they see as reflective of the real-life
views of the author. This often leads them to note that these ideas are
contradictory, at best, if not downright mad and dangerous (although,

as the "narrator" notes, "Mailer's" dangerousness and potential for dem-
agoguery is somewhat mitigated by the fact that it never seems to fail
that for every idea he puts forth that elicits assent from a crowd he seems
immediately to put forth another that enrages them).[3] In these realist
readings then, the ideas of the character "Mailer" are privileged, are
taken to be definitive of the text.

At the other end of the critical literature *Armies* is taken more seriously as fiction, as a novel. These critics read the text through such notions as character, point of view, style, plot, and so on. Among these readings the most interesting for my purposes is that of Mas'ud Zavarzadeh
in his *The Mythopoeic Reality: The Postwar American Non-fiction
Novel.*[4] Zavarzadeh's approach is the most thoroughgoing challenge to
the realists. He characterizes Mailer's text as "post-modernist," "anti-
interpretive," and "non-totalizing," in other words, as a total rejection
of realist assumptions. He notes the "surface interpretations" offered by
"Mailer" and the other characters and "actants," but argues that these
interpretations are superseded "verbally or actionally" by a "meta-
interpretive" level. The result is thus an "absurdist" text in which all
interpretations of the events represented in the text are negated. This
meta-interpretive level is that which I have identified with the "narrator,"
and from my perspective Zavarzadeh has merely inverted a monological
reading by privileging the narrator's voice over that of the "character,"
by once again resolving them into one. Indeed, the irony of Zavarzadeh's
postmodernist reading is that it becomes a realist, reflection theory vis-
à-vis a really absurd postmodern reality.

These differing critical stances entail differing political and epistemological stances as well. *Armies* is structured through/as a double interpretive framework in which Mailer as participant-interpreter in/of the
events of the march (in which he played a minor part) is portrayed in the
third person by a narrator-interpreter who further mediates the reality
represented (*The Education of Henry Adams* is perhaps the most important precedent Mailer draws on for the narrational form of *Armies*).
Like the realist critics, I too will at various times take "Mailer" to task
for his views, but I think the text allows us also to see through and past
those views, because the doubling of narrator-character distances even
Mailer from some of them.

The two "books" of the text treat the relationship between these two
Mailers somewhat differently, and are formally distinct in other ways as
well. The longer of the two parts, Book 1, "History as a Novel: The Steps

of the Pentagon," resembles a novel, and is written in the third person about a "character" named "Norman Mailer." This section also relies fairly heavily on such novelistic devices as imagined dialogue, literary allusion, elaborate conceit, and so on. Book 2, "The Novel as History: The Battle of the Pentagon," resembles contemporary mainstream historiography or journalism by attempting to step back and view the events related in Book 1 from a panoramic, "objective" viewpoint rather than that of individual, embodied consciousness.

In my reading, this twofold structure, along with other mediating devices, throws into question the authority of the author/text, and thereby grants a certain degree of autonomy to the demonstration as a drama that itself enacts and embodies certain representational problematics. In other words, *Armies* is constructed in such a way that the problem of reading the text and the problem of reading the event illuminate each other. My attempt to analyze these hermeneutical questions will be interwoven, as they are in Mailer's text, with an attempt to point out some of the theoretical, rhetorical, and strategic questions facing the New Left (and its successors) that this particular event/text brings to the fore.[5]

Real metaphoric relationships between political strategies and certain "literary" strategies structure the text/event that is the Pentagon demonstration / *Armies*. The text can illuminate the extent to which and the ways in which questions about interpretation and representation are not external to but are rather crucial to an understanding of the political actions of oppositional movements in recent times. One key task faced by a dissenting political movement like the New Left is that of influencing the conditions of interpretation or reception of its activities. This is perhaps most obvious in the case of a movement's relation to the mass media. The media, through the ideological constraints of reporting/editing practices and formal limits structured into electronic media, habitually shape American political culture in ways detrimental to nonmainstream political activity. In turn, the political movement obviously needs to create conditions of interpretation and forms of representation that foster a dialogue in which its viewpoints are taken seriously. In this light the Pentagon march itself is a representational form, one with its own internal structures of mediation. Subsequently those forms are subjected to mass-mediated representation. Mailer's text is, among other things, a strategic attempt to outflank mass media accounts of the march by claiming a more comprehensive and more profound reading of the event. And my account will, of course, in turn attempt in certain ways to outflank previous readings of the text (*Armies* / the Pentagon demonstration).

HERMENEUTICAL SURROUNDINGS:
THE TEXT AS EVENT

In the same way that a text is detached from its author,
an action is detached from its agent and develops
consequences of its own.

—Paul Ricoeur

He had succeeded in fashioning therefore an action
which was at once penned and open-ended.

—Norman Mailer

The central purpose of the march on the Pentagon in 1967 was to protest
and call for an end to U.S. involvement in the Vietnam War. But this particular protest had a more grand objective as well, at least for many of
the participants. The march was an attempt to assert democratic control
over the course of America's political life through a collective reinterpretation of the meaning of the building said to embody the nation's "defense." For some this also meant a collective symbolic reclamation of the
defense building itself through what became known as the "siege of the
Pentagon." The plan was for the demonstrators to surround the building
while some sought to enter it, in order, as Mailer put it, to "wound the
Pentagon symbolically," to show it vulnerable to the "people" in whose
name it was carrying out its policies.

The event was described in New Left organizing literature as the
chance to "meet the warmakers face-to-face." But the precise reasons or
likely results of such an encounter were left vague. The march was
planned (by the National Mobilization Committee to End the War in
Vietnam, or MOBE) to allow a variety of antiwar positions to be expressed and enacted by a broad coalition of liberal, left-liberal, pacifist,
Old Left, and New Left groups. Each group and individual within the
group would presumably face the warmakers in their own fashion. Thus
the Pentagon march presented itself to the demonstrators and the wider
audience that heard of it partly as a hermeneutic problem: What is to be
the meaning of this event? The answer cannot be given fully in advance
but is precisely dependent on the acts, including the interpretive acts, of
the participants and observers. And the originality of this particular
demonstration was that it was designed to provide more than one degree
of participation/observation.

One of the main MOBE coordinators for the Pentagon march, Dave
Dellinger, explains it this way:

> At the Pentagon there [will be] first the traditional law-abiding march and rally, with their inspiring message of diversity and strength. These [will be] followed by more forceful methods of mobile action and civil defiance, with their message that the strength must not only be made visible but deployed and activated. In such an arrangement, those who are not ready to commit civil disobedience have an important role to play. They are not kept home by a monolithic program of direct action. Before the day is over, they will observe and evaluate the direct action on the scene rather than have it filtered to them through the daily press (which is apt to caricature and discredit it) or through movement accounts (which are apt to glamorize and romanticize it). Their presence as outside, semirespectable observers can be crucial to restraining the police; their proximity as sympathizers and potential recruits for the next action can also have a salutary effect on the protesters, giving them some of the courage that comes from feeling themselves part of a larger, broader movement but also restraining those who might be tempted [to violence].[6]

Thus the Pentagon demonstration is to include, like Mailer's text, a double hermeneutic—a group of activists who attempt through a form of real political theater to engage the warmakers in dialogue and/or (symbolic?) battle, and a larger group of participant-interpreters who surround the more militant of the protesters in a way that positions them to interpret the events for themselves (and for others they may converse with subsequently), while also allowing them to be drawn further into the dialogue and struggle if they so choose. The underlying assumption here, a fundamental one of the New Left, is that people are changed primarily by action, not by the passive consumption of information or of action consumed in the form of packaged "spectacles."[7] Mailer has a good deal to say directly about these questions, about the "aesthetic" of the march, as he calls it, some of which I deal with below. But my concern now is to suggest some ways in which the form or style of Mailer's text itself becomes part of the strategic action of the march. At one point in *Armies*, Mailer writes that "the clue to discovery was not in the substance of one's ideas, but in what was learned from the style of one's attack" (37). I'll have cause later to point out some of the dangers of this position, but for now I want to explore, with this authorization from the text itself, what can be learned from the style of its attack on the Pentagon.

The beginning of the second of *Armies*' two "books" provides an explicit commentary on the method or strategy of the text. In a section entitled "A Novel Metaphor," Mailer writes:

> The Novelist in passing his baton to the Historian has a happy smile. He has been faster than you think. As a working craftsman, a journeyman artist, he

is not without guile; he has come to decide that if you would see the horizon from a forest, you must build a tower. If the horizon will reveal most of what is significant, an hour of examination can yet do the job—it is the tower which takes months to build. So the Novelist working in secret collaboration with the Historian has perhaps tried to build with his novel a tower fully equipped with telescopes to study—at the greatest advantage—our own horizon. Of course, the tower is crooked, and the telescopes warped, but the instruments of all sciences—history so much as physics—are always constructed in small or large error; what supports the use of them now is that our intimacy with the master builder of the tower, and the lens grinder of the telescopes (yes, even the machinist of the barrels) has given some advantage for correcting the error of the instruments and the imbalance of his tower. May that be claimed for many histories? . . . The method is then exposed. The mass media which surrounded the march on the Pentagon created a forest of inaccuracy which would blind the efforts of an historian; our novel has provided us with the possibility, no, even the instrument to view our facts and conceivably study them in that field of light a labor of lens-grinding has produced. Let us prepare then (the metaphors soon to be mixed—for the Novelist is slowing to a jog, and the Historian is all grip on the rein) let us prepare then to see what the history may disclose.

(245–46)

The passage is notable in several respects,[8] but for now I just want to note two related aspects: first, that the author suggests he is not an infallible authority on the meaning of the event or even on the meaning of his text; and second, that Mailer is concerned to counter the mass media accounts that "surrounded" the event and created "a forest of inaccuracy."

As I will show below his method of doing this is more complex than this passage overtly suggests (and even here I'd note that the title of the chapter, "A Novel Metaphor," plays against the simple dichotomy of history/novel it proffers, and that the Historian and Novelist must already be mixed since they have metaphorically moved from tower to horseback). Mailer structures the text in such a way that he can be both a "semi-respectable" observer (precisely the role the organizers assigned to him and such fellow notables as Dwight Macdonald and Robert Lowell), and an active participant (partly through the act of writing the text). But as this passage already suggests, the two roles are not neatly separable. Indeed one of the functions of the text is to undermine, not only through overt argument, but through the strategic movement of the text as well, the ideologically loaded split of participation from observation.

Part of the complex epistemological stance of the text is suggested by the word "disclose" that occurs near the end of the passage. It suggests not only a revelation, an event that cannot be summoned, but a dis-

closing, an opening. Both of these meanings evoke the coming together
of event and actor-interpreter (or writer-interpreter) that opens, discloses, new possibilities that somehow inhere in some space between the
two. Thus the event/text can be seen as an ongoing revelation, requiring
continuing acts of interpretation. Similarly, the word "perhaps" stresses
the nature of the text as an event that is unfolding; that is, even the author
is not sure what it will disclose and has only just learned that the novelist
was in secret collaboration with the historian.[9] The text does not claim
to be authoritative, yet it nevertheless seeks an "advantage" (i.e., both a
vantage point and a superior strategic position) over the mass media's
"forest of inaccuracy." Thus, I suggest that Mailer surrounds the media's
surrounding of the event with a text that claims not so much greater ac-
curacy as greater semantic and political richness. But even this claim is
significantly qualified in the ongoing revelation of the text. In character-
izing Dellinger's plan for the march, Mailer writes: "He had succeeded
therefore in fashioning an action which was at once penned and open-
ended—for the character of the civil disobedience . . . remained unde-
fined" (271). The pun "penned" further suggests that event and text are
somehow parallel, that Mailer's "penned" text is nevertheless in some
way "open-ended" as well.

NOVEL/HISTORY/EPIC

Armies is simultaneously a history and critique of the Pentagon march
and its "aesthetic," a theoretical reflection on interpreting political action, and a self-consciously aesthetic object embodying formal concerns
seemingly supplemental to the task of describing and analyzing the
march. The two voices Mailer alludes to above, the "Novelist" and the
"Historian," seem on the surface to be the dominant presences in Book
1 and Book 2 of *Armies*, respectively, but this relationship is actually con-
siderably more complicated. Book 1 follows Mailer through the four
days during which his involvement in the march unfolds, and consists
primarily of a series of (often extraordinary) encounters and dialogues
with a range of participants from all sides. Book 2 fills in the larger picture of the event, its organizing, and its culmination in an imagined
(though not wholly imaginary) collective dialogue between the army of
protesters and the guardians of "technology land."

While the two books differ in vantage point, the text is structured as
a twofold "rite of passage." The first rite, which prefigures and prepares
the second, is Mailer's, and as related in Book 1 climaxes in his experi-

encing a moment of "grace" upon "transgressing a police line" in an act of solidarity with the protest. The second rite of passage, dramatized in Book 2, is collective, involving the most committed of the demonstrators who win a moral victory by together withstanding a brutal assault from the guardians of the Pentagon during a night of vigilance on the steps of the building.

Mailer's act of solidarity with the protesters is a precondition for his understanding the march; indeed that act in an important sense *is* his understanding of the Pentagon march. The "character" Norman Mailer as participant-interpreter moves in the course of Book 1 from ironic distance to engagement, passing through (and never wholly losing) a certain ambivalence. It is a strategy that, unlike say one that begins from an already decided stance, leaves room for the reader. Indeed, in Book 1 especially, Mailer is a reader, a reader of rhetorics and of events who, like the reader of the text, searches out the unfolding of the plot of the march. And what the plot unfolds, on one level, is a displacing of Mailer's ego by the event. Mailer's very egotism (much vaunted by the narrator and much in evidence in the participant) becomes, as Warner Berthoff puts it, no longer "an instrument of self-promotion but a theme of discourse," a dramatic backdrop that enhances the reader's sense of a self being "gradually burned away as the full objective dimensions of the event are revealed."[10] The text initially portrays Mailer as a *grand conservateur* (staying appropriately in the Hay-Adams Hotel), as one impatient with such "idiot mass manifestations" as the march. He is resistant at first to the request of his friend Mitch Goodman that he take part in the march. But gradually through the course of Book 1 Mailer develops a grudging respect, then a real admiration, for some of the young protesters. Thus his rite of passage entails a transformation from a reluctant spectator-participant to a full-fledged participant who commits an act of civil disobedience that, at least temporarily, transfigures him: "It was as if the air had changed, or light had altered; he felt immediately more alive" (149).

But as the "he" in this passage reminds us, the participant-interpreter is not the authorial voice of the text. Our picture is complicated by the fact that the text is told in the third person, through a rather shadowy narrator-interpreter.[11] That these two figures are both in some sense Norman Mailer creates a strange kind of self-reflection in the text. It is a device that can be seen as guarding against the reification of self-reflection itself. The narrator's mediated position is frequently and confusingly merged with the presumably more immediate experience of the participant. In the scene in which the description of Mailer's civil disobedience is related, for example, he is described as looking like a "banker run amok," and there is no way to be sure if this was "his" sense as the event was taking place or "his" ironic reflection upon it later (150).

Throughout Book 1, this double structure continues to suggest a certain distance between the actor in the event and the author of the text. But it is not a difference that can be sorted out, hierarchized, such that the later reflections are somehow more true or sound than the more immediate ones. The participant-interpreter and the narrator-interpreter embody two different moments in the event, or serve in effect to double the event. However, as the second term ("interpreter") in my descriptions of these roles is meant to suggest, they also meet in some third function. Generally one could argue that Mailer as narrator-interpreter keeps the text open, critically mediated, while Mailer the participant-interpreter embodies the necessity of engagement, of choosing to act politically in the face of uncertainty. But in a further twist one can see that the act of writing the text, the act performed in some sense by the narrator, may be, in a society dominated by the media, the more powerful political contribution Mailer makes (just as the act of narration in *Invisible Man* belies the passivity of the character invisible man). And each role involves acts of interpretation, acts which once enacted develop unforeseen consequences and become open to interpretation by others (including, in this curious case, oneself as other).

In Book 2, the character Mailer largely disappears, leaving only the narrator. It is not entirely clear if the reader is supposed to identify the voice of the historian in Book 2 with that of the narrator in Book 1, but the ambiguity is sufficient to cast shadows back on the former since, in the circular movement of the text, we realize that our firsthand, novelistic account was in fact mediated, while, as we'll see, the high, not to say, phallic perch of the historian proves highly unstable. Moreover, throughout Book 1 "Mailer" is also referred to alternately as "the Novelist," "the Historian," "the Participant," "the Ruminant," "the Existentialist," and by a scattering of other designations, all of which give a cumulative sense of the author being somehow eccentric to himself and enmeshed in a web of events, roles, and languages.

In any event, the transition between the two books provides a moment in which the authorial voices or functions seem to collide. With a circularity that momentarily removes the text from time, Mailer ends Book 1 with a representation of the moment he began (begins) its writing:

Then he began his history of the Pentagon. It insisted on becoming a history of himself over four days, and therefore was history in the costume of a novel. He labored in the aesthetic of the problem for weeks, discovering that his dimensions as a character were simple: blessed had been the novelist, for his protagonist was a simple of a hero and a marvel of a fool, with more than average gifts of objectivity—might his critics have as much!—this verdict disclosed by the unprotective haste with which he was obliged to write, for he wrote of necessity at a rate faster than he had ever written before, as if the accelerating history of the country forbade deliberation. Yet in writing his personal history of these four days, he was delivered a discovery of what the march on the Pentagon finally meant, and what had been won, and what had been lost, and so found himself ready at last to write a most concise Short History, a veritable précis of a collective novel, which here now, in the remaining pages, will seek as History, no, rather as some Novel of History, to elucidate that quintessentially American event.

(241)

Note that the "novelist" and his "protagonist" are still not quite collapsed into one as "he" discovers "his dimensions as a character." Yet the time of the writing and the time of experiencing the march seem to fuse as the act of writing is accelerated at the rate of history itself. And the act of writing itself "discloses" the meaning of the event, the meaning emerging in some "here now" of the text rather than inhering in the past or the event as past. Finally, even when "what the march on the Pentagon finally meant" is "disclosed" it is disclosed to the third person Mailer, not offered in some presumably more authoritative first person. And, as I argue below, "what the march . . . finally meant" is "disclosed" to neither of the Mailers, but only by the reader participating in the text of the Pentagon event.

This doubling of the "author" into participant and narrator is related to another formal doubling in the text. In my initial characterization of the dominant voices of the two books of the text, I spoke of the second book as "attempting" to achieve a panoramic, objective viewpoint. I said "attempting" because soon after the "Historian" is said to take over in Book 2, he encounters problems of interpretation, or more precisely of sympathetic imagination, that take him beyond the disciplinary boundaries of historiography: Mailer writes that "[Book 2] while dutiful to all newspaper accounts, eyewitness reports, and historic inductions available, while even obedient to a general style of historical writing, at least up to this point, while even pretending to be a history (on the basis of its introduction) is finally now to be disclosed as some sort of condensation of a collective novel—which is to admit that an explanation of the mys-

tery of the events at the Pentagon cannot be developed by the methods
of history—only by the instincts of the novelist" (284). We will have to
deal with this curious break in the text later (i.e., why does the author
initially "pretend" to be writing a history?), but for now it is enough to
note that a certain tension between the forms of the novel and of history
is indicated even in the putatively historical section.

This is merely one of the more manifest points at which the novel and
history-writing are placed in conflict. Throughout the text the terms
"novel" and "history" are fused and confused self-consciously until they
seem to lose their autonomy as concepts, becoming some hybrid that
questions the existence of novel and history as discrete writing forms,
and that, in turn, questions the epistemological bases of these forms. The
subtitle of the text, *History as a Novel, The Novel as History*, is emblematic of this questioning in that it does not resolve itself into some syn-
thetic new term like nonfiction novel but is instead presented as an unstable chiasmus.[12]

Essentially developmental, realist stories are told in each book (inter-
rupted only by occasional flashbacks and theoretical digressions). But
these stories are defamiliarized, are mediated and distanced, through a
foregrounding of literary technique, particularly through an extended
metaphor of the event as aesthetic object (see chapter titles "A Palette of
Tactics," "An Arbitrated Aesthetic," "An Aesthetic Tested"). And while
the novel and history may be the most apparent forms at play in the text,
there is a third form also present that in effect comments on and to an
extent synthesizes the cognitive claims of the other two. Several critics
have noted the "epic" aspects of *Armies*, but none has suggested how
they function in the text except as providing, in their "mock-heroic" dimension, moments of comic relief.[13] Taking their clue from the narrator's
occasional remarks about the participant as a "mock hero," and from
the numerous epic similes and metaphors that do indeed serve to make
fun of Mailer the participant—even his urination, for example, is treated
in heroic battle simile—critics have stressed the important comic service
the epic dimension offers at the expense of a more general role it plays.

The persistent use throughout the text of epic conventions, devices,
and allusions—the text begins, like the classical epic, *in medias res;* it is
centered in "battle"; the event is surrounded by "pageantry"; the stories
of the "hero" and of the "nation" are paralleled; the text includes at least
a couple of Homeric catalogues of battle forces, and so on—recalls a time
when story and history were not two forms but one. The attempt to re-
vive such an archaic form is of course doomed, and that is not Mailer's

ultimate aim. Indeed, critics are not wrong to see much of the epic element as "mock epic." But that is only part of the truth. The epic elements,
existing only as fragments, like shards from some literary dig, also stand
as a measure of something lost. Georg Lukács once referred to the novel
as "the epic of a world without God"; in *Armies* it is not God that is lost
but something akin, a social order capable of articulating itself in a coherent moral and political vision (this, I take it, is the Edmund Burkean
dimension of Mailer's "Left Conservatism" [208–9] that leads him to
bemoan the fact that the "two halves" of a schizophrenic America were
not coming together [179]). As Alasdair MacIntyre has cogently argued,
the narrative form we call "epic" was the product of a political culture
that understands the orderly, mutually obligated relation of each citizen
to his or her compatriots and to the community, a relation modernity
has, for better and for worse, rendered largely inconceivable.[14] To his
credit, Mailer resists the desire to will such coherence into being through
aesthetic form alone, but he also seems to suggest that if he can just find
the right story to tell, find the right cutting edge of style, the sense of
communal purpose he sees buried in the democratically heroic dimensions of our past could be brought back to life (178–79).

The epic element in the text represents a necessarily failed attempt to
figure history in such a way as to emerge out of the novel/history into
something new. That is, the novel/history that is the text knows itself as
a failed epic. But that failure is a failure of the culture, not of the writer.
It is the political failure to create a meaningful dialogue about our shared
and splintered multiculture, a failure of liberal pluralism intensified by
the "accelerating," fragmenting force of what Mailer sees as technology
gone mad and what Habermas was around the same time describing as
the invasion of the "life-world" by instrumental rationality.[15]

Mailer notes approvingly at one point that organizer Jerry Rubin
hoped the march would be an "epic of disruption," an epic disruption of
political business as usual in the United States. And, to mix our classical
metaphors, it is a disruption aimed at transforming a business establishment (in the business of war making) into a marketplace, an agora
(mythic originary site of democratic debate in the "Western" tradition).

In a Whitmaniacal gesture, "Mailer" as meta-rhetorician attempts to
encompass and analyze the divergent voices of America in 1967, from
the "grandma with orange hair" who would rather play slot machines
than contemplate the war, to the marshals supervising arrests at the Pentagon and the young guardsmen surrounding it, to the pacifists and revolutionaries who were there to "wound it" symbolically or literally. As

"Mailer" and the narrator move through the text encountering and in-
terviewing (directly or in his/their imagination) a variety of participants
and their opponents, the event and the text become, ever so briefly, an
arena of citizenship, a real metaphor prefiguring a possible rebirth of
American democracy, embodying the attempts of the early New Left to
(re)invent a democracy of direct, equal participation. But just as
"Mailer" is only a mock general and a mock hero, so too *Armies* and the
march are ultimately (or as yet) only a mock epic, a pastiche of an epic,
because the dialogues reach an impasse.

CARNIVAL/TIME

The awareness that they are about to make the
continuum of history explode is characteristic of the
revolutionary classes at the moment of their action. The
great revolution introduced a new calendar. The initial
day of a calendar serves as an historical time-lapse
camera. And, basically, it is the same day that keeps
recurring in the guise of holidays, which are days of
remembrance. Thus the calendars do not measure time
as clocks do; they are monuments of a historical
consciousness of which not the slightest trace has been
apparent . . . in the past hundred years. In the July
revolution an incident occurred which showed the
consciousness still alive. On the first evening of fighting
it turned out that the clocks in towers were being fired
on simultaneously and independently from several
places in Paris.

                                        —*Walter Benjamin*

A month before Columbia, in an action foretelling the
confrontation in Chicago, we held a Yip-in celebration
at midnight in Grand Central Station. Our leaflets
called for a joyous equinox mating, a pre-Chicago
festival of life with balloons, roller-skating and
dancing. Six thousand people showed up and frolicked
under the vaulted ceiling. Everybody was enjoying
themselves when one eager beaver scampered up on the
information center and yanked off the clock's hands.
Could this gesture prevent the trains from running on

time? Was this equal to tearing down the flag?
Obviously it was of major importance, for the act
resulted in the cops going berserk. They began bashing
heads without warning. . . . The place had become an
enclosed tomb in which the cries of the people were
magnified increasing the horror. The scene was worse
than anything that was to happen in Chicago.

—*Abbie Hoffman*

Armies of the Night opens with the narrator quoting an account in *Time* magazine of Norman Mailer's exploits during a rally the night before the march on the Pentagon. The magazine's account begins, "Washington's scruffy Ambassador Theater, normally a pad for psychedelic frolics, was the scene of an unscheduled scatological solo last week in support of the peace demonstrations. Its antistar was author Norman Mailer, who proved even less prepared to explain Why Are We in Vietnam? than his current novel bearing that title" (13). The account continues on in this vein, mocking Mailer and the absurdity of the protest he is made momentarily to symbolize. After quoting the account, Mailer comments, "Now we may leave Time in order to find out what happened" (14). This punning phrase neatly joins two important themes of the text: the problem of historical consciousness (time) and the problem of mass mediation (*Time*). The play with ways of writing history described above is in part a response to the way those forms have been reshaped by modern electronic media and by the cultural economy of late capitalism generally.[16]

One of Mailer's tasks in *Armies* is to rescue the march on the Pentagon from time, from dissipation, by placing it in a "quintessentially American" continuum. This he attempts through a brief but incisive history of the American left, and through a linking of the New Left to the history of democratic struggle in the United States generally. But he also wishes to preserve the event's power to shatter *Time*, shatter the mass media continuum of pseudohistory packaged by consumer society. The mass media's accounts of an event like the march are, from the participant's viewpoint, in a rather literal sense surreal, the layering of another reality over the face-to-face (i.e., differently mediated) reality they experienced. And the form that those accounts take is one in which context and continuity are largely destroyed. Both the daily press and, more fully, the televised press make news as discontinuous bits, rendering it nearly impossible for a political movement to convey a sense of itself as an ongoing, historical development motivated by an elaborated critique. Thus it may at points be imperative for movements of social change to stress precisely those continuities that are effaced by the mass media.[17]

In an earlier short story, one of Mailer's characters announces that he cannot write a realist novel because "reality is no longer realistic." Indeed, there is a sense in which reality, especially as filtered through television, has become for many surreal (in the sense that it appears in the form of discontinuous, seemingly unmotivated images).[18] In such a world "realism" may become a critical force once more, but it will be a realism with a difference.

Traditional realist stories are told in each of *Armies'* two books, but, as I suggested above, these stories are defamiliarized, are mediated and distanced, through a foregrounding of literariness (the epic allusions, especially) and through an extended metaphor of the event as aesthetic object. Were Mailer a less political and less ambitious novelist, this literariness might have become an end in itself (as it has for many contemporary writers). Mailer's ego drives him to be not merely a great writer but a great writer who changes the world. That means attending to the aesthetic of history itself, attending to social texts that are crossed by but not confined to literary performances.

My reading of *Armies* suggests that the text/event at the Pentagon takes the path of both intensifying and replacing the (sur)reality of everyday life. The event is not only drama itself but also includes some self-consciously surrealist theater by the American version of the situationists, the Yippies, whose antics Mailer records "realistically." Such surrealist play was one mode of action among many in the march, one with an important but limited audience. Mailer's treatment suggests that neither realism nor surrealism remain critical modes when pursued purely, but work best when set alongside or against one another.

Mailer calls up images from the past and links those images to the present, not as empirical history but as genealogical events charged with energy to incite, to deepen, but also sometimes to chasten, the cause of the moment. The struggle with and for American history takes the form of an attempt by the text to bridge what became known in the sixties as the generation gap, a gap that was due in part to the influence of new cultural media. As the first generation raised fully under the hegemony of the new medium of television, the sixties children are to Mailer's eye socialized as surrealists:

> They had had their minds jabbed and poked and twitched and finally galvanized into surrealistic modes of response by commercials cutting into dramatic narratives, and . . . flipping from network to network—they were

forced willy-nilly to build their idea of the spacetime continuum (and therefore their nervous system) on the jumps and cracks and leaps and breaks
which every phenomenon from the media seemed to contain within it. The
authority had operated on their brains with commercials, and washed their
brains with packaged education, packaged politics.

(103)

Mailer partly qualifies the McLuhanesque aspect of this analysis. He
applauds the surrealist moment, the new nonlinear mode, but sees its
limits, sees its complicity in the maintenance of the system that needs to
be overturned. In a surreal world, a world in which reality is carved up
into commodity chunks placed between but indistinguishable from commercials, a sense of narrative, of history, becomes a powerful and necessary element in a subversive movement. And Mailer worries that already signs of a "packaging" of surrealist politics are on the horizon.

But this sense of a nonlinear reality is also for Mailer what "was good
about" the young; "their belief was reserved for the revelatory mystery
of the happening, where you did not know what was going to happen
next." This utopian, presentist mood is one important source of the New
Left's critical spirit, of their great refusal of a secondhand, representative
democratic politics. But it also cuts the young left off from empowering
roots in traditions of revolt and from a developed sense of the root causes
of the current malaise.

In the United States of late capitalism, where mass-mediated
(sur)reality seems at once to be random and utterly programmed, spontaneity may be an essential subversive quality or it may be part of the
program.[19] Therefore, the need is for what Rosa Luxemburg identified as
strategic spontaneity. In celebrating the "revelatory mystery of the happening," Mailer reinforces a tendency among the "action faction" of the
post-1967 New Left to assume that strategy will emerge from action itself. But as Luxemburg knew, even spontaneity has forms; as was true
of the happenings themselves, political spontaneity without imaginative
strategy quickly devolves into highly conventional, passively consumable, co-optable forms.[20]

The new mode of consciousness of the youth also limits their capacity
to sustain the long-range task of changing things (Mailer notes that the
Pentagon march is part of a "war" that may go on for "twenty years" or
more [105]). Thus some of the celebration of spontaneity as strategy is
offset by the narrator's description of "Mailer's" political position as that
of a "Left Conservative," one who finds it necessary to use "the style of
Marx in order to attain certain values suggested by Edmund Burke"
(208–9). One of the ways "Mailer" embodies this Left Conservatism, an

echo perhaps of Henry Adams's self-definition as a "conservative Christian anarchist," is by dividing his loyalties between the worlds of the youth and of the elders. Then the text overlays this generational discontinuity with an attempt to articulate forms of imagined historical continuity, forms that link the march to exceptional moments in the history of American democratic struggle. This primarily takes the form of an effort throughout the text to call up metaphorically the ghosts of "the Union Dead." As he reaches the site of the premarch rally, for example, Mailer writes that as he took a turn "to the right to come down from Washington Monument toward the length of the long reflecting pool which led . . . to the steps of the Lincoln Memorial, out from that direction came the clear bitter-sweet excitation of a military trumpet resounding in the near distance, one peal which seemed to go all the way back through a galaxy of bugles to the cries of the Civil War. . . . The ghosts of old battles were wheeling like clouds over Washington today" (108). As is perhaps apparent here, Mailer's storytelling is made more complex by the self-consciously symbolic nature of the events themselves. The events themselves are charged with self-conscious symbolism: in the Civil War passage above, for example, Mailer's reading is partly the result of the theatrical organization of the rally, which quite consciously used the figure of Lincoln as a backdrop.

The link between the generational and the more broadly historical levels of continuity making is also achieved in part through character, particularly through the character of Robert Lowell (who along with Dwight Macdonald was Mailer's closest comrade-in-arms during the march). (And, of course, also through the character "Mailer," who had in some measure helped to form the hip culture from which the counterculture had grown.) Lowell not only links the two levels of history, but embodies the role of language as mediator of the process of making history. Lowell (whose very name suggests the word "loyal") is both the keeper of American history (as a descendant of the long line of Boston Lowells) and a keeper of the American language (as poet). And as author of *For the Union Dead*, a collection of poems whose title echoes at several points in Mailer's text, Lowell unites both roles. Mailer uses him to symbolize both the power and the current fragility of the American legacy. The poet is portrayed as a sensibility from another age buffeted by the shocks of modern experience and always on the edge of a crack-up. For all his dignity and the depth of character suggested by what appears to Mailer as the face of a "man paying the moral debts of ten generations of ancestors," Lowell too is touched by the mad modern moment. Thus when Mailer tries to capture the complex instability of the poet's mind he draws his metaphor from the counterculture: "Lowell's brain at its most painful must have been equal to an overdose of LSD on Halloween" (99).

Lowell is a symbol of the symbolic war waged for generations by writers trying to rescue America from itself. And the Civil War allusions themselves often have unmistakable literary echoes: Mailer felt

> the slow sweet filling of a long unused reservoir and intimations of all the Armies of the past which had gathered on a field like this believing their cause to be grand and just and heroic, and therefore amazingly sweet—the long promenade sweeping the circle of the long reflecting pool and gathering the thousands on its banks had seemed to capture that sense of long-gone Armies, that fine strain of love which hovers like some last lavender in the dying echo of a superbly played string, there was a love of evening in the warm morning air, a violet of late shadows, a ghost of Gettysburg and the knowledge that a sense of danger had finally come to the American Left, not to the brave students who had gone South years ago to hunt for Negro rights, but to the damnable mediocre middle of the Left, and that stirred a tenderness which lifted like a thin smoke of battle, tinted rose-color in legend, to honor the light in the blood welling from the fallen brave.
>
> (114)

I hear echoes of Faulkner, both in diction and rhythm, and of Whitman in mythic scope. This is Mailer's own attempt to bridge the generations, to link the cause of the young protesters to all that is laudable in the American literary/historical tradition (while also, of course, aggrandizing that literary history for himself). Perhaps these historical linkages can even help give courage to the respectable "damnable mediocre middle of the Left" that is now taking to the streets with the youthful rebellious rabble.

On the other side, much of Mailer's ambivalence regarding the youthful participants who are spearheading the protest stems from his sense of their lack of any developed sense of history. Mailer writes that to the young the past is just something "assembled from all the intersections between history and the comic books, between legend and television, the Biblical archetypes and the movies" (109). He sees this attitude epitomized and embodied especially by the representatives of the countercuture:

> The hippies were there in great number, perambulating down the hill, many dressed like the legions of Sgt. Pepper's Band, some were gotten up like Arab sheiks, or in Park Avenue doormen's greatcoats, others like Rogers and Clark of the West, Wyatt Earp, Kit Carson, Daniel Boone in Buckskin, some had grown mustaches to look like Have Gun Will Travel—Paladin's surrogate was here!—and wild Indians with feathers, a hippie gotten up like Batman, an-

other like Claude Rains in The Invisible Man—his face wrapped in a turban of bandages and he wore a black satin top hat. A host of these troops wore capes, beat-up khaki capes . . . or fine capes, orange linings, or luminous rose linings, the edges ragged, near a tatter, threads ready to feather, but a musketeer's hat on their head. One hippie may have been dressed like Charles Chaplin; Buster Keaton and W. C. Fields could have come to the ball; there were Martians and Moonmen and a knight unhorsed who stalked about in the weight of real armor. There were to be seen a hundred soldiers in Confederate gray, and maybe there were two or three hundred hippies in officer's coats of Union dark blue. . . . There were soldiers in Foreign Legion uniforms and tropical bush jackets, San Quentin and Chino, California striped shirt and pants, British copies of Eisenhower jackets. . . . Turkish shepards [sic] and Roman senators, gurus and samurai in dirty smocks.

(108–9)

Mailer is both charmed and appalled by this appropriation of all the world and its history. A kind of glittering sediment in some meta-imperialist imagination, the scene also reflects real joy and exudes critique of the drabness of middle-class culture. The young festive marchers are a walking figuration of postmodern pastiche, but Mailer must throw his "allegiance" to them anyway because these young women and men have come to end the war, or rather they have come to battle against "technology land" and against their own parents who are preparing "(often unknown to themselves) for some sexo-technological variety of neo-fascism" (110).

While announcing that his "allegiance was with the . . . hippies," Mailer also senses something disturbing in their apparently joyful carnival, "something sinister" beneath "the play of costumes":

[There are] nightmares beneath the gaiety of these middle-class runaways, these Crusaders going to attack the hard core of technology land with less training than Armies were once offered by a medieval assembly ground. The nightmare was in the echoes of those trips which had fractured their sense of past and present. [The] tissue of past history . . . was . . . being bombed by the use of LSD as outrageously as the atoll at Eniwetok, Hiroshima, Nagasaki, and the scorched foliage of Vietnam. The history of the past was being exploded right into the present: perhaps there were now lacunae in the firmament of the past, holes where once had been the psychic reality of an era which was gone.

(110)

This fantastical rumination joins a number of themes. The connection of LSD to the technologized violence of modern warfare (a connection, incidentally, moved from the fantastic to the empirical by the subsequent revelation of the U.S. Army and CIA's involvement in the early development of the drug) implicates the youth in the very "technology land" they seek to transform. They have not escaped history ("indeed the history of all eras [is] on their backs as trophies"), and their LSD is to Mailer only a kind of internalized TV, mind technologized. But the allusion to the "medieval assembly ground" and "Crusades" reminds us that Mailer too is complicit in the appropriation of history. Through his epic gesture he, too, explodes the past into the present. And the crimes of the historyless children are ultimately more the fault of the technocratic parents who "brainwashed the mood of the present" and buried the past beneath a pile of time-machine gadgets, while the hippies are in some sense hipster Mailer's semilegitimate offspring. In any event, Mailer's allegiance overcomes his doubts about the youth because, for whatever reason, the "aesthetic at last was in the politics," the "dress ball was going into battle" (109).

The counterculture carnival, the "dress ball," goes to battle at first in the Pentagon event through magic. And Mailer goes with them, first personally, then textually. In what must be one of the most extraordinary negotiating sessions in the history of diplomacy, the ambassadors of radical hipdom and the guardians of Washington, D.C., haggled in the autumn of 1967 over just how far the protesters might be permitted to levitate the Pentagon. Soon-to-be-Yippie! Abbie Hoffman and other hippie-left organizers requested a permit for an attempt to raise the building one hundred feet as part of an effort to exorcise the evil spirits contained within it. The government negotiators would agree only to an effort to raise it ten feet. They would not, however, consent to an encirclement of the building, thus putting the magicians at a decided tactical disadvantage.

Attracted by the sounds of the rock group the Fugs, Mailer finds himself in the midst of this levitation and exorcism in progress. He is handed a mimeographed piece of paper that "had a legend that went something like this":

> October 21, 1967, Washington, D.C., U.S.A., Planet Earth. We Freemen [*sic*] of all colors of the spectrum, in the name of God, Ra, Jehovah, Anubis, Osiris, . . . Bacchus, Isis, Jesus Christ, Maitreya, Buddha, Rama do exorcise and cast out the EVIL which has walled and captured the pentacle of power and perverted its use to the total machine and its child the hydrogen bomb. . . . We are demanding that the pentacle of power once again be used to serve the interests of GOD manifest in this world as man. We are embarking on a motion which is millennial in scope. Let this day, October 21, 1967, mark the beginning of suprapolitics. *By the act of reading this paper* you are engaged in the Holy Ritual of Exorcism. To further participate focus your thought on the casting out of evil through the grace of GOD which is all (ours).
>
> (139–40; my emphasis)

A voice, Mailer tells us, then intones the names of yet another long list of gods and goddesses (including Allah, Isis, and Tyrone Power) and "in the name of the flowing living universe, in the name of the mouth of the river, we call upon the spirit . . . to raise the Pentagon from its destiny and preserve it" (141).

Thus simultaneously this highly symbolic event is surely also the most literal enactment of *Aufhebung* in political history. Theory practiced, the abstract trying to raise concrete. (Abbie Hoffman, incidentally, claimed that the exorcism was expected to be taken far more seriously in the Buddhist spirit world of Vietnam than at home; the apparent failure of the exorcism can be traced to the fact that in the United States most of the exorcists and the audience were lacking in the faith and substantial knowledge of the spirit world and its ways.)[21]

Mailer's direct participation in this magic theater, not only by "reading" the ritual but by joining in a chant of "Out demons! Out!," is foreshadowed and overlain by a similar but significantly different spiritual language that appears intermittently from the beginning of the text. Mailer's initial characterization of the march is as an attempt to "invest the Pentagon" (24), and throughout the early chapters the archaic meaning of "invest" (to surround) and the religious notion of "investiture" are played against the contemporary narrowing of the term "investment" to fit only the financial sphere. In a style that inverts the technique of the "Economy" chapter of an earlier nonfiction novel, Thoreau's *Walden*, Mailer, as narrator, attempts to translate the terms of political economy into those of a moral economy. Through textual magic he attempts to invest the Pentagon with new meaning, or rather he implicitly joins the effort to "invest the Pentagon" by trying to reassert the claim to moral meaning of a term now hopelessly confused with such things as the tax investment in the real war being waged from inside the building under symbolic attack. And by the "act of reading" his text we are invited to new surroundings, renewed attempts at exorcism.

THE CUTTING EDGE OF RADICAL STYLE: EVENT AS TEXT

I want to argue now that the literary strategies examined above serve on the formal level as an equivalent to what Mailer calls the "aesthetic of the New Left," and thus that these strategies enable *Armies* to dissolve back into the social text that in turn enabled it. The narrator's characterization of the New Left's "aesthetic" includes an explicit paralleling of it to the problem of a writer's style (or at least to the style of a writer like Norman Mailer):

> The New Left was drawing its political aesthetic from Cuba. The revolutionary idea which the followers of Castro had induced from their experience in the hills was that you created the revolution first and learned from it, learned of what your revolution might consist and where it might go out of the intimate truth of the way it presented itself to your experience. Just as the truth of his material was revealed to a good writer by the cutting edge of his style . . . so a revolutionary began to uncover the nature of his true situation by trying to ride the beast of his revolution. The idea behind these ideas was then obviously that the future of the revolution existed in the nerves and cells of the people who created it and lived it, rather than in the sanctity of the original idea.
>
> (104)

The implication here is that a text is a kind of beast that the writer can try to ride but that has a will of its own. And this relationship is further mediated by "style," a "cutting" tool, that is nevertheless dependent on or entwined with a revelation of the truth of the material. This latter image is either a paradox, or it means that the cutting is a kind of cutting away that uncovers some truth already existing beneath the surface. In either case, the text, the material, is semi-autonomous—the writer can ride the revolution, the revelation, but can never master it, never know it fully. There is a tautology here, or more generously, a kind of hermeneutic circularity that militates against reifying event or author, but sees them as shaping each other.

And if the "truth of his material [is] revealed to a good writer by the cutting edge of his style," what is revealed by the curious break in the text of *Armies* noted earlier, the moment when the "history" falls back into novelness? Let's return to the passage and look at it in full:

> Doubtless it has been hardly possible to ignore that this work resides in two enclaves, the first entitled History as a Novel, the second here before us called The Novel as History. No one familiar with the husking ambiguities of English will be much mystified by the titles. It is obvious the first book is a history in the guise or dress or manifest of a novel, and the second a real or true novel—no less!—presented in the style of a history. (Of course, everyone including the author will continue to speak of the first book as a novel and the second as a history—practical usage finds favor in such comfortable opposites.) However, the first book can be, in the formal sense nothing but a personal history, which while written as a novel was to the best of the author's memory scrupulous to the facts and therefore a document; whereas the second, while dutiful to all newspaper accounts, eyewitness reports, and historic inductions available, while even obedient to a general style of historical writ-

ing, at least up to this point, while even pretending to be a history (on the basis of its introduction) is finally now to be disclosed as some sort of condensation of a collective novel—which is to admit that an explanation of the mystery of the events at the Pentagon cannot be developed by the methods of history—only by the instincts of the novelist. The reasons are several but reduce to one. Forget that the journalistic information available from both sides is so incoherent, inaccurate, contradictory, malicious, even based on error that no accurate history is conceivable. More than one historian has found a way through chains of false fact. No, the difficulty is that the history is interior—no documents can give sufficient intimation: the novel must replace history at precisely that point where experience is sufficiently emotional, spiritual, psychical, moral, existential, or supernatural to expose the fact that the historian in pursuing the experience would be obliged to quit the clearly demarcated limits of historic inquiry. So these limits are now relinquished. The collective novel which follows, while still written in the cloak of an historic style, and therefore, continually attempting to be scrupulous to the welter of a hundred confusing and opposing facts, will now unashamedly enter that world of strange lights and intuitive speculation which is the novel.

(283–84)

On one level, this is the moment in which it is revealed to Mailer that the politics of his "existential" aesthetic prevents the writing of a putatively objective history, even one prefaced by a novel: if he is to participate in this "revolutionary" moment he cannot let history drain the moment of its open-endedness, its mystery. And thus he tries to fall back on the to him more familiar terrain of the novel. But to do so is to undercut the interplay of forms he has just set out. Hence he can only offer a quasi-mystical appeal to the "instincts" of the novelist and the "strange lights" of the novel, creating a conflict between a positive history based on "the instincts of the novelist" and novelness as precisely disruptive of history, as rooted in a contingent subjectivity displaced by the beastlike text.

In the transitionary writing between the two "books" of *Armies*, Mailer (and "Mailer") had acknowledged what he here interrupts the text to note: he had described the second book about to begin "as History, no, rather as some Novel of History" (241). But the moment must still be enacted because Mailer can keep alive a sense of the event as event only by keeping alive a sense of the text as event. Early in Book 2 he notes the tendency of historiography to "assume that . . . dramatic issues were never in doubt" (276), and this is clearly one of the reasons Mailer eventually abandons the pretense of writing a history. The original idea of the event or of the text is not sacred, but must be open to reinscription, open to the discovery of new meanings in the event that is the encounter between actor and text, event and writer, just as the meaning of the "revolution" must be recreated as it develops over time.

If the event is to be understood, the text implies, it must be experienced, lived through: "political action whose end was unknown" is contrasted with the effort to "comprehend." Thus Mailer's text can only fail to comprehend the event unless it makes the text itself an ongoing, revelatory event (though no purely textual strategy can guarantee that the text will be experienced as an event, rather than comprehended as a "book" "about" an event).

The textual break occurs just at the moment when the narrator is about to recount the face-to-face encounter between the protesters and the troops sent to protect the Pentagon. And the test of the text's eventness, openness, would seem to lie in its account of this climactic second "rite of passage":

> How many of these demonstrators, certain at the beginning of the night by the firm conviction of their ego that they would not leave till morning, must have been obliged to pass through layers and dimensions and bursting cysts of cowardice they never knew existed before. . . . Yes, the passage through the night against every temptation to leave—the cold, the possibility of new, more brutal, and more overwhelming attacks, the boredom, the middle-class terror of excess . . . yes, the passage through the night brought every temptation to leave, including the thundering schisms of muttered political argument in the dark . . . what unseen burning torch of which unknown but still palpably felt spirit might expire? no, this passage through the night was a rite of passage, and these disenchanted heirs of the Old Left, this rabble of American Vietcong, and hippies, and pacifists, and whoever else was left still afloat on a voyage whose first note had been struck with the first sound of the trumpet Mailer had heard crossing Washington Monument in the morning. "Come here, come here, come here," the trumpet had said, and now eighteen hours later, in the false dawn, the echo of far greater rites of passage in American history, the light reflected from the radiance of greater more heroic hours may have come nonetheless to shine along the inner space and caverns of the freaks, some hint of a glorious future may have hung in the air, some refrain from all the great American rites of passage when men and women manacled themselves to a lost and painful principle, and survived a day, a night, a week, a month, a year, a celebration of Thanksgiving—the country had been founded on a rite of passage. Very few had not emigrated here without echo of that rite, even if it were no more (and no less!) than eight days . . . of steerage on an ocean crossing (or the eighty days of dying on a slave ship) each generation of Americans had forged their own rite, in the forest of the Alleghenies and the Adirondacks, at Valley Forge, at New Orleans in 1812, . . . at Gettysburg, the Alamo, the Klondike, the Argonne, Normandy, Pusan— the engagement at the Pentagon was a pale rite of passage next to these, and

yet it was probably a true one, for it came to the spoiled children of a dead and de-animalized middle class who had chosen most freely, out of the incomprehensible mysteries of moral choice, to make an attack and then hold a testament before the most authoritative embodiment of the principle that America was right, America was might, America was the true religious war of Christ against the Communist. So it became a rite of passage for these tender, drug-vitiated jargon-mired children, they endured through a night, a black dark night which began in joy, near foundered in terror, and dragged on through empty apathetic hours while glints of light came to each alone.

(310–11)

Some critics have found this passage convincing, others have found it overblown and bombastic. I would argue that Mailer means it to be a true forgery, part of the epic not quite achieved. It is littered with equivocation, with "may" and "perhaps" and other words of far from epic dimension. And the section in which this passage takes place is entitled "An Aesthetic Forged," a pun designed to draw attention to the author's forgery in attempting to reach for an epic tone, as well as the sometimes strained quality of the action itself.

At one point in *Armies*, Mailer refers to the march on the Pentagon as "an ambiguous event whose essential value or absurdity may not be established for ten or twenty years." As we have seen, there is a parallel ambiguity built into the text's form so that the question of its realism is suspended rather than answered. Or rather, the question of realism is for the text a political question, not merely an epistemological one. Mailer's attempt to counter the "forest of inaccuracy" about the march provided by the mass media, takes the form of a kind of existential historiography or "participatory journalism" that parallels the striving for "participatory democracy" on the part of the New Left that is its most admirable feature.[22]

But this search for an existential historiography also sugggests how Mailer's style as revealed in this passage parallels some of the limitations of the New Left. One of the labels used by the narrator to describe "Mailer" is "the Existentialist,'" and I use the word existential above because it recurs throughout the text in key passages. What Mailer seems to mean by it is something like openness of the moment to an act of will. It seems to be a simplified shorthand for the positions of Camus and of the early, pre-Marxist Sartre upon whom history weighed rather lightly (as opposed to the older Sartre for whom Marxism provided a notion of necessity and historical limits). Numerous New Leftists were similarly weaned on this notion of willful transcendence of the historically given, and the fluidity of the decade seemed to reinforce that sense of nearly infinite possibility.[23] Indeed, numerous acts of personal heroism, moral and physical, grew out of such faith. But an overemphasis on the possibilities of the pure moment, the willed contingency, weakened strategic thinking in the New Left, eventually and ironically leaving it open to wild ideological swings having little connection to the possibilities available within the field of (not infinite) possibility. As Fredric Jameson argues, that feeling of free will and willed freedom was itself in part determined by cracks in hegemonic ideology created during the uncertain shift to a new mode of political economic organization—called by Jameson "late capitalism" and by others "post-Fordism," or "postindustrial society."[24]

At its best, the text's play with form, its calling attention to its artifice, and its critique of various "bureaucratized" and "technologized" radical rhetorics can be read as a call for greater self-reflexivity on the part of the New Left. Foregrounding style provides periodic reminders that interpretation is a political act, a shaping that is a being shaped, an ongoing act in which the reader (for who is the author but a reader?) is participating, while in turn suggesting that political actions are always partly open forms whose interpretations must themselves be struggled over.

When introducing Book 2, Mailer speaks of it as a "veritable précis of a collective novel" (241). Besides the manifest reference to Book 2 itself as a condensed collective novel, I believe he means by this at least two other things: first, that it is a précis in the sense of a condensation of the "collective novel" that was the march on the Pentagon itself; and second, that it is a précis in the sense of a prospectus or "prefiguration" of a collective, novel, re-writing of American political reality. This latter reading includes the realization that the text is part of the event it recounts, and that, conversely, the text will be reinterpreted as the event is reinterpreted through subsequent critical action in the world. Text and event share a similar fate. In this sense then, Mailer's text can be read as a contribution to the re-making, re-writing, of American reality, but one that acknowledges that project to be a collective one beyond the scope of the novel as a totalizing form rooted in limited, individual experience. It is a history that runs into limits, falls into novelness, but only to fall once more into History itself, into the political struggle to reinterpret and remake the world.

PREFIGURING A NEW LEFT AESTHETIC

As I noted above, Mailer suggests that the Pentagon march was an "ambiguous" event whose meaning might not be known for "ten or twenty years." More than twenty years after the event/text, its meaning is still ambiguous because it is still contested by Americans. The New Left, and "the sixties" more generally, continues to be a key signifier in ideological struggles in this country. Indeed, the very use of the periodizing term "the sixties" serves as a depoliticizing move, implying as it frequently does that radical politics had been tried once in those years but the frame of decades now seals us off from such activities. What can we make of *Armies* / the Pentagon march as a moment in the ongoing contest for a New Left? How do we read these particular textual events into the ongoing struggle to define the political meanings set in motion in that time period?

To begin to answer these questions, let's return to *Armies'* crucially ambiguous characterization of the "New Left aesthetic":

> Revolutions could fail as well by Castro's method as by the most inflexible Comintern program; what seemed significant here, was the idea of revolution which preceded ideology; the New Left had obviously adopted this idea for the march. The aesthetic of the New Left now therefore began with the notion that the authority could not comprehend nor contain nor finally manage to control any political action whose end was unknown. They could attack it, beat it, jail it, misrepresent it, . . . but they could not feel a sense of victory because they could not understand a movement which inspired thousands and hundreds of thousands to march without a coordinated plan.
>
> (104–5)

On the one hand, the idea of a revolution that "precedes ideology" can be read as a perfect description of the need for ongoing democratic openness, experimentation, ideological flexibility—that which was best about the New Left. On the other hand, such a position can be read as a move toward the mystification of a communal ethos that is the opposite of such democratic openness. The subsequent history of the New Left suggests that both of these "readings" of the Pentagon text found an audience.

The Pentagon march was a turning point, a moment in which the New Left could either clarify its real symbolic confrontation with the hegemonic forces, or confuse that confrontation with some imminent (and immanent) revolution (the Pentagon is not the Winter Palace). *Armies* leans toward the former of these positions, but the narrator/"Mailer's" masculinism as revealed in numerous homophobic, sexist passages in the text but also as embodied in his celebration of the dangerous air of violence he felt enlivening the march, and his related contempt for the pragmatic organizing efforts of "damnable, mediocre" middle-class radicals, made possible a reading that rendered his intervention less effective than it might have been in clarifying the New Left to itself and to the wider community at the time it was penned.

Just as "Mailer's" appeal to "the instincts of the novelist," to some higher or deeper knowledge, can be read as freezing the dialectic of the text by reasserting a higher- or deeper-level objectivity rather than a still-open collective hermeneutic, the parallel appeal to an experience or a revelation beyond ideology led some in the New Left to posit an "actionist" mystique that cut off dialogue inside and outside the movement community. Too great of a reliance on communal ethos to the neglect of strategic and theoretical positioning left the New Left ironically vulnerable to what "Mailer" called "the solid-as-brickwork-logic-of-the-next-step" offered by Old Left–style groups like the Progressive Labor party. The claim to have no ideology, or an ideology emerging spontaneously out of practice, became itself a rigid ideological position that was easily flip-flopped into its opposite. Like "Mailer's" "instincts," such a position merely ironically mirrors hegemonic notions of objectivity.

Above I've kept Mailer in quotes in order to suggest that it is possible to place a distance between the text and the author/character. Doing so, it is possible to see how the larger structure of the text can be read as mitigating the tendency toward mystification and exclusivity. "Mailer" and "Mailer," the "Ruminant" and the "Participant," can be seen, for example, as dialectically synthesizing the split developing in the mid-sixties between a mostly older, "praxis axis" of the New Left (that sought to think through the contradictions of democratic practice) and a younger, emerging, "action faction" (closer to Mailer's notion of the New Left's "Cuban" aesthetic).[25] The text as ruminating act implicitly sets limits on the ideological mystique of participatory revelation. But as a specific intervention into the charged political atmosphere of 1968, the text's ambiguities were not always strategic ones.

On the one hand, *Armies* offers a critical portrait of "Teague" (201–4; 216–24), a dedicated Leninist, who prefigures the New Left's takeover by and regression into a parody of the Old Left. But on the other hand, the narrator is also clearly drawn to certain elements in the hypermilitant "Revolutionary Contingent" that appointed itself leader of the "siege" of the Pentagon. In his account of their activities ("A Perspective of Battle"), as in his description of the "rite of passage," Mailer mirrors them by sometimes confusing physical with moral courage, violence with meaningful confrontation, mediated with literalist assault on the defense fortress.

Mailer's characterization of the "aesthetic" of the Pentagon march and siege captures a portion of the New Left in transition to the confrontation-based politics of its late phase (roughly 1968–70). In that phase a small but influential component of the "action faction" began to make "action for action's sake" the aesthetic of the movement, arguing that revolutionary action would speak for itself. But action seldom speaks unambiguously—it too must be read. A revolutionary reading is not an inevitable consequence of proximity to or even immersion in the event itself, but comes only through a careful interplay of rhetorical strategy and context (of the kind initially planned into the march by MOBE organizers). "Actionism" or "confrontationism" in the late sixties was for a time successful in dramatically increasing the size and notoriety of the movement. But those successes were not generally accompanied by, and often undermined, serious attempts to cultivate the roots, to build a critical democratic community through collective political (re)education.

These shortcomings of the New Left, or rather part of the New Left, are serious ones, but they are also ones many New Leftists tried to counter as they emerged, and they have been exaggerated by a spate of recent histories and memoirs of the sixties.[26] As Ronald Grele has noted, these new history/memoirs seem to have "copied again and again" Mailer's form.[27] But for the most part, despite impressive elements and despite the fact that their authors were far more deeply enmeshed in the New Left than Mailer ever was, these texts precisely lack the sense of eventness that remains crucial to understanding the New Left and political movements generally. Most of these memoir/histories emplot a classic "decline and fall" pattern of tragedy in narrating the story of the late New Left, and thus become (inadvertently) quite conservative by closing down the New Left moment. They are the tales of older, wiser men (and the maleness is important because the "decline" phase doesn't look so much like decline from the perspective of the simultaneous "rise" of the women's movement). They are men mesmerized by and critical of their too often "irresponsible" youth. While sympathetic to the New Left, the new memoirists nevertheless stress many of the same causes for decline earlier given by hostile critics: violence and revolutionist adventurism, and unrealistic, undisciplined personal utopianism/moralism. And they attribute the "implosion" of the best-known national New Left group, Students for a Democratic Society (SDS), to its excessive democracy and failure to become more centralized, more disciplined, and more representative. As explanations of the New Left's putative "fall" afer 1967, these readings tell too little of the story.

The dominance of the younger, putatively less responsible and less in-tellectual "action faction" over the more measured "praxis axis" of the New Left became amplified after the Pentagon march, degenerating in short time into complicity with the Chicago convention "police riot," and into its farcical reenactment, the Weathermen "days of rage." A handful of former New Leftists even became involved in a spate of bomb-ings, aimed mostly against property associated with the war effort, some of which became inadvertent murders. The lesson that you can't blow up hegemonic social relations (though *agents provocateurs* will always be there to help you try) is a crucial one that the memoirists are certainly right to underline. Indeed, the desire of agencies of repression to provoke violence remains the most eloquent testimony to the necessity of non-violent strategies in the context of liberal democratic states. So long as those states disguise their violence in successfully legitimating rhetoric, counterhegemonic violence is strategically suicidal (and internally de-structive to movements as well). But the vast majority of the New Left engaged in at most rhetorical violence, and even the scattered acts of physical violence can in no way be compared to the vast violence un-leashed by the American empire in Vietnam, Newark, and Chicago, or to the violence of the repressive counterintelligence apparatus directed especially against black and Native American but also against white rad-icals in the late sixties. This far greater violence was pursued precisely by those "reasonable," "responsible," "disciplined," "representative" men the New Left had done so much to expose as morally bankrupt.

Similarly, while the demise of SDS in a hail of ideological babble in 1969 was a loss to the movement, becoming more like the parties and institutions that upheld and uphold American racism, sexism, classism, and imperialism would hardly have been a more effective strategy. Rather than being read as a tragic fall of what could have been a national center for the movement, the end of SDS should be read as also a diffusion of energy that helped usher in a host of new movements (women's, gay, en-vironmental, etc.), a diffusion that sent most dedicated New Left activists not off to revolutionism or Wall Street (as media stereotypes would have it) but back to the grass roots to help form hundreds of participatory democratic community organizations across the country that less dra-matically but often effectively continue movement work.[28]

A more useful reading of the issues raised by the new memoirists can be found in Wini Breines's book *Community and Organization in the New Left, 1962–1968: The Great Refusal*, and in her critical review of literature on sixties movements.[29] Breines uses the term "prefigurative politics" to describe the attempts by the early New Left to anticipate, through the community structure and model personal relations within "the Movement," the new society they sought to bring into being. Breines notes the difficulty of this task, indeed the theme of her text is the conflict between this internal, trans*form*ative concern and the seemingly more instrumental task of inducing structural political change. But she defends it as an essential strategy for radical change under late capitalism:

> The effort to build community, to create and prefigure in lived action . . . the desired society, the emphasis on means and not ends, the spontaneous and utopian experiments that developed in the midst of political actions whose goal was a free and democratic society—all were central to the movements of the sixties and among their most important contribution. A central organization [i.e., a more tightly structured SDS] could neither have "saved" the movement, nor was it congruent with the New Left's suspicion of hierarchy, leadership, and the concentration of power. The movement was not simply unruly and undisciplined; it was experimenting with anti-hierarchical organizational forms.[30]

Moreover, the ongoing nature of these experiments, Breines notes, belies the exaggerated "decline and fall" stories told by the memoirists: "Most of the democratic and hopeful elements in American society even today have roots in the sixties: feminism, countercultural perspectives in the arts; the contributions of people of color finally acknowledged by white society; a distancing from . . . militaristic, and nationalistic sentiments; and the decentered political organizations and projects attempting to build a more equal, less competitive, multicultural and tolerant society."[31]

Breines doesn't note that there is also a significant "aesthetic" ambiguity within the term "prefigurative" itself, one that links her analysis to the one I am offering here. She clearly intends the term to signify a preconception of the future society experienced within the movement itself. But the term also suggests *pre*figurative, not yet figured, not yet locked into form. And this latter definition is nearly the precise opposite of the former. If a movement community is in some sense the form of prefigurative politics, prefiguration requires a reflexive questioning of this form. It requires a delicate balance between community and inclusivity, ethos and critical consciousness. This is in part an ambiguity built into American democracy itself—a form at once calling *for* open, collective decision making, and calling for equal protection of all individuals *from* collective decisions; it is this tension that has led insurgent group after insurgent group to use calls for democracy against the American state that perpetually claims falsely to have achieved it.

The problems the New Left and *Armies* had in achieving and maintaining this delicate balance can be explored further by looking at another dramatic demonstration, the Women's Pentagon Action. Though only indirectly commenting on the earlier Pentagon march, the Women's Action sheds light on the limits of that text and offers further developments of the attempt to articulate a collective political hermeneutic process.

Dramatic Ecofeminism

*The Women's Pentagon Action as
Theater and Theory*

A NEW STAGE OF THE MOVEMENT

In this chapter I want to do two things: first, continue the exploration of demonstration dramaturgy begun in the previous chapter; and second, extend my genealogy of social movement cultures toward the present. I combine these two elements through a reading of the "text" of the Women's Pentagon Actions of the early 1980s, two exceptionally dramatic political demonstrations that raise a host of issues about the relationship between theory and theatrics, politics and representation. My argument is that the Women's Pentagon events form a significant advance in radical dramaturgy that is made possible in large part by the significant advances in radical theory and method that have been developed most fully by contemporary feminism(s).

The Women's Pentagon Actions enact an interplay of theory and performance that suggests new ways to perform theory as well as new theories of political performance. The theories performed in these actions draw on the work of a number of recent social movements, movements that are challenging the American left to examine what one might call its politico-epistemological foundations, challenging the left to democratize leadership, theorizing, and the production of movement power/knowledge generally. In reading the Women's Pentagon Actions I trace these ideas as they are expanded by a group of antimilitarist women, but I also draw on my own experience in the Livermore Action Group, an antimilitarist network of women and men whose ideas and actions have built upon the theory and practice embodied in the Women's Action.[1]

Throughout this chapter, I use the terms Action, Actions, Pentagon Action(s), Women's Action(s), and Women's Pentagon Action (WPA) interchangeably to refer to two women-only theatrical demonstrations, one in the fall of 1980, the other in the fall of 1981, that involved the ritual (re)enactment of Mourning, Rage, Empowerment, and Defiance, concluding with the encirclement of and civil disobedience against the Pentagon complex.[2] For convenience' sake, I discuss the two "performances" of this "play" as if they were one text. The first action involved approximately two thousand women, the second roughly twice that number.

These particular actions are important not only because they were exemplary radical theater, but also because they note a turning point for an important strand of the left. They were one key transitionary moment that contributed to the resurgence of American and European peace, ecology, and feminist movements in the eighties as well as helping to trigger a re-imagining of movement theatrics/tactics that fostered, for example, the women's encampments at Seneca Falls, Greenham Common, and elsewhere; the Pentagon Actions also inspired numerous mixed gender, mixed media theatrical actions here and abroad around a host of other issues including apartheid and U.S. intervention in Central America.[3] Precipitated by first candidate, then President Reagan's efforts to reheat the Cold War, these Actions also mark the public emergence of the sometimes problematic but always interesting strand of politics known as ecofeminism.[4]

At one level, the Women's Pentagon events embody a radically transformative critique-in-action of the New Left of the 1960s and their style of demonstration politics. While one should acknowledge that the Second Wave Women's Movement (at least initially) drew on the successes and failures of the New Left,[5] it is not possible, as some male leftists would have it, to view feminism as something added onto the kind of radical democratic politics advocated by the New Left (i.e., adding in "women's issues"). Rather feminism will be used here to designate an elaborated ensemble of political theories, methods, and practices that itself critiques, incorporates, and goes beyond earlier radical theories.[6] To the extent that some feminisms have managed to focus on issues of race, class, colonialism, sexual orientation, and environmental devastation, as well as and as intertwined with analyses of gender, they have become the most important radical perspectives from which to undertake future political thought and action. In this chapter my concern is with how a strand of feminism does this at the level of collective political education and collective political expression through the theatrical enactment of certain theoretical, methodological, and strategic positions.

In offering a reading of the events of the Women's Pentagon Action I am writing consciously as an outsider (as a nonparticipant and, to re-mark the category, as a nonwoman). Thus I think it is important to underline a caveat offered by Ynestra King as a preamble to her narrative account of the Women's Action. She wrote that her effort was "not an attempt to represent the group [of participants]. Each of us has her own story, and our collective story could only be written collectively."[7] What follows likewise does not presume to be such a story of the Pentagon Action(s). Nor does my version of these events pretend to be an empirical history (I do not assume that all or even any one individual who partic-ipated in the Action experienced it as I describe it). Rather, as with my other readings, I am attempting to construct something new from and with this text/event, in this case something of an "ideal type" of the event(s) that can draw out some themes and ideas about theater and pol-itics to make those ideas more readily available for political discussion.

I speculate on meanings in the event for both the immediate and me-diated audiences of the Actions, though eventually that distinction breaks down as I argue that the "direct experience" of the events (as op-posed to experiencing them theoretically) should not be privileged. This latter point is meant to underscore what I take to be one crucially im-portant theoretical stance built into the Action—a dialogical critique of essentialist or overly generalized notions of "woman" and "women's ex-perience."[8] Such a critique has become increasingly important in recent feminist theory as early claims about "women" and "experience" have been challenged by Third World women, working-class women, lesbi-ans, and others marginalized by the mostly white, mostly middle-class representatives of Second Wave feminism in the United States.[9] In offering such an interpretation, I am consciously working against reductive read-ings of the Pentagon Actions that portray them as precisely deploying such essentialism.

My general interpretation is mediated through several written ac-counts of the events, with particular attention given to two articles about the Women's Action that appeared in *Socialist Review* in 1982. As rep-resentational extensions of the Pentagon Actions, these two texts are of special interest to me because they enact certain rhetorical strategies that are also strategies I see in the WPA proper. It is interesting and I think more than coincidental that two of the most thoughtful analyses of the Women's Actions have multiple authorship, one an interactive interview, the other a full-scale dialogue in which eventually it becomes impossible even to tell which of the two speakers is talking.[10] I say it is more than coincidental because both these articles as well as other accounts of the Actions make it clear that from the organizing stages onward, the events were created out of and evolved into multilayered dialogues (as Ynestra King's claim above that an account of the event could only be written collectively also testifies).[11] I read this collective authorship as an important corrective to the element of masculinist narcissism I have tried to underline and undermine in the three other "literary" texts examined above.

While drawing on these written accounts, my main interest is in reading the Women's Pentagon events themselves as text. This is not a claim that the events speak unambiguously or without mediation, but precisely the opposite: I want to show that the event inherently acknowledges its textuality, its polyvocality, that it explicitly opens itself to conflictual collective and individual interpretation, and that it thereby raises theoretical issues about the construction of power/knowledge within movements as well as questions about the politics of interpretation.

MOBILIZING EMOTION

Methodologically, much of the dramaturgical logic of the Women's Pentagon Actions can be seen as emerging from a twofold extension of the idea of consciousness-raising: it extends the method to issues that are not normally considered feminist; and it extends it to theatrical public space. Consciousness-raising, the name given to attempts by women meeting in small groups to discuss personal experiences in order to transform them into the basis for the collective, structural, political analysis of sexist oppression, was a key element in the early period of Second Wave feminism. Most historians and theorists of feminism agree that consciousness-raising was an important political method in the early stages of the rebirth of feminism in the sixties and seventies, but they disagree as to its ongoing usefulness and importance.[12] In recent years, "cr" has been implicated in the essentialist debate for seeming to base itself on naively empirical notions of a common "woman's experience," thereby at once glossing over differences of race, class, nationality, sexuality, and so on, among women and seeming to privilege psychology over action, pure experience over mediated theory. As I suggested above, I think these critiques are crucial ones, but there is another way of formulating them. The critiques are aimed more at limited experiences than at the limits of experientially based theorizing (after all, even reading Louis Althusser or Donna Haraway is an experience, albeit one that challenges naive conceptions of experience). As a number of feminist critics have begun to argue, something like a common womankind plays a necessary heuristic role in feminism. The problem arises with the rush to give that heuristic concept a specific content. Some participants in the WPA can be justly accused of this kind of essentializing, this attempt to create what Audre Lorde has called "the friendly face of cheap alliance." But there is also in the WPA a way of drawing on experiences and a way of using consciousness-raising that suggests a path through this dilemma. Rather than simply replacing consciousness-raising, the Action attempts to re-place it into a more varied public space where conflicting and complementary experiences can begin to serve as the basis for the kind of political alignment amidst diversity that is the only sound basis for theorizing and practicing feminism (or any other contemporary radical struggle).

One can picture the Actions as a series of concentric dialogues or polyphonic encounters modeled on and transforming the basic consciousness-raising group developed by Second Wave feminists. What this series or layering of "cr-groups" suggests is both a confirmation and a transformation of claims about the centrality of consciousness-raising as *the* feminist method. Consciousness-raising, as *one* feminist method, proves able to illuminate the limits of particular feminisms while also expanding the terrain of "proper" feminist concerns.[13] The Pentagon Action is an important moment in a general process through which consciousness-raising as method and feminism as theory are becoming integral to the general project of building an oppositional, alternative social-movement epistemology and politics. Consciousness-raising and the closely related decision-making method called "consensus process" (which I will discuss later in this chapter) are becoming key elements of a new, collective political hermeneutics.[14]

From the beginning the Action had a complex sense of movement over the boundaries of traditional feminist concerns that is at the same time an effort to deepen those concerns. The event drew not only on the feminist movement and community but also on the environmental, solidarity, lesbian/gay, antiracist, peace, and antinuclear direct action movements, among others. Both ideologically and tactically it sought to cross

boundaries, creating new formations and formulations. As one participant put it: "We observed an exciting cross fertilization of ideas from
different movements: the tactic of civil disobedience came from the black
civil rights and anti-nuclear movements; guerilla theater, used by the yip-
pees [sic] and the 1960s feminists; collective process and decentralized
organization, developed by feminists and anarchists; a commitment to
working with women and discussions about the politics of lesbianism,
originated with the feminist and lesbian-feminist movement; and affinity
groups, associated with the anti-nuclear movement."[15] One direction of
the Women's Action is outward toward the wide spectrum of ecological,
antimilitarist, anticapitalist activities, while another impetus sought to
deepen the connection of women as women to one another by making
the action a women's-only event. The two directions then come together
in the notion that the Pentagon events would enact a specifically feminist
analysis of militarism that would illuminate it in new ways: by drama-
tizing the centrality of gender for military ideologies, by showing the connection of militarism to patterns of male violence against women, and so
forth. In turn, this activity would also provide new insights about the
nature and scope of feminism: by showing the necessity of global, mul-
tiethnic, multiclass perspectives, and by challenging stultifying dichotomies between cultural and materialist feminists.[16]

The plan for a Women's Action at the Pentagon grew out of a discussion following a conference on feminism and ecology held at Amherst in
spring of 1980. As one of the early organizers put it: "We knew that we
wanted it to be a women's action, to reflect feminist values; to represent
as many constituencies as possible; and that, while we were going to the
military's headquarters, we wanted to address a wide range of concerns,
pointing to the Pentagon sometimes literally, sometimes symbolically."[17]
The tone and intent of the initial efforts included the desire to direct the
action both outward in an "ordinary language" that participants'
"mothers could understand" and inward toward involving and transforming the participants themselves. Early organizing centered around
the collective creation of a "Unity Statement" that would provide tone
and vision for the action. More than two hundred women took part in
the process of drafting the document, achieving agreement on its content
through a series of small and larger consciousness-raising sessions meant
to articulate and deepen the themes of the event. Thus the drafting of the
statement was an event itself, one that engaged some women who did
not attend the Action (just as later publication and circulation of the
statement has led to discussion and debate among many other "indirect

participants"). The statement continued to be revised even after the first successful Action in fall of 1980, keeping alive a sense of the openness of the event, a sense of the meaning of the Action as in-process.

The "Unity Statement," given final literary polish by writer Grace Paley, was presented less as a manifesto than as a focus for ongoing discussion.[18] Among other things, the statement aimed to link the new militarism to sexist violence against women and to degradation of a "feminized" and othered Nature; to raise issues of racism, sexism, and heterosexism as they shape our interventionist foreign policy; and to expose links between the military budget and domestic poverty as it falls unequally upon women, particularly women of color. The list of issues it raises are presented for the most part in everyday language, and the points are often simply juxtaposed rather than hammered into some seamless ideological system, thus inviting readers to formulate some connections on their own.

The desire to find an accessible language free of leftist jargon was paralleled by organizing efforts outside the normal leftist channels in laundromats, beauty parlors, PTA meetings, and other venues frequented by women who might not think of themselves as activists or feminists.

In a similar spirit, the action was not planned as a coalition event—organizations were not formally represented—but rather as an effort to create a new, perhaps temporary but nonetheless rich political community in/as the Action. This opening up of a distance between organizational identity and more general political identity accounts for the apparently pervasive feeling of participants that they were able to achieve real dialogue with other ideological viewpoints. These dialogues were further facilitated by workshops on the day before the Action treating "ecology, militarism, work, racism, artists, childcare, health, sexual orientation, poverty," and a range of other topics.[19]

FORGING (COLLECTIVE) IDENTITIES

The overall theatrical structure of the Action was also culled from cr-style planning meetings in which women were asked to reflect on their thoughts and emotions when confronted with the spectacle of militarism on all of its complex levels. The results of these smaller sessions were then externalized, theatricalized as the four stages of the action. The theater-in-action was structured around the ritual collective (re)enactment of feelings of Mourning, Rage, Empowerment, and Defiance, with each stage marked by a change in the tempo of accompanying drumbeats, and by huge papier-mâché puppets (provided by the Bread and Puppet Theater) that expressively embodied the particular emotion and served as orientation points for participants.

Through this theatricalization of emotion, a complex and truly social psychology in-forms the action. Personal emotions are revealed to be social and historical emotion-structures (or "structures of feeling" as Raymond Williams calls them) inter-subjectively reformulated, expressed, and reflected upon. These emotions are enacted thoughtfully and pointedly. As Donna Warnock puts it, "Instead of giving into the sexist stereotype that emotion should not be part of rational thinking and should not be shown in public, we demonstrated that being in touch with our emotions makes us strong and intelligent."[20] In contradistinction to America's mania for indulgent, individualist therapies, the events dramatically demonstrate collective use of and transformation of emotions, a translation of emotion (back) into public discourse, a kind of (partial) catharsis embedded in, not substituting for, thoughtful action. At the level of feminist theory, this mode of action symbolically and practically complicates and synthesizes the political-analytic, materialist strength usually identified with socialist feminisms with the emotional empowerment skills and sense of ritual developed most fully by cultural feminists.[21]

The "mobilization of emotions" into the four main categories is part of a more general dynamic in the Action that sought to deepen each participant's personal, individual identity and responsibility, while at the same time constructing or acknowledging larger, collective identities and a sense of structural power to counter the alienating and divisive individualism so prevalent in the United States (even on the left). One of the ways this dynamic worked was through the issuing of collective names to all the participants; they were asked upon entering the pre-Action encampment to add the last name of either (antinuclear activist) Karen Silkwood or Yolanda Ward (a black feminist activist murdered just before the Action) to their own first name. As one participant noted, the names crossed racial identity, and also linked corporate violence to state violence. Every woman wore a large name tag that both individualized her (with a first name) and made her part of a larger collective (with her new last name).[22]

Rhoda Linton remarks on the effects of these and related efforts: "I was very conscious of moving back and forth from being an individual to being part of a huge piece of the world. It's nothing like the kind of feeling I got from the demonstrations I participated in in the past. I'm not trying to put those down; I'm simply trying to show the way that this was different."[23]

Women in the Action were also encouraged to play certain generic female social roles: Mother, Daughter, Sister, Victim of Male Violence, Healer, and so on. By assuming these social identities, women did not give up their "personal" experience, but in acting another role that experience is given a creative distance (creative in the sense that it becomes a re-source for acting the role, and in the sense that such distance can make room for reflection on the social construction of one's "own" experience). As in consciousness-raising groups, putatively individual identity is tested against, displaced into, a sense of social identity-structures. The fact that participants were mostly not professional actors enhanced this distancing process since their performances would not be smoothly naturalistic;[24] by re-presenting social gesture and language without the "naturalness" of everyday behavior, the possibility of socially changing the self is opened up. The theatrical is/becomes the political.

A similar process of individualizing, personalizing, balanced against a sense of collective, structural identity was enacted in the creation of a Women's Cemetery on the Pentagon lands, the key event in the Mourning phase of the Action. Participants were asked to make a cardboard headstone and to place upon it the name of a woman or women who died at the hands of patriarchal violence. The name could either be a highly personal one (a family member or a friend or a lover), or one felt from a distance (a Latin American woman "disappeared" by a death squad). Some wrote collective names ("For the many women who have been murdered as a result of battering, rape and abuse"), but most apparently were more personal ("My Grandmother [who] died of a self-induced abortion in 1932"). Or as in the case of one woman, the personal and the global became one as she wrote of "Three unknown Vietnamese women. Killed by my son."

This process allowed collective power to emerge from the placing of so many individual cases side by side. Women moved through this theater of death drawing their own interpretations and discussing with other women the collective sources of so many kinds of violence. In such a context, a nuclear power plant is revealed as "domestic" violence, and a battered woman in Argentina is a matter of international concern.

More generally, the cemetery ritual enacted the making of history. On their way to the Pentagon, participants walked through the horribly anonymous yet putatively heroic Arlington National Cemetery, where "even the tombstones stand at attention in neat military rows."[25] At the

Pentagon their cemetery countered the still deeper anonymity of the women in history who gave or had their lives taken in constructing and resisting the militarist, patriarchal culture of the present. Lines across geography but also across time were established as the names of mothers and grandmothers made history, made a genealogy that deepened awareness in the present of the terrible costs of militarism.

Painting the tombstones, weaving a collective braid with which to encircle the Pentagon, baking bread for those who were to go to jail for civil disobedience, these events were part of a Preparation day that preceded the Action proper. Like the glimpses of the material production process in a Brecht play, these preparations emphasize the hidden, unrewarded domestic production that fuels patriarchal capitalism, while at the same time reinforcing the sense that not someone else but the participants themselves were making this event, making this history.

These are powerful, symbolically rich enactments, but as some participants realized, the symbolism contains some problematic aspects. Both the general role-playing and the preparation phase of the Action highlight a potential danger in the symbols chosen by many of the participants. In contrast to the political strength emanating from assuming the collective identities of activists like Silkwood and Ward, much of the role-playing and preparation work risked reinforcement of traditional women's roles and women's work (weaving, breadmaking, etc). The promise of such symbolic gestures is that they can help bring traditional (nonactivist, nonfeminist) women into the Action and the movement; and they offer public celebration of the kind of private lives most women have lived for centuries. This can be an important part of a re-writing of women's (and men's) history. But the danger is that such traditional symbolism will inadvertently further entrench limiting definitions of "women's roles" and "women's work."

One particular danger resides in the use during the Action of what Micaela di Leonardo has criticized as "Moral Mother" symbolism,[26] the tendency to identify women as morally superior to and inherently less militaristic than men by virtue of their roles as mothers and nurturers. Di Leonardo grants the drawing power of this rhetoric to many women, but she sees it as an ultimately disempowering, dead-end strategy (even when it relies on social rather than biological determinations for its basis). She argues that the Moral Mother position glosses over the complicity (nearly always exploited complicity, but complicity nonetheless) of women in militarism (as military personnel, workers in civilian defense production, etc.); obfuscates questions about the construction of gender as a contribution to militarist culture; and downplays the specifically political (as opposed to moral in a narrow sense) nature of resistance to militarism. Di Leonardo adds that "using the Moral Mother image to enter the public world also meant that it could be used against women to push them back into the home."[27]

Concerns similar to di Leonardo's were expressed as part of the dialogue in the Action from the beginning, but her analysis is a particularly lucid reminder of potential limits to certain symbols and representational strategies used in the movement. Some participants in the Pentagon Action also critiqued the emphasis on the mother/traditionalist roles on the related grounds that it tended to discriminate against women who had no interest in being mothers or who had chosen to do nontraditional female labor.[28]

The danger of the "moral mother" position is reinforced when an ecological component is added in the form of the notion that women are closer to and thus more able to defend "Mother Earth." For some feminist critics this fusion or confusion of feminism with ecology or other issues is dangerous because they believe only some essentialist notion of "the feminine" can justify "a woman's perspective" on nuclear weapons or American interventionism.[29]

But there are some other ways to explain the choice of an all-women's Action that do not fall into this trap. One is the simple but important point made by a number of participants that being free for a time from the sexism they often encountered in their respective mixed-gender organizations was liberating and illuminating. A second argument contends that socialization, not biology, has placed some (not all) women in a position to see through militarism by virtue of their forced distance from it. Finally, and to me most importantly, this question can be reformulated not in terms of the inherent pacifism of one gender and the inherent militarism of the other but of the necessity of militarism to rely on the deployment of gender differentiation. That is, one can make a specific historical argument, of the kind called for by Joan Scott, for gender (as well as class and race) as a necessary category for any full analysis of militarism as a system or subsystem of capitalism. The kind of connections made in the "Unity Statement" and in the Action between violence against women and war, between militarism and masculinity, between the violence of poverty and the costs of military build-ups are key elements of such an analysis.[30]

In response to an interviewer's question about this nurturant "women as saviors of the earth" stance, Pentagon Action participant-organizer Warnock offered the following analysis, summing up both the dangers of the position and the possibility that it can be clarified and made useful as a small part of a larger strategy: "There are two sides to [the earth saviors] line. The notion that women are more nurturing and, therefore, should participate to save the earth is usually sexist. That's our sex role stereotype. The fact is that everyone has the capacity to nurture. That women have been socialized to do so is a reality, and it is an asset we have going for us. But at the same time we recognize it as a strength, we must deplore it as a mandate."[31]

With these cautions in mind, it is possible to return and re-read the "traditional" symbolism in the Action in another way. As I suggested earlier, the public enactment of normally "private" roles and activities of women is a significant re-contextualization. And because the entire Action was infused with a spirit of collective play, of festivity, and of defiance, the mindful transgression of the putative boundary between public and private life makes the acts of baking and weaving something else, something quite other than traditional.[32] Moreover, the "Unity Statement," as well as workshops in the Action, stressed nontraditional occupations for women alongside respect for roles traditionally defined as women's work.

Participant-organizers of the Actions also sought to avoid the "star system" that is one key element in the alienating "spectacularization" of most demonstrations; there were no speakers and thus no audience. And "there were no 'stars' in this entire demonstration. I could never identify from one day to the next, or from one event to the next, the same people doing whatever leading needed to be done."[33] Or as Ynestra King put it, "All of us were the theater, the actors."[34]

Linton remarks on how different the event seemed from the large mass rallies she'd participated in, where what I've called "spectacularization" precisely undermined a sense of continuity, stressed an extraordinariness that could inadvertently discourage ongoing action. Contrasting the events with the usual elite-planned demonstration, Linton and Michele Whitham exchange these observations:

> In the past it seemed as though we limited what we could experience through our political actions by limiting ourselves in time and space, by designing short-term events that focused on themselves, on their own moment.
>
> And by surrendering ourselves to the mass also. How can you experience if you're not there as an entity?

> Right. Not to be someone who contributes my piece and sees what every-
> body else's piece is, but limiting ourselves to the words of selected individuals
> who "represent" us or who somehow lend legitimacy to us because of who
> they are, not because of who we are.
> At many of those demonstrations, others spoke for us.
> Right.
> I'm really understanding the power of planning together now, because in
> planning for someone you conceptualize the experience for them. You do the
> thinking and the interpreting.
> You take away from their opportunity to create themselves. To name their
> own reality.[35]

These remarks "represent" a growing realization in new social movements that the structure of demonstrations (not to say of many movement organizations) too often replicates the liberal representative system
against which the activists are working and whose rhetorical traps poststructuralist theorists have been unraveling.

The New Left and other sixties movements provide numerous examples of how easily an apparently deep commitment to internal democracy can be eroded by representatives, and of the high cost to movements when that erosion occurs.[36] Many postsixties movements have
tried to keep this important question of political form and content,
means and ends, constantly on the agenda, and this critique of representation along with developments of the idea of consciousness-raising as
an active, open-ended form of internal, equalizing political education
have so far been key to this process.

The Preparation stage of the Action (along with the final Empowerment stage and its closing ceremony) can be seen to serve another important function. By not allowing a radical break between Preparation
and Action, the general sense of political-cultural process preceding and
continuing beyond the Action was reinforced. This sense of ongoing action was also fostered by the fact that the women who chose to go to jail
for acts of civil disobedience continued their learning process and their
organizational outreach through dialogue with the "regular" women
prisoners whose illegal actions, while not recognized as such, should
often be read as (un)civil disobedience to a racist, sexist, economically
exploitative social formation.[37]

STRATEGIC RAGE

Each phase of the planning and acting of the Women's Pentagon events
passed through something like a consciousness-raising session—some-

times formalized, other times not, but utilizing the basic cr-group model with its antihierarchical, radically participatory structure. One important aspect of this "feminist process" (as it is called in the antinuclear direct action movement) is that intellection and emotion are not allowed to be conceived separately; in certain key ways the two become intertwined and transposed, making it clear that intellection without emotion is frequently irrational.

The choice of and movement into the Rage stage of the Action bears particular contrast with the New Left. For some in the New Left, rage was seen as empowering and useful, but mostly in empowering a break out of putatively "bourgeois" reticences and useful primarily for intimidating opponents. This contributed eventually to the sophomoric and sectarian squandering of much of SDS's political capital through actions like the street-trashing "days of rage." These New Left demonstration theatrics may have offered the classical theatrical experience of catharsis, but, as Bertolt Brecht argued, that experience frequently reinforces dominant emotion structures rather than clarifying or changing them; catharsis provided a venting of emotion that takes the place of rather than extends thinking. How, for example, did many New Left demonstrations formally differ from the venting of emotions in a football rally? Indeed, a pep-rally structure no doubt played into New Left mobilizations; but that structure could and did as easily provide a way out of the movement when a new or rather old content was poured into the form.

By contrast, in the Women's Action the connection between emotions like Rage and Empowerment was a more mediated, analytic, though deeply felt, connection: "Unless you deal with your emotions you just don't think clearly. Witness the militarists: are they rational? Unrecognized emotions are like a fog veiling the brain; because vision is distorted, misinformation is believed. At the Pentagon we were attempting to lift that fog. We were dealing with emotions that we, in fact, had and, consequently, needed to deal with, in order to get to our power and to think intelligently."[38] Such a perspective sets up a dialectical play in the Action between militarism as external, material force and militarism as an internalized mode of consciousness from which even movement members themselves are not immune.

To argue that Rage was strategically mobilized in the Action should not be to neglect its transgressive power. The public enactment of decidedly "unfeminine" Rage and Defiance was a real violation of patriarchal decorum. I have generally argued against "spectacular" demonstrations, but there is one sense in which the Women's Pentagon theater was legit-imately (illegitimately) spectacular. As Mary Russo has pointed out, women are not supposed to "make spectacles of themselves" in public but rather be available as spectacle to the male gaze. Thus when women participate en masse in an unsanctioned carnival of transgression it can be a politically forceful spectacle that can threaten patriarchal imagery and power. Since public and theatric space have traditionally been denied to women, to simultaneously reclaim them both is strategically vital.[39]

Because the "external," instrumental effects of demonstrations have been previously overemphasized, I have here concentrated primarily on the effects of the Action on the participants to the neglect of questions about the wider audience of nonparticipants, but I want to make a couple of remarks about this more distant audience. Mainstream coverage of the Pentagon Action did not significantly break through the media stereo-types of activist women that Alison Young has analyzed (with regard to the newspaper coverage of the women at Greenham Common peace camp).[40] But for the many who heard about or saw the Pentagon Actions on television, the spectacle of women collectively invading, surrounding, "penetrating," and blockading the sacred stronghold of the military es-tablishment was a strikingly disruptive symbol. Ynestra King, for one, attests that even the jaded, patronizing reporters sent to cover the Action seemed shocked, moved, and impressed by the drama of the event.[41] And in the interactive interview I have been analyzing, nonparticipant Whit-ham becomes as engaged by/in the text as her interlocutor who was there "in person."

I want to stress that in the long run movements need *both* effective openings onto the wider society and places to make their own meanings. The WPA no doubt could have been more effective than it was with re-gard to confronting the so-called mainstream. But it is exemplary with regard to the internal movement dynamics it suggests, and the form of theorizing and political education it embodies. Such examples are crucial because, given the capacity of postmodern capitalism to incorporate de-fiance as spectacle, the creation of alternative public spaces in which the oppositional movements largely determine their own meanings is central to any counterhegemonic project. The precedence of this dimension over the external media effects is suggested eloquently by the gesture of one participant who had been assigned the task of interacting with the me-dia: at a certain point in the Action she felt moved to drop her media badge and her role as interpreter in order to enter more fully into the drama unfolding around her.[42]

DEFYING CONSENSUS

Consciousness-raising was also very much at play in the Defiance stage of the Action. Participants in the civil disobedience dimension of the action used a more formalized method partly derived from but extending cr that is similarly designed to dialectically synthesize cognitive and affective moments. These civilly disobedient participants (as well as many others in the Action) were part of "affinity groups" of 8 to 15 people who made decisions together by "consensus process" rather than parliamentary or representative procedures. Consensus process as developed in the contemporary direct action movement builds on and gives more self-reflexive form to radical democratic discussion styles in the Civil Rights movement and New Left, and formalizes consciousness-raising as developed in the Women's movement (as well as drawing on components derived from the Quakers and other sources).[43]

Sometimes misconstrued by outsiders as coercive and requiring unanimity, the goal of consensus is just the opposite—to maximize and then mobilize a diversity of opinions. Consensus process is based on the premise that because liberal, patriarchal capitalism enforces a variety of hegemonic, unreflexive forms of consent, movement decisions need forms that allow each participant to give active, not merely passive, assent to the outlines of the group's action, an assent that should ideally emerge from scrutiny of numerous levels of thought and feeling, from the most strategically instrumental to the most affective/aesthetic. The goal is to bring forth hidden dissensus in order both to strengthen any basis of cooperation that can be achieved and to ensure that the broadest range of factors is brought into play in any decision. The proliferation of semi-autonomous affinity groups further allows for a range of actions from a range of principles within a basic, collectively determined set of guidelines (usually ones having to do with prohibition of various kinds of violence).

Alongside some of the cr-style procedures used in formulating and preparing the Action, consensus process lays the groundwork for, or rehearses, the larger enactment of thoughtful emotions that shapes the Action overall. In this small group process one's emotions are both given weight and recognized as something other than one's personal property. In a similar way, the four acts of the Pentagon drama call for participants to express their personal, private sense of mourning, rage, empowerment, and defiance, but in a context in which private meanings are transformed, recontextualized, revealed to be publicly political.

Consensus process, in more or less formalized versions, is widely practiced in new social movements in the United States, Europe, and elsewhere. It can be thought of as a theorized and practical attempt to create
the lineaments of what Jürgen Habermas elsewhere heuristically posits
as a domination-free communication structure that can do justice to the
multiple dimensions of experience.[44] Habermas's theory has striking parallels with feminist and feminist-influenced recent social movement practice, but from the heights of "malestream" theory he seems nowhere to
have acknowledged the connection.[45] As Donald Beggs has argued,
consensus/feminist process is structurally related to recent shifts in social
and political theorizing: "consensus is a collective practice which closely
corresponds to the epistemological paradigm shift now happening in late
capitalist human sciences."[46] For theorists of the human sciences and social movement participant-theorists there is a questioning of the object/
subject relation and recognition of intersubjective, ideological processes
in which both instrumental rationality and expressive-affective rationality are at play.

Consensus decision making is at once a recovery process and the creation of something new, a recovery of communal bonds made ever more
tenuous as capitalism has evolved, and the prefiguration of new, radically
democratic social relations. The very necessity of having to resort to the
conscious creation of techniques for building and sustaining community
is made into a virtue in consensus as tacit assumptions, a source not only
of affections but also of prejudices, become available for collective review. Consensus is a process for the self-conscious, reflective construction of community because, as Beggs puts it, consensus "constitutes political obligation, not as a contract theory (which limits itself to strategic
rationality), but as intersubjective bonds that ground action imperatives
through a specific decision process. Groups are unified consensually in
the collective generation of meaning contexts and interpretations of the
world."[47] Like Habermas's early heuristic concept, "the ideal speech situation," consensus is never fully or finally achieved; it is always a pro-
visional agreement of those present and thus subject to transformation
by those not yet included in the polis-in-process. What this means for the
WPA (and any similar action) is that the truth or continuing truthfulness
of its (unavoidably) representative actions depends on an ever-expanding
circle of participants whose differences must necessarily displace, refor-
mulate, the collectivity-in-difference. If the texts examined in Chapters
2, 3, and 4 have a tendency to recoup collective processes in the individual ego, the Women's Action represents the danger of premature univer-
salization, a fact brought home most vividly by women of color, some of

whom protested their marginalization and underrepresentation in the event.[48]

In the Women's Action a sense of collective thinking and collective interpretation seems to have been extremely strong, no doubt in large part because the layering of identities was both subtle and starkly clear: the (relatively) undistorted communication[49] aimed at by use of consensus process can only occur when respect for each participant's contribution is offered even as that contribution is decentered in the collective process. The creation of consensus entails a subtle sacrifice of one's position, an attempt to create a new entity that arises from no one particular contribution but that is only possible because of those varied contributions. This collective determination arises only with the active consent of each member of the "consensing" group, each of whom has potential veto power over the proposal. While obviously vulnerable to abuse, this process also ensures a very serious form of self- and collective reflexivity, a searching for the deepest levels of strategic and interpersonal agreement and disagreement.

The formalization of consensus process by feminist and direct action movements has made the process far less subject to abuse than was the emerging version used by the early Student Nonviolent Coordinating Committee (SNCC) and the New Left, but it remains to be seen how well this process can be translated to an evergrowing mass of constituents (or rather whether it can prevent the "massing" of such a constituency and maintain its radical democratic ethos). In the Women's Pentagon Action, consensus is a key part of the process through which various political identities and identity politics are forced to confront one another amidst the practical imperatives of acting in (some degree of) concert. That action/Action imperative serves to illuminate those differences that matter and those that do not, and to create theory in the moment of clarifying goals, working out strategy, and improvising tactics.

The contemporary movements that use these processes and forms are already beginning to face the test presented to the New Left, the task of maintaining democratic integrity while integrating an ever larger and more diverse membership. But to date consensus and its attendant ethos is the closest approximation I have seen to a union of democratic form and substance, collective determination and individual responsibility, community and critical self-reflexivity.

I have emphasized the cerebral, even philosophical, dimensions of these processes and of the Action generally because I think they have been distorted by analyses (even by some feminists) that have been based on stereotyped dichotomies of emotion and rationality. But I don't wish to add a new distortion by overemphasizing the hermeneutic dimensions, for the purpose of consensus process was to lead not just to interpreting the world but to changing it, changing it through direct action. The dramatic movement of the defiance stage moves from the mind to the body, or rather to the body as mind, the body as a political statement against militarism. And defiance through civil disobedience is an experience of the political, bodily pleasures of transgression. We spend most of our lives in a state of compromise, particularly political compromise in which the body of our actions is always less than we desire. But the act of blocking the entrance to the Pentagon, or of entering it illegally, entails the often frightening but also erotically charged sense of throwing one's full being into one's political actions (Thoreau called it casting your "whole vote" in contrast to the compromised voting among relatively bland alternatives that is the incomplete democracy offered by the state).

Encouraged by all the women around them, affinity groups attacked the center of violence nonviolently, physically enacting their dissent, publicly defying the false consensus that allows imperialism, racist wars, and domestically impoverishing military build-ups to go on under the cover of "representative" democracy. They took yarn (another traditional symbol of feminine labor) and used it to weave webs to close the entrances to the Pentagon, adapting those domestic(ated) labors to a disruption of the smooth operations that hide the deadly "business" that is transacted there. As Noël Sturgeon writes, "The webs woven by women across military gates represent [an] attempt . . . to redefine the growing interconnectedness of the world on a basis other than that of internationalized capital. The magic of witches . . . opposes the 'magical' characteristics of a nuclear technology which maintains the balance between life and death through arcane, secret operations known only to the initiated."[50] Moving out from the allegedly private domestic sphere to a clearly public one, the civilly disobedient actions of women at the Pentagon aimed to bring "home" the effects of the secretive, private workings of an indefensible system that uses the cover of "national security" to spread insecurity across the land and around the globe.

DRAMATIC THEORIES

The Women's Actions can be placed in and seen as a critical extension of ideas on radical theater encapsulated in German playwright-theorist Bertolt Brecht's notion of an epic, didactic, defamiliarizing drama—ideas used, critiqued, and developed further by feminist dramatists and performance artists over the course of the last two decades.[51] Put in terms of theatrical theory, the WPA can be read as, among other things, a feminist/Brechtian critique of aspects of the Artaudian politics of the New Left (as well as a challenge to the commodification and containment of Brechtian theater itself).[52] That is, if the New Left drew much of its sense of drama from the contemporary "happenings" and total-immersion theater of the sixties (forms that owe much to Antonin Artaud's multimedia "theater of cruelty"), the Women's Pentagon Action seems to have drawn its dramatic sense from the more thoughtful and thought-provoking notion of a "defamiliarizing" theater associated with Brecht. As feminist theater critic Jill Dolan suggests, Brecht and Artaud both sought to "uncover the political and aesthetic myths of realism," the former by "distancing spectators from the theatre's lulling narrative," and the latter by "total physical immersion in a theatre experience of sensual gestures free of narrative authority."[53] Thus both of these critical theatrical modes have their place in radical dramaturgy, and the New Left and the WPA drew from them both (among others), but their respective historical moments drove the former more toward Artaud, the latter more toward a Brechtian mode.

Despite critical perspectives developed by Artaud, the situationists, and other theatrical and media-minded theorists, much of the sixties left ultimately could not resist fully the then emerging "society of the spectacle." Allowing and even encouraging the transformation of political actions into "spectacles" for media consumption, New Left dramatism was eventually absorbed into the flow of the late capitalist imaginary.[54] Learning from this experience, the Women's Action tried to be antispectacular from its inception.[55] Where spectacular theater seeks to be totally involving ("be-in" as being), the Pentagon Action aimed also for a moment of distancing or estrangement that allowed for and called for reflection, reflection on the fact that all the world's a stage wherein the actors have mostly forgotten that their social scripts are produced by authorial forces that can be challenged.

That moment of distance is precisely the moment of theory, and I want to suggest that in this case the very "stagedness," the elaborate theatricality, of the Women's Pentagon Action set the basic context for such reflection by carefully transforming real experience into real theater. Thus, far from theater being less real or a diversion from the real, in this context the Action's theatricality was a way of moving closer to real possibilities of transformation by dislodging mere realism, thus engaging reality more deeply and thoughtfully, and contributing to a more profound dramatics of resistance. In turn, this greater thoughtfulness emerges in part because the event, as serious theater, also engaged the participants' emotions profoundly.

Many of us on the left like to theorize about the dialectical play of theory and practice, but in practice the two activities are usually remote from one another. The beauty of the Women's Action to me is that it enacted the faith of the organizers that a stronger theoretical understanding would indeed emerge out of the practice of confronting a variety of participants with a new strategic context. The Women's Pentagon events enact a radically open-ended polyphonic conversation drawing on and displacing several major "schools" of feminist theory, while also addressing other issues not generally thought of as feminist. The events consciously enacted the creation of a collective subject or subjectivity that did not (could not) exist before the Action itself. The events enact not a synthesis but instead a heterogenous logic of collective experiencing/ thinking that is vital to the ongoing re-writing of feminist politics and central to the feminist re-writing of left theory and practice generally.

The Pentagon Actions are also an important moment in a wider process through which consciousness-raising as a method and feminisms as theories are becoming central to the project of building an oppositional, alternative social movement politics. Consciousness-raising and the closely related consensus process, when understood as necessarily dependent on always expanding the diversity of the movement constituency, can be key elements in a new, collective, radically democratic political epistemology.

The women of the Pentagon Actions opened a rift in the seam of militarist and patriarchal imagery that is at the same time an opening toward new possibilities of acting in the world. Their Defiance has found resonance in a host of subsequent Peace Camps and resistance actions fueled by women inspired directly or indirectly by the Women's Pentagon Action. And much of that continuing energy has coalesced around the political stance known as "ecofeminism," a left "green" movement combining feminism and environmentalism with analyses of racial and class oppression.

The Women's Pentagon Action is exemplary theater, exemplary political education, because reflective, collective determination was at work in a variety of ways and at every level of the action. The events of the Action externalized, dramatized elements of consciousness-raising and consensus process, and self-consciously expressed an interplay of political thought/emotion that challenged dominant rhetorical and political paradigms. The Actions projected these challenges into the public sphere while simultaneously maintaining a sense of their importance at the most intimate levels of internal movement activity. The Women's Pentagon play was a powerful (if imperfect) dramatization of possibilities for radical theater and theatrical radicalism; the events form a text worth reading and re-reading as democratic movements search for the next stage of political struggle.

SIX

Toward Some Postmodernist Populisms

A Prescriptive Postscript

Viewed from one perspective the trajectory of this book has brought us ever closer to the (con)text of social movements and political action; and that is surely one of my intentions. But on another level that trajectory is an illusory one, since we have never really left the realm of academic, literary critical discourse—even this kind of "politerature" is still only polite *rature*, only a limited erasure of domination that can but does not automatically lead to wider domains of political action. Thus I want by way of conclusion to summarize some of the strategies emerging from my readings and suggest ways that they might be implemented in broader arenas of democratic contestation. I start with questions about the current roles of the literary intellectual in society and about certain currently dominant literary critical gestures that circumscribe those roles. Then I move into an analysis of various attempts to characterize our "postmodern condition" as a way into an argument for the kinds of counterhegemonic cultural/political activities I think we need in this particular and peculiar historical moment. My aim is to resist various kinds of critical and political sectarianisms by suggesting that certain habitually counterposed strategies actually need one another. To do so requires that I bracket some substantive political and theoretical differences, but I have no doubt that partisans of particular positions will be quick to resurrect those differences that matter. My hope, however, is that I can provoke them to do so in more creative, less debilitatingly agonistic ways.

W(H)ITHER INTELLECTUALS?

What is to be (un)done in order to bring literary theory and criticism to bear more cogently on political questions? As I hope my readings have demonstrated, I do not think there is a simple or singular answer to such a question. But surely if a tendency toward theoreticism has sometimes been part of the problem, anti-intellectualism will not be part of the solution. As Frank Lentricchia has argued, calls for a more engaged literary and cultural criticism must not and need not lead to anti-intellectualism or even anti-academicism, for it is illusory and self-denigrating for academic intellectuals to ignore the fact that we are situated in universities where there is much work to be done.[1]

At the same time, we need to think and act on the basis of a concept of the "literary" intellectual that is multileveled, that recognizes that there are a number of different audiences toward which we can and should address ourselves, perhaps beginning but not ending with the academy.[2] We need, on one level, to be what Foucault called "specific intellectuals," fighting on the important ground of our own particular, academic turf, as teachers teaching critical modes of reading, thinking, and acting, as colleagues struggling to dismantle professional, disciplinary, and institutional barriers to radical action, and as employees struggling within the hierarchical educational apparatus. But just at the moment when many have sought to use this notion of the specific intellectual to replace the older, indubitably sullied notion of a "universal intellectual" (one who presumes to speak for Humanity but tends in fact to speak only for a privileged portion of it), political conservatives have embraced the figure of the public intellectual as a base for a popular assault on the (limited) gains made by groups marginalized by race, gender, ethnicity, and/or sexuality. Setting these "special interests" against universal principles, conservatives have revealed how the solidification of the margins into "specific" "identities" and "communities" have made them vulnerably isolated. This suggests that without some horizon of public interest, based in certain (more legitimately) universalist claims, it may be impossible to create a counterhegemonic bloc. Every local site opens onto some set of universal(izing) principles; what matters is which particular universals get deployed and in whose interests. This need not entail the positing of a *single*, universal set of principles or values, however, but could instead posit a play of particularity and universality at work within a variety of semi-autonomous political movements whose interaction could provide insurance against *reductive* universals even as they sought tentative consensus on mutually enabling general principles.[3]

Moreover, as a number of critics have suggested recently, the choice between "specific" and "universal" intellectual is not a simple either/or; there is no easy way out of the multiple positions "we" (variously, unevenly) inhabit.[4] "Western" intellectuals, for example, like other citizens of the world, are caught in transnational capitalism's universalizing webs as well as in specific locations of power/resistance. Thus while we may wish to abandon a false universalism, that universalism may not be about to abandon us.[5] Indeed, the pressures of hegemony may be asserting themselves most fully just at those points where privileged white males claim with such abandon to have become decentered, or claim to celebrate (without representing) heroic marginals and minorities. And the disciplinary apparatus may be at work most forcefully at those points where the most brilliant critical minds of a generation cross every intellectual border except the one policing the boundaries of academia and its discourses.

Thus Janice Radway, Edward Said, and Cornel West, among others, are quite right to call for academics to seek out wider, popular audiences whenever possible, to accept responsibility for putting our theories and rhetorical skills into practice in the test of public dialogue.[6] We need to be more insistent in using our academic positioning to open space for the voices of social movement resistance. We also need to involve ourselves (or involve ourselves more fully) in those movements, neither denying nor exaggerating the particular intellectual skills we possess but offering them in contexts that will inevitably also reveal the blindnesses our knowledge has produced in us. Edward Said publicly advocating the rights of the Palestinians, Cornel West bringing his counterhegemonic voice into African-American churches, Janice Radway engaging in dialogue about feminism with romance-novel readers offer three very different but equally suggestive models of "literary" intellectuals breaking out of professional confines in order to profess more efficaciously.

In talking this way I realize that I risk the danger of further entrenching the false notion that the university is a wholly otherworldly place, or at least that it is not part of what I have been calling the wider world. This notion is false both because it occludes the work of universities as servants of the state and of corporate capitalism and, more importantly, because it hides the ways in which social movement resistance does take place on campuses. Of course universities have been the site of social movements; indeed in many instances they have played key roles in their development and diffusion. It is even possible to argue that there are social movements at the level of knowledge going on in universities. But while various kinds of political struggles go on in the university on a variety of levels, they are all to one degree or another forced to compromise with institutional structures designed to reproduce existing social relations. I have defined social movements by contrast as always extra-institutional, as structured by a certain refusal to settle for compromise solutions and by a resistance to all final acts of representation. The academic institutions of today are very different from what they were thirty years ago, and those changes were made possible by events outside as well as inside the university that employed non- and sometimes even anti-academic modes of struggle. My point is simply that these changes are now in danger of being lost if that history is forgotten and the battle is restricted to the realm and modes of academic contest alone.

The proliferation and intertextual elaboration of theory has at times led us to forget that this recent period of rich theoretical activity itself was to a great extent enabled by first the rise and then the relative decline of the first wave of new social movements in the 1960s. The new theory was enabled initially by social movements in the sense that the agenda of anticolonial, antiracist, antisexist concerns that animates much recent theory, as well as the critique of leftist orthodoxies and the distrust of centralized institutions and totalizing discourses, were the core of the radical democratic activity in the sixties.[7] While not all the new theoretical work was openly or progressively political, all of it benefitted from space opened up in the academy by concrete struggles by anticolonial movements, by women, by African-Americans, and by a host of others who asked new questions that forced reconceptualizations of virtually every field in the humanities and social sciences.

The new work was enabled by these movements in a second sense in that their (relative) decline in the seventies sent people back to the drawing board of theory, and led them to begin the "long march through the institutions" that has done much to strengthen the academic base of the American left. But the march through the institutions also has taken its toll by helping define "Theory" in narrowly philosophical terms, cutting it off from various other forms of critical thinking (including literature itself as theory), and by institutionalizing theory in ways that draw it within disciplinary matrices that isolate it from social movements (which are themselves theorizing entities).[8] The very success of Theory within the academy has tended to give it an illusory aura of autonomy that further insulates theorists from social movement activists and deepens the suspicions of some activists that theory is not of practical importance.

When confronted with such claims many of my colleagues resort to the one (and usually only) theory they share with Ronald Reagan—the "trickle down" theory—in this case, the theory that theory eventually trickles down from the heights of academic conferences and abstruse books to water the grass roots. I think there is some truth to this, but surely we can do better than we have done at facilitating this process: and surely part of the problem of this model is that it describes a one-way flow of knowledge. We need a model of our enterprise that recognizes academia as one crucial site of political activity and protects it as one crucial site of theoretical activity, but a model that guards against the complacency that emerges when we in universities imagine ourselves to have a monopoly on theory or exaggerate the importance of our academic battles.

FORMALISMS AND THEIR (DIS)CONTENTS

Let me make these criticisms more specific by looking at five interrelated, overlapping theoretical and rhetorical tropes or "moves" that have contributed to complacency, that have made it difficult to connect theory to social movement practice and social movement theory to critical practice in recent years. All five of these moves have been and can still be quite productive (indeed I have used all of them to one degree or another in previous chapters). But I believe that as currently practiced they often provide more distraction than illumination and insight.

The first and overarching move has been carelessness in how we extend the notion of "text" out of the literary into other social realms. This projection of text into the wider social landscape has been an immensely useful rhetorical gesture for countering naive, unmediated empiricism, and for uncovering the discursive construction of objects, facts, events, practices. But this process, intended to help rescue the social world from reification, has too often instead subsumed the social into a reified, formalist notion of literature (or textuality). This is a tempting move for those of us whose main action in the world is the manipulation of words, but exaggerating the importance of textual criticism (narrowly conceived) tends to divert attention away from those points where textual power is deployed in the wider world, and away from strategies for deconstructing the linguistic and extralinguistic institutional bases of discourses. Even institutions can sometimes fruitfully be seen as the instantiation of metaphors, but the key word here is instantiation not metaphor. Deconstructing *Moby-Dick* can be part of, but should not be confused with, deconstructing the Leviathan of the American state.

The "virtual reality," video game war in the Persian Gulf provides a graphic example of how important "textual," semiotic warfare has become. In the form of representational strategies carefully constructed by White House media experts to fit into existing media storytelling, a "literary" war of signs was crucial in enabling the very real, very deadly effects of the more literal war.[9] But even as this confirms the emphasis of recent theory on the textual construction of reality, it points up how useless such analyses are if they are not also tied to theories and strategies for gaining access to the social means of reality reproduction, and theories and strategies for expanding the constituency of resisters.

A second, related set of critical miscues entails certain fusions or confusions of "literary" representation with political representation. This problem has two dimensions working in rather opposite directions. One consists of arguments that attempt to aestheticize politics by projecting allegedly "antirepresentational," avant-gardist strategies (literary/critical) onto larger sociopolitical realms.[10] While I am sympathetic to these efforts (they are akin to and inform what I have been doing here), it seems to me they greatly underestimate the inherent conservatism of everyday life (even under "postmodern" conditions), ignore those moments when relatively stable representations serve struggles against domination, and fail to take seriously enough the fact that different social domains work by different logics. At least in the hands of epigones, such positions seem to degenerate into celebrations of difference for difference's sake, ambiguity for ambiguity's sake. What is needed is not the elimination of ambiguity and certainly not of difference but a more careful search for those points where ambiguities are strategically necessary to specific political contexts and where differences arise from the need to differentiate specific oppressions.

The equally dangerous reverse side of this trope conflates literary representation with political representation by projecting the latter onto the former. Getting literary representation for the previously invisible can be one step toward changing the political balance of powers (and thus projects like the truly canon-challenging *Heath Anthology of American Literature*, for example, are immensely important). But this kind of representation does not translate automatically into representation in the political sense. There is even a danger that this new representation of "minorities" will be used as a substitute for serious challenges to those wider systems of power. The new discourse of "multiculturalism," for example, can either be used to force a total reconceptualization of the narrow version of the literary and cultural past called "the Western tradition," or it can be used to confirm marginalized peoples in subcultural ghettos that divide and conquer, offering separate, but not equal, representation. Terms like multiculturalism are already being used by those who wish to "administer" and "manage" diversity to create a more pliable student body and work force. And they are being used to "integrate" selected representatives of "minority" groups into the cultural and economic system without significantly altering the power ratios that keep most group members in the underclasses. Literary representation can serve either to create multicultural elites and the illusion of political progress, or serve as one wedge for broader social change. It can accomplish the latter only if we do not exaggerate the connection between the literary and the political.

The next three rhetorical moves I want to criticize all concern the radical questioning of the individual subject as social agent in recent theory. One dimension of this move entails the effacing of historical actors by translating them into abstract "Others" or abstract forces of "difference" that putatively challenge Western metaphysics or Man or the West itself. This move has been useful in undoing a number of reified categories of "Western" thought, but it is an extremely imprecise, even evasive, strategy at the level of sociopolitical action. This vagueing and vogueing of the "Other" has a tendency to efface those historical "subjects" who have been actively "decolonizing" the West during the last three decades thereby further distancing academic critics from the only forces capable of actually, not just textually, deconstructing domination. Even some "organic intellectuals" associated with liberation movements have been confused by this theoretical slippage, but I think it is primarily those removed from the stakes of lived and theorized (as opposed to merely theorized) marginality who have perpetuated this effacement (sometimes going so far as to play "marginal" the way some Westerners used to "go native" in the not-distant-enough past).[11]

Part of this confusion has arisen from a failure to translate fully from the political and cultural (con)texts of France into the very different (con)texts of the United States. Particularly among younger scholars, textual Otherness has become not only a substitute for but an obfuscation of "other," more consequential political struggles. Cornel West puts the issue this way:

Americans are always already in a condition of postmodern fragmentation and heterogeneity in a way that Europeans have not been; and the revolt against the center by those constituted as marginals is an oppositional difference in a way that poststructuralist notions of difference are not. These American attacks on universality in the name of difference, these "postmodern" issues of Otherness (Afro-Americans, Native Americans, women, gays) are in fact an implicit critique of certain French postmodern discourses about Otherness that really serve to hide . . . the power of the voices and movements of Others.[12]

We need, therefore, a far more (con)text-specific sense of centrality and marginality, otherness and the dominant, one that continually seeks to trace textual heteroglossia back to its origins in specific social sites of contestation for meaning and/as power.

A fourth move that a number of theorists are re-thinking is the related critique of "essentialism" that has become normative, indeed seemingly essential, in many "postmodern" discourses. As Diana Fuss argues, essentialism (a belief in the "real . . . invariable and fixed, essence" of a category, an object, or an identity) is "deeply and inextricably co-implicated" with its supposed opposite, constructionism.[13] There are very important political stakes in bridging the gulf between essentialists and constructivists, because the two are often equated with social movement activists and academic theorists, respectively, a move that reinforces a debilitating theory/practice split.[14] As Fuss suggests, we must avoid asking reductive questions like, is this text or argument essentialist (and therefore "bad"), and ask instead, for what purposes is a seemingly essentialist position put forth. Terms like "strategic essentialism" that have been used to challenge this kind of questioning are helpful, but only if they do not make the condescending assumption that those deploying these strategies do so unintentionally. The deployment, for example, of a collective identity (woman, gay, African-American, native) is *most* likely to be recognized as strategic from inside that collective where intimate knowledge of internal difference is greatest; it is on the outside that such gestures are most likely to be mistaken as essentialist. Seemingly essentialist gestures are a necessary, recurring epistemological moment in organizing, one that is never wholly superseded by the equally necessary moments when internal diversity must be stressed.

The fifth and final theoretical move in need of re-envisioning is a complex corollary of the essentialist and "Other" questions: the problem of the dissolving "subject" in relation to political agency. This generally entails replacing an exaggerated notion of subjective self-creation with an exaggerated notion of determination of self by language. The postmodern critique of "Western Man" as heroic bourgeois individual has been essential in undoing "essentialist" positionings that have been politically counterproductive. But it is far from clear that a politics without a subject, or without an active notion of human agency, can be a politics at all. Those who theorize a "decentered subject" and who are anxious to further this decentering must face the contrary fact that for many of those "subjects" marginalized by current hegemonic structures, achieving subjecthood is a key moment in the radicalization process. Truly decentering the straight, white, male, Western, capitalist self may well depend on a strengthened sense of subjecthood on the part of those who have for so long been subject to that dominant Self.

As Chela Sandoval has argued, in one of the first and most lucid reconceptualizations of marginalized subjects, this does not mean a reconstruction of the centered Western Self because those on the margins have never had the luxury of such a unified self. In Sandoval's specific example, women of color have always had to engage to one degree or another in a complex negotiation of identities or layers of identity in order to survive in the interstices of straight, white, male power. Like W. E. B. Du Bois's notion of "double consciousness," Sandoval's argument acknowledges that multiple subjectivities are virtually structured into the consciousness of those "othered" by the dominant. But she suggests that realization of an "oppositional consciousness" is achieved only through active political engagement in which identities shift to fit specific, tactical, and strategic needs, possibilities, and limits. Oppositional consciousness entails a constant creation and re-creation of identity, but it is a far more active and self-conscious form of being than that conceptualized as the decentered subject. It is less a question of being centerless than of having multiple tactical centers from which to resist both marginalization and the co-optive centerings offered by dominating forces.[15]

As a number of theorists have suggested, a new social movement politics is needed that creates and maintains an irreducible plurality of subject positions even as it seeks to articulate "equivalences," points of discursive alliance, across collective subjects.[16] But this means seeing both representation and identity as ongoing processes that sometimes must be strategically stabilized, that cannot always be in a state of deconstructive transformation. Those in positions of privilege need to see marginalized "subject positions" as real, active, self-conscious, theorizing, resisting, embattled, unstable, collective, and individualized political actors, not abstract resisting force-fields or subjects-in-process of becoming some-one's avant-garde fantasy.

If recent critical revolutions have not exactly taken place "in the realm of Pure Spirit," the five theoretical moves I have just outlined do seem to have led at times to discourses full of sound and sometimes fury but sig-nifying (almost) nothing. By contrast, the best of recent theoretical and literary work seems to me to have emerged from critics and writers who experience oppression on a daily basis and who tend for that reason to have fairly direct ties to ongoing movements. Recent efforts by feminist critics, for example, to interweave class, race, gender, sexual orientation, and the domination of nature into their analyses, while also evolving a range of strategies to deal with different levels and sites of struggle, from the seminar to the streets, have been spurred largely by demands from movement constituencies that the diversity of women be acknowledged and theorized (a fact, again, sometimes effaced by the fetishizing of fem-inist theory as an autonomous force). What I read as the relatively greater political clarity and power of much feminist and antiracist criticism sug-gests that the context of an ongoing social movement is a key element needed to shape literary and cultural criticism, not in the narrow sense that one must write always for an audience of social movement activists, but rather in the sense that contact with movements can generate ques-tions that remind theorists of the difference between changing theories and theorizing change.

THROUGH A GLASS BUILDING DARKLY

The critique of theoretical moves just outlined can be seen as part of a broader effort that attempts to rethink and resituate the concept(s) de-noted by the term "postmodernism." I want to clarify the wider political-theoretical base for my critical position by briefly engaging several American critics whose differing but overlapping perspectives on the "postmodern condition" make clearer the political stakes of that debate and the political stakes of my advocacy of "postmodernist realism."

Fredric Jameson's essay "Postmodernism, or The Cultural Logic of Late Capitalism" provides a particularly provocative point of entry into the debate since, as his title suggests, Jameson sees postmodernism not as one style among others but as nothing less than "the cultural domi-nant" corresponding to and aiding the (re)production of "late capital-ism." For Jameson, postmodernism is the culture that emerges from mass-mediated, multinational capitalist production, a culture he reads as a virtually seamless web of hegemonic form. He argues, therefore, that "every position on postmodernism in culture . . . is also and necessarily an implicitly or explicitly political stance on the nature of multinational capitalism."[17] I think this latter argument is largely correct, and I want here to explore the political implications of various readings of postmodernism, beginning with the politics implied in Jameson's own position.

For Jameson the symptoms or elements of postmodernism as they appear in aesthetic forms and everyday life include the waning of affect; the fragmentation of subjectivity; and an effacement of history that results in a preference for nostalgic, "retro" art forms that "mimic" or "cannibalize" earlier styles and stylistic eras. Time becomes lost in space; history becomes a history of styles without reference to any social grounding. The central generic postmodernist term for Jameson is "pastiche," a "neutral" form of parody, one without satiric, critical content. As with all forms of postmodernism as he defines them, "pastiche" lacks a norm, let alone a utopian possibility, against which to measure itself. Postmodernism is at once full of all histories and cultures, and utterly empty, having transformed them all into interchangeable codes with no more meaning than the disconnected sentences of a schizophrenic.

At the level of theorizing, postmodernism is characterized by the replacement of depth/surface models with the structural play of surfaces. Jameson offers five examples of what has been lost or challenged: the "hermeneutic model of inside and outside," the "existential model of authenticity and inauthenticity," the "dialectical [model] of essence and appearance," the "Freudian model of latent and manifest, or of repression," and the "great semiotic opposition of signifier and signified." For Jameson what has been lost with these models is the purity, if not the very possibility, of critical distancing from capitalism as the site of domination.

While somewhat anxiously acknowledging the danger of inducing passivity or despair through such a "totalizing" analysis, Jameson claims that it is only by positing such a dominant that one can identify, using Raymond Williams's terms, "residual" and "emergent" forms of resistance to this dominant. In this regard, Jameson's most provocative thesis is no doubt that various forms of postmodernist and poststructuralist "theoretical discourse" bear all the markings of this cultural dominant, that in celebrating a certain aleatory heterogeneity of textualized images and "intensities" these writers are in fact celebrating the "logic" of multinational capitalism. Postmodernism is the cultural logic of multinational capitalism, a new mode of production wherein, in Guy Debord's phrase, "The image has become the final form of commodity reification."[18] The cultural or superstructural sphere, according to Jameson, is at once greatly expanded and totally eliminated. One can either see the cultural as swallowing the political economic, or the reverse. The result, he claims, is the same: a process of near-total reification. Jameson's most striking metaphoric emblem for this process is the mammoth Bonaventure Hotel in Los Angeles, a postmodern monolith that at once repels the city around it by creating within its walls a self-sufficient minicity cum fortress, and simulates the surrounding city on its mirrored surfaces. Inside such a disorienting edifice "our now postmodern bodies are bereft of spatial coordinates and practically (let alone theoretically) incapable of distanciation."[19]

Jameson includes among the victims of postmodernism the very possibility of any even "semi-autonomous" cultural sphere, the possibility of any critical "aesthetic distancing." Instead he posits a situation in which all "critical distancings" including "specifically political interventions" are immediately reabsorbed into the postmodern, late-capitalist system. The anxiously repeated assertion near the end of his essay that he does not want his totalizing analysis to be seen as encouraging passivity before the inevitably long march of the dialectic only confirms to me that, despite a final rather obscure gesture toward some new "as yet untheorized" didactic art, political paralysis is precisely what Jameson's logic would seem to dictate.[20]

Jameson's analysis provides one of the most powerful negative readings of postmodernism, and he is therefore right to say his perspective can be made useful as a backdrop against which to posit attempts to define resistive forces in postmodernity. But there are several aspects of Jameson's position that make it a less than ideal vantage point for observing and furthering such resistance. To begin with, his position is ultimately (in the last instance) economistically reductive and undialectical. Seeing postmodernism as the extrusion of a new phase of capitalist production needs to be balanced against the internal evolution of aesthetic forms and representational practices, which themselves act upon economic and social relations. Similarly, his strong privileging of class relations leaves little room for such elements as race, gender, and nationalism as independent or at least semi-autonomous causal factors. Moreover, even within the realm of political economy Jameson's model is not the most useful one; in *The Condition of Postmodernity*, a book that is to a large extent an elaboration of Jameson's general thesis, David Harvey argues that postmodernism more closely resembles the relative chaos of an as yet still experimental new regime of "flexible accumulation" than some homogenous third stage of capitalism. Yet, Harvey joins Jameson in too quickly shutting down rather than opening up debate about new political economic developments, a closure that in turn short-circuits possible new configurations of the cultural sphere.[21]

Jameson's position has also been criticized as unduly globalizing. A number of Third World and postcolonial intellectuals have questioned the theoretical hubris in finding postmodern cultural imperialism everywhere in such a way that various local knowledges and anticolonial discourses are seen as merely mirrors of Western hegemony. Indeed, from the point of view of these critics it is Jameson who is the bearer of cultural imperialism rather than its critic as he postmodernizes realms that may seem to share certain features but that serve very different purposes in Third World (con)texts, including in the domestic Third Worlds within the United States. Stuart Hall has quipped that postmodernism is how the world imagines itself to be America.[22] While this is surely true in part, particularly of certain well-publicized French postmodern thinkers, it is equally true that often postmodernism has been about how America imagines itself to be the world; that is the danger raised by sweeping gestures like Jameson's.

In order to posit his wholly incorporated postmodernism, Jameson must also homogenize and exaggerate the oppositional quality of "high modernism" (a position that does not bother to distinguish between the politics of Dada and of T. S. Eliot, for example, is homogenizing in the extreme). In a rather stark, binary opposition modernism plays hero to postmodernism's villain. This is misleading on both ends, for surely if modernism had been as oppositional as he suggests it could not have so easily become canonized, and if postmodernism allows "no distanciation" from the ideological, it is difficult to account for the obvious, ongoing oppositional effects of Jameson's own powerful writings.

Thus, the problem with Jameson's otherwise highly suggestive and useful story is that, rather than making it possible to clarify the resistive power of the "residual" or the "emergent," as he claims is his goal, these possibilities are often obscured by the very brilliance of his presentation of the incorporative powers of postmodernism. To find such resistance one must look both more carefully inside and more widely outside of the postmodernism he analyzes. While keeping in mind Jameson's cautionary tale of the cunning of postmodernism, one must also ask whether,

while all of us may in some degree be caught in the webs of the postmodern cultural dominant, some may be less entangled than others
(webs are, after all, traps riddled with holes). We can begin to locate these
possible pockets of resistance by first looking at the opposite side of this
question, by asking: who is *most* caught in the webs of postmodernism?

WE SHALL NOT BE MAUVED

Critic Fred Pfeil, partly in response to what he calls Jameson's "magis-
terially" performed reading of postmodernism, has offered an alternative
perspective on postmodern culture, one that attempts specifically to answer the question of who produces and who consumes the bulk of postmodernist texts.[23] Pfeil suggests that Jameson's extremely abstract version of a political-economic analysis of the forces shaping the "cultural
logic of late capitalism" will simply leave readers, as he puts it, waiting
"to catch the next Kondratieff wave," the next great crash of capitalism
against the shores of its own internal contradictions. He accepts much
in Jameson's phenomenology of the postmodern, but he wants to discuss
it with greater particularity as to its origins, and greater sense of possibility regarding its resistability:

> For underneath the apparent naturalness and inevitability of "postmodern-
> ism" and "late capitalism" . . . lies another level of unnatural, willed and con-
> tingent reality—the reality of the "conjuncture." And such a distinction is cru-
> cial for us as cultural and political agents, for the "organic" in all its achieved
> naturalness is always the effect of innumerable conjunctural struggles won
> and lost, on the cultural, political, and economic levels alike. . . . What fol-
> lows is an analysis of postmodernism not as an inevitable effusion of an entire
> mode of production but as a cultural-aesthetic set of pleasures and practices
> created by and for a particular social group at a determinate moment in his-
> tory.
>   Specifically . . . postmodernism is preeminently the "expressive form" of
> the social and material life experiences of my own generation and class, re-
> spectively designated as the "baby boom" and the "professional-managerial
> class" or PMC.[24]

Pfeil offers the following definition of the "PMC," drawn from the work
of Barbara and John Erhenreich: the professional-managerial class consists of "salaried mental workers who do not own the means of production and whose major function in the social division of labor may be
broadly described as the reproduction of capitalist culture and capitalist
class relations."[25] Pfeil goes on to demonstrate that the PMC, made up
of perhaps as much as 80 percent of the employed 35–45-year-olds in

the United States in 1990 (and a similar proportion in most advanced capitalist states),[26] remains a politically ambivalent, ideologically fluid population whose indecision produces and is produced by ambiguities in the class position of its members. That ambiguity can perhaps best be indicated by noting that different critics have referred to this same group as either "the new working class" or "the new middle class."

Where Jameson's analysis characteristically does not rise to the level of the concrete in which empirical readership of postmodernist productions could be an issue, Pfeil argues convincingly that the professional-managerial class finds its "structure of feeling" expressed in and partly produced by the kind of works Jameson calls postmodernist. Raised for the most part in a world saturated with mass-mediated images, amidst a "ceaseless process of the consumerized self's construction, fragmentation, and dissolution at the hands of a relentless invasive world of products," as the "primary target . . . of the commodified messages . . . beamed out by the U.S. culture industry," reality comes to the PMC "pried loose from its point of origin in any genuinely social discourse or personal experience, distorted and crystalized into an infinitely manipulable, reproducible fragment which . . . may be rubbed up and recombined with any other and then returned, as intrusively and insidiously as possible to the consciousness of the privatized consumer/viewer to be recognized and chosen [as his/her own]." Eventually such mass-mediated reality becomes for many a substitution of "the always-shifting pseudo-collectivity of 'life-style' . . . for the public realm lost."[27] In this context, recognition, at the level of "high cultural" postmodernism, of an aesthetic of fragmentation, confirms reality for the PMC. But Pfeil's point is that it is often not a wholly comforting or comfortable recognition.

While not disproving the hypothesis that postmodernism is our cultural dominant, Pfeil's analysis raises certain political strategic possibilities obscured in Jameson's picture. Where Jameson sees postmodernism as a generalized condition of late capitalism, as a more profound penetration of capitalism into cultural realms still left semi-autonomous in the earlier era of "high modernism," Pfeil sees a more dialectical logic at work in postmodernism. Noting that postmodernism is in many respects the successor to the sixties counterculture, he sees in its products many of the same ambivalent gestures toward incorporation and resistance found in the counterculture itself. Drawing on the work of the Birmingham school, Pfeil views the counterculture as a utopian prefiguration (as in other contexts has Jameson himself), and he finds that logic still at play in postmodernist works like those of performance artist Laurie Anderson or the rock group Talking Heads. Where Jameson sees aimless pastiche, Pfeil sees anxious ambivalence, a gesture toward utopian redemption of cultural refuse that knows itself to be a failed gesture, that precisely senses but does not wholly succumb to the immense forces of incorporation Jameson elaborates. What the baby-boom PMC will make of that knowledge is an as yet undecided political and cultural question.

A number of important strategic implications (mostly left unstated) flow from Pfeil's line of argument. Most obvious of these is simply the fact that struggle over the political direction that the PMC is to take is of immense importance. Leftists should now once and for all shed their guilt about organizing among this class (often their own). One key component of such organizing will be the revival of a strategy begun (too) late in the sixties by the New Left, the strategy of forming political organizations in all the various professional or vocational sectors of the PMC.[28] One aspect of this struggle needs to begin at the most basic level of countering the discourse of the "yuppie," a term that obscures the less affluent lives of the vast majority of members of the PMC by assimilating them into the upper class, and contributes to the suppression of insight into the more fruitful class alliances open to the PMC (alliances with those other groups who own little but their actual or potential labor power).

In all the industrial countries the PMC has contributed a great deal to the growth of radical democratic new social movements.[29] It is also this class that has contributed most to the new modes of mass-mediated mystification that do so much to maintain domination. Thus, an important contest needs to be waged in particular for the hearts and minds of those members of the PMC who work in the consciousness industries (advertising, mass media, etc.) that do so much to shape imagined reality not only for their class but for other classes as well.

Pfeil's "conjunctural" analysis is an improvement on Jameson's more Hegelian version of class struggle because, though he is reluctant to speculate or make recommendations about "the aesthetico-political future of postmodernist cultural works," Pfeil points out that the "possibility that much of what we now call postmodernism might be turned and engaged in more progressive political directions is finally a function of the extent to which [alliances with lower classes] are constructed . . . [along with a] concomitant new public sphere."[30]

One need not raise the specter of banal political art to argue for more engaged versions of postmodernism. Indeed, as a number of critics close to the scene of postmodernist production have noted, such works already exist and critics have an obligation to further such work and to call for more work like it.[31] Craig Owens, for example, has analyzed one of the figures who figures prominently in Pfeil's account, Laurie Anderson, as a kind of crypto-feminist whose work is becoming less crypto and more feminist all the time, in part because of the responses to her work by feminist critics. This kind of argument helps open up the "inside" of postmodernism I mentioned above by distinguishing between differing postmodernisms and postmodernists, suggesting certain strategic arenas where postmodernist works have been and can be politically affective and effective. Owens cites Jameson as a critic whose protection of Marxism as the "master narrative" of History makes it impossible for him to see in many works of postmodernism a much-needed dismantling of oppressive aspects of the Western tradition, oppressive traditions with regard to race, gender, and the exploitation of nature in which Marxism itself is also implicated. Owens shows, for example, how the pastiche-like use of mass-mediated images in much feminist art is quite distinct from and opposed to the flatly ironic use of such images in Warholian postmodernism. Where Jameson sees in postmodernism an attack on the very capacity and will to theorize and totalize, critics like Owens see (in some versions) the strategic deployment of postmodernist devices to attack particularly oppressive totalizing theories that assign marginal roles to all but white male theorists.[32]

OF CYBORGS AND SALT EATERS

As a number of feminist critics have suggested, the discourse on postmodernism has until recently been dominated by men, both in the most obvious sense that men have tended to monopolize the verbal space of the postmodernism debate, and in the more important sense that much of the discourse on postmodernism itself can be seen as an evasion of feminist critical concerns (Owens and a few others notwithstanding).[33] As Meaghan Morris has argued, this elision works on at least two planes. On the one hand feminist contributors and precursors to the postmodernism debate have been ignored or effaced, and on the other hand the debate itself has tended to diffuse feminist critique into the vague concerns with Otherness, difference, marginality, and so on that I discussed above.[34] Each of these terms has more politically specific meanings within feminist theory, and that ground has been obscured by the kind of discussion presented in such postmodern theorists as Lyotard, Baudrillard, Deleuze, and Derrida. The efforts of Jameson, Pfeil, and others to polit-

icize the postmodernism debate have not fully overcome these initial eva-
sions. But work by feminist, antiracist, and postcolonial critics has begun
to specify some of the political possibilities and limits of postmodernity
as condition and postmodernisms as strategies.

Feminist theorist Donna Haraway, for example, has offered in her "cyborg manifesto"[35] a seriously witty and ironic political myth to take advantage of certain features of postmodern culture that might be and to
some degree are being turned against multinational, patriarchal capitalism. While accepting much of Jameson's analysis, she reads late capitalism more dialectically as a mode that in the process of trying to create a
high-tech postmodern "informatics of domination" has destroyed many
of the naturalizing, reifying constraints of liberal humanism, especially
the constraints upon women entailed by their "encodation" as "natural."
She argues that the current stage of transnational, postmodern capitalism includes a radical restructuring of social relations of science and technology. Chief among these restructuring processes are transgressions of
boundaries between humans, animals, and the techno-mechanical that
have important destabilizing effects on a number of repressive humanist
ideologies, particularly on ideologies of "nature" that have policed gender boundaries.

Haraway sees gender boundary transgressions as particularly important in the light of the increasing centrality worldwide of women's labor
in emerging political economic structures, a transformation that makes
it more imperative than ever that feminist analysis be at the center of any
counterhegemonic political struggle. Her metaphor for the ambiguous
relation to technology structured into this process is the "cyborg," the
cybernetic organism that is part human, part machine, an entity that
marks our inextricable entwinement with technological systems but also
our potentional liberation from "classed," "raced," and "gendered" notions of human nature. Cyborgs can take the menacing form of robo-
cops, but they can also become forces of quite dramatically nonessen-
tialist resistance that can take advantage of liberatory possibilities in this
period of transition to some new high-tech political economy.

Haraway's argument that the "informatics of domination" has integrated women into the printed circuits of the new high technologies is
not a return of the repressed "labor metaphysic" of Marxism with its
guaranteed link between class and consciousness, however, but rather
one that sees semiotic and material struggle as inextricably integrated. It
is necessary, for example, if sources of resistance are to be found, to understand not only the economic matrices but also the various indigenous

cultural traditions and constructions of gender identity that shape Malaysian or Mexican women on the high-tech assembly line.

If one refuses to engage the forms of postmodern technoculture altogether, Haraway suggests, one has eliminated the possibility of talking to the large numbers of people deeply shaped by those forms. Yet if one accepts those forms as thoroughly dominant, one also runs the equal risk of ignoring sources of resistance partly outside the postmodernist dynamic. Haraway is aware of this problem and thus takes some care to suggest that hers is only one among many possible "myths" and strategies. Following in the path of a number of Third World critics, her work acknowledges that hypothesizing a seamless, universal postmodern condition may simply be a kind of inverted rebirth of Western Man. While she is not always as clear as she might be about the extent to which her analysis applies to only certain arenas of the current world system, Haraway clearly understands that the postmodern condition is subject to uneven development and capable of manifesting itself very differently among different social sectors and actors in differing cultural matrices.

What critics who wish to find liberatory possibilities in postmodernism tend to slight in their sometimes fruitful attempts to appropriate the appropriators is the political potential of what Raymond Williams has called "residual cultures." Just as the original Luddism was not simply reactionary but also anticipatory and prefigurative of future labor struggles, elements of high-tech Luddism are called for alongside, and sometimes in place of, "cyborgian" struggles to democratize elements of the high-tech political economy. If we can no longer, after a period of important theoretical self-examination, point to and appropriate traditions with epistemological innocence, we can nevertheless find numerous ways to (re)construct "traditions" as arguments against the current, imperfectly dominant system. The powerful political impact of recent work recovering/creating women's, ethnic, and gay histories, for example, is evidence against overly generalized notions of postmodern ahistoricity.

There is real danger in positing a relentless postmodernity that has swept away all previous traditional knowledges and cultures. It is one thing to argue that postmodern conditions have blurred or eliminated a number of "borders" (national, ethnic, cultural, etc.), but quite another to argue that the subjects and objects crossing those borders are thereby hegemonically homogenized or transformed into heroic postmodern nomads.[36] The cultural "deterritorialization" process of transnational capitalism is an uneven, multilayered set of developments, full of resistances and transformations as well as incorporations.[37] Haraway, for example, finds in such diverse sources as science fiction literature, recent theoretical/autobiographical works by women of color, and ecofeminist direct actions, the creation of new spaces at once inside and outside the cultural dominant, spaces marked by a creatively "monstrous" acceptance of elements of the dominant that ironically inverts its values, while also drawing sustenance from the reinvention of subjugated knowledges and traditions.

A dynamic of intertextual, interactive residual-dominant-emergent moments is at work in these processes as it is in each of the "literary" texts I examined in earlier chapters. And a similar process is at work in what seem to me the most vital recent works of postmodernist realism, a new wave of texts by feminists of color. In novels like Toni Cade Bambara's *The Salt Eaters*, in multigeneric, cross-lingual texts like Cherríe Moraga's *Loving in the War Years: lo que nunca paso por sus labios* and Gloria Anzaldúa's *Borderlands/La Frontera: The New Mestiza*, in the films and autobiographical/theoretical writing of Trinh T. Minh-ha, in the massive community murals of Judy Baca, multiple, fractured identities and multiple, fractured histories are played against desires for connection and integrity.[38] These texts, like the work of Chela Sandoval discussed above, see identity as at once given and constructed, as something to be used against domination (a map to the interstices of power) and as an opportunity for self-(re)fashioning. Their "otherness" emerges from a history of oppression, and (re)turns that oppression into historically specific differences that provide solidarity for resistance and liberation. These theoretical texts are also clearly rooted in oppositional counterpublics where they play an active role in articulating and furthering acts of collective self-definition as a basis for collective action for change. Texts like these interactively arise from and create social movement audiences that prevent their dissemination into postmodern babel. They are exemplary reminders that it is in the struggle to create collective subjects-in-resistance that what I call postmodernist realism is doing its work.

POP GOES THE AVANT-GARDE

Just as claims about the postmodern collapse of national, ethnic, and cultural differences are exaggerated, so too is the oft-heard claim that postmodernism has collapsed the distinction between "high" and "popular" culture. Fred Pfeil, in the article cited above, offers a subtler analysis of this process. While noting that elements of popular culture increasingly have been drawn into high art forms, he suggests that high-, middle-, and lowbrow planes of postmodernism exist ("Einstein on the Beach," the David Letterman show, TV commercials). This seems undeniable, and because each of these different levels generates different kinds of cultural capital for different groups, we need to contest differently on each of these planes based on analysis of the varying audiences and aesthetic logics they entail.[39]

That analysis begins with a reassessment of the era of what Jameson calls "high modernism." As Andreas Huyssen has argued, "modernism" and "mass culture" arose simultaneously at the turn of the last century, with the former acting in part as a symptomatic response to the apparent banality and conservatism of the latter.[40] While not all modernist art was politically weighted to the left (sometimes as in Eliot or Wyndham Lewis it moved rightward), virtually all of it was antibourgeois. And included in modernism was a powerful left avant-garde position (Dada, surrealism, Brecht, etc.). In the postmodern era lines between high and low culture have become blurred (but not erased) both because much avant-garde technique has been absorbed by mass or popular culture, and because the avant-garde itself has become canonized in conservative ways.

What has occurred is not the total collapse of modernism and the avant-garde but rather a recognition that "art" has become inextricably entwined with "commerce," leading to two quite different, equally "postmodern" responses. One response, represented best perhaps at the level of aesthetic production by Andy Warhol and in theory by Jean Baudrillard, in effect accepts and celebrates the transformation of all art into capitalist hyperreal image commodities such that all the world becomes a kind of kitschy aesthetic playground.[41] A second, resistive postmodernism, represented by artist/activist/theorists like Hans Haacke, Barbara Kruger, and the Guerrilla Girls and much AIDS art-activism, takes the utter commodification of even the most avant-gardist art as a problem that can be solved only by political-economic as well as cultural transformation. Work like Haacke's and Kruger's remains avant-gardist in the sense that it is often formally innovative and is directed primarily at a relatively small audience of connoisseurs, but it has lost the avant-garde faith in the revolutionary potential of aesthetic form in itself to effect change and turns instead (or in addition) to questions of aesthetic function (questions about the transformation of art into cultural capital for corporations, for example, are at the core of Haacke's work). I think this kind of work is quite important (as my attention to some "elite" texts in the chapters above suggests), but this should be seen as only one plane of "postmodernist realism."

Political contestation is needed not only on the level of a (redefined) avant-garde, but also at the middle- and lowbrow levels of popular culture. As John Fiske points out, while the cultural avant-garde has sometimes been and can continue to be more politically radical than popular culture, it has also, virtually by definition, been more politically contained:

> Popular culture is progressive, not revolutionary. Radical art forms that oppose or ignore the structures of domination can never be popular because they cannot offer points of pertinence to the everyday life of the people, for everyday life is a series of tactical maneuvers against the strategy of the colonizing forces. It cannot produce the conditions of its existence, but must make do with those it has, often turning them against the system that produces them. Radical art tries to create its own terms of existence, to free itself from the status quo. It has an important place in the system of culture, and some of its radicalness may filter through to, and increase the progressiveness of, popular art, but it can never, in itself, be popular. Indeed, Bourdieu (1984) argues that radical art is bourgeois and lies outside the bounds of popular taste, while Barthes (1973) suggests that avant-garde art can only cause conflict between fractions of the bourgeoisie, but can never be part of class struggle. The political effectivity of radical art is limited by an inability to be relevant to the everyday life of the people, and, by the same token, any radicalness of popular art is equally limited by the same requirement of relevance.[42]

The conditions of postmodernity may at once have transformed (or perhaps only clarified) the role of the avant-garde and opened up more radical possibilities for effective aesthetico-political intervention.[43]

In the struggle over the future of the baby boom generation the avant-garde may have an important role to play, especially where avant-garde artists (like Laurie Anderson or Keith Haring) seek out wider audiences. But formalist elitisms among avant-garde artists and critics continue to inhibit their effectiveness through exaggerated stress on formal innovation in which avant-garde cultural production is portrayed as the only valid form of cultural representation, and through exaggerated claims for the political efficacy of such formal experiments.[44] Particularly in the more modest role of intraclass agitation, radical forms can prove progressive if articulated to particular political struggles (as, for example, in the work of some New York artists to resist the gentrification of certain neighborhoods by members of the "yuppoisie," among whom were some putatively avant-garde artists, or the adaptation of Barbara Kruger's graphic style by the Gran Fury collective of the AIDS Coalition to Unleash Power—ACT UP).[45]

Alongside and intertwined with this cultural agitation is the generally less radical but much more far-reaching struggle over the meaning and direction of "popular culture." As Michel de Certeau, Pierre Bourdieu, and, following them, Fiske have claimed, much popular culture represents a constant, if usually moderate, state of counterhegemonic rebellion against various powers that be. Looked at from the point of view of reception/articulation, rather than only from the point of view of production/distribution (which is clearly a mass-market, capitalist process that does have real constraining effects), popular culture is full of populist (especially anticorporate, antihierarchical) energy. This energy, like populist sentiment in general, is not inherently progressive, however. And unlike Fiske, I think that more often than not this disruptive energy is hegemonically redirected into safe forms of rebellion. But my argument is that this need not be the case, especially if more energy from the critical and aesthetic avant-garde were to be directed toward contesting the articulation of the popular.[46] As Andrew Ross has convincingly argued, the failure of intellectuals to contest on the ground of popular culture has been politically disastrous.[47]

Obviously serious difficulties stand in the way of realizing such a project, for the forces of postmodern incorporation of resistance *are* formidable, though not as densely woven as critics like Baudrillard and Jameson (from very different positions) suggest. In a culture where the production of "differences" has become highly commodified, the production of substantive representations of difference is a fraught task. The monopoly mass media and other forces of (post)modernization relentlessly transmute and absorb older value systems and current positive differences, but they do so unevenly and imperfectly. When a new source of resistance emerges, as in the rich ghetto culture of graffiti art, break dancing, and rap music, for example, the system's mass media are quick to cannibalize the phenomena as a source of stylistic renewal, as a new form to use to sell its products and as a new "image product" in its own right. But such acts of incorporation are always incomplete, stimulating in turn new sources of resistance.

Hip-hop culture is a complex hybrid that is at once recognizably postmodern and deeply rooted in African-American traditions. The struggle is in using the latter to direct the energies of the former. Two typical responses vitiate such possibilities. One response tries to portray hip-hop as some authentic, folk form beyond criticism. The other points to its use in commercials and sees it as already totally incorporated. Stressing the former tends to leave unchallenged the sexist, homophobic, anti-Semitic, and narrowly nationalistic dimensions of some hip-hop productions, whereas stressing the latter ignores the very real moments of antiracist resistance still alive despite commercial incorporation of some aspects of hip-hop style. Both sides have part of the truth but each exaggerates the uniformity of an extremely mixed phenomenon.

Rap music, to take one example, is a complex layering of sounds that is also a complex layering of residual, dominant, and emergent forms. Rap uses contemporary technology to pastiche white and black popular culture in ways that can be appropriately labeled postmodern. But it does so to create communally and politically charged texts of resistance, ones that have not only politicized much of America's inner-city youth but have also to some degree helped politicize elements of the PMC's cultural avant-garde whose attempts to appropriate some of hip-hop's energy often led to an education in the realities of ghetto-barrio life.

At the same time, rap builds on and sometimes educates its audience about a rich history of black musical and oral art that has been a source of resistance to racist white power for four hundred years. Rap is deeply rooted in older black vernacular forms that are themselves part of a tradition of resistance working through counterincorporation of dominant forms, a process of counterhegemonic appropriation at least as old as the adaptation of Christian hymns as codes for the underground railroad's resistance to slavery.

That the tradition of resistance behind hip-hop culture is not always known to hip-hop audiences or to the artists themselves (though some hip-hop texts include Afro-centric history lessons and others patch in, for example, excerpts from the speeches of King and/or Malcolm X) is a sign not of some inevitable postmodern loss of historicity but of a general amnesia in American culture that has long served to erase all (unpleasant) memories of resistance. The proper response is not despair at inevitable postmodern incorporation, but the intensification of work to create movement (con)texts that provide both historical genealogies and clearer political directions for these strong new efforts to define and "fight the powers that be."

BEYOND ACTUALLY EXISTING POPULISMS

The importance (as well as the limits) of cultural radicalism can be seen by looking at the history and future of political radicalism in the United States generally. In an analysis that dovetails interestingly with Michel de Certeau and Fiske's characterization of cultural resistance in everyday life, Richard Flacks has argued that the "left tradition" of democratic radicalism in the United States has been more successful through cultural than through traditionally political modes of contestation. In his brilliant reinterpretation of American radicalism, Flacks argues that the left has often exhausted itself in pursuit of revolutionary forms of action/rhetoric in nonrevolutionary situations, situations in which the immediate appeals and problems of everyday existence have kept ordinary people from achieving the degree of political engagement called for by the left. One ironic effect of this process has been that the American left has underestimated its own accomplishments by failing to note more incremental or delayed transformations brought about by radical activity. In effect, the left has failed to see through the smoke-screen thrown up by "mainstream" politics to hide its impact, and it has failed to look for changes in the right places (i.e., at the socio-cultural level rather than at political institutions).[48]

What the parallel analyses of the avant-garde and the left tradition suggest is that both have often squandered progressive cultural and political possibilities (and failed to credit themselves for victories) through the search for large-scale "forms" of dramatic, revolutionary change. At the most obvious level of comparison, this has meant a homology between avant-garde aesthetics (including much postmodern theory) and vanguard politics, though of course these two tendencies have imagined themselves to be worlds apart. It has meant a homologous revolutionary elitism that has amounted to a peculiar self-disciplining and self-limiting of radical energies. Radicals have thereby failed to take seriously the opportunities offered by a series of populist moments, both at the level of culture and at the level of more explicitly political action.[49]

What this suggests to me is the need for a new cultural/political "populism," new in the sense that it must deal with the particular postmodern conditions we have been examining, and populist in the sense that it seeks to become a truly counterhegemonic, popular force. Populism, of course, is a complex, ideologically contradictory political concept. The left has been rightly suspicious at times of populism because its progressive and reactionary versions have often been intermingled. But I would argue that this desire for ideological clarity or purity has contributed much to the left's marginalization, and should be replaced by efforts aimed at re-accenting moderate and perhaps even right populist moments in more progressive directions.

To suggest an agenda for exploring these issues, I want to begin by looking at what one might call, with fully appropriate irony, "actually existing populism" (i.e., a self-identified contemporary American left populist movement).[50] As is true of the actually existing socialism I am invoking, this self-identified populism is a contradictory, problematical, rather than an unambiguously exemplary, model (though in a very different way than existing socialisms). The "new populism," as defined by its most prolific spokespersons, Sara Evans and Harry Boyte, refers to the resurgence of localist, community-centered organizing in the 1970s and 1980s in the United States.[51]

In Evans and Boyte's construction the new populism is distinguished from other leftist organizing by claiming greater commitment to building on existing community ties, through churches, neighborhood groups, civic organizations, and so on. Though many are socialists, these theorists/organizers claim to strive for a less "ideological" approach, building analysis up from concrete circumstances. Believing the prime source of America's antidemocratic, "antipolitical" politics to reside in reliance on the technocratic elites of the liberal, interest-group pluralist state, they eschew petitioning of the state and stress instead self-reliant political organizations in the realm of civil society.

The strength of this position (as evidenced by the numerous large and small citizen activist networks laboriously chronicled by Boyte) is in the ability to build on (while transforming) existing (and usually eroding) community groups. They also build philosophically upon a popular tradition of liberal and radical American antistatism and anticorporatism that can be a real resource for the left. And they turn assaults by "modernization" on the family, the church, the neighborhood, and the workplace into sources for criticism of capitalism (as opposed to the "new right's" efforts to blame these things on feminism, welfarism, etc.). Evans and Boyte, and the populist left position they represent, make the significant point that much of the left, immersed as it is in the language of relentless critique, has cut itself off from important "traditional" sources of resistance. Both Boyte and Evans have activist roots in the Civil Rights movement, and they understand that much of the power of that movement came from the ability of Southern blacks to adapt existing cultural institutions, particularly black churches, to the purposes of a movement of radical transformation. Building on and re-directing, rather than severing, roots was a key to the vast mobilizations accomplished. One need only point to the extent to which Catholic and Protestant churches have proven themselves the backbone of virtually every major left movement in recent years to see that this remains an important lesson for organizers.

But as Boyte and Evans have admitted, communitarian groups with strong traditional ties are also vulnerable on a number of fronts. In particular, they are in danger of two kinds of co-optation. They can either be transformed into the kind of liberal interest groups they attempt to replace, given that, as we saw with the New Left, the eschewal of "ideology" often leaves little room for long-range social analysis. Or they can become defensive, conservative communities bent on excluding others from their new-found power. This danger is particularly strong when, again, in the interests of being "nonideological," abstract appeals to community insufficiently acknowledge what Boyte and Evans to their credit admit, that "communities can be open, evolving, and changing—or static, parochial, defensive and rigid. They can encourage new roles for those traditionally marginalized or powerless within their midst or they can reinforce traditional patterns of patriarchy, racial bigotry, homophobia, and exclusivity."[52]

A third, still more devastating possibility is not mentioned by Boyte and Evans: that even if successful at maintaining their independent, non-interest-group status, citizens groups may be serving the state inadvertently by helping to stabilize sectors of the poor and marginalized. Moreover, confinement to locality may be as much an effect of transnational capitalism as a form of resistance to it. As David Harvey argues it:

> The . . . dilemmas of socialist or working-class movements in the face of universalizing capitalism are shared by other oppositional groups—racial minorities, colonized peoples, women, etc.—who are relatively empowered to organize in place but disempowered when it comes to organizing over space. In clinging, often of necessity, to a place-bound identity, however, such oppositional movements become a part of the very fragmentation which a mobile capitalism and flexible accumulation can feed upon. "Regional resistances," the struggle for local autonomy, place-bound organization, may be excellent bases for political action, but they cannot bear the burden of radical historical change alone.[53]

The closeness in language between the "new populism" and Reagan's "new federalism" has led to exaggerated attacks from the left on the "new citizens movement," but such critiques are not without ground.[54] A more fruitful approach than simply attacking this position, however, would stress the way that the complementary counterforces of feminist and class- and race-conscious populisms with more national and even global perspectives are key to making this new localist populism truly democratic. And it would acknowledge that many "new populists" themselves call for such global thinking and acting alongside and amidst localism.[55]

Nevertheless, parallels between right and left populisms should give pause. In effect, the left "new populism" is in as much danger of embracing dominant forms (from a different angle) as are some uncritical proponents of the postmodernist ethos. They are in danger of playing into the new conservatism as the strategic deployment of a nostalgic version of America's past (including many elements celebrated by left populists) as a cover for the relentless (post)modernizing forces of transnational capitalism. There is delusion in any localist, ground-up communitarian organizing that believes it can ignore ideology or state and global capitalist forces. It is extremely doubtful that localities can ever generate the economic resources for such ground-up social reorganization; decentralization must proceed simultaneously with a strategy of democratic struggle over the central economic institutions of the state and "private" sectors, and no contradiction should be seen in using existing institutional structures of the welfare state (which provide vital services to many people) as part of a protracted transitionary process.[56]

At the same time, the similarities between right and left populisms make it crystal clear that so long as the new right struggles to cynically utilize "residual" elements (i.e., "traditional family values"), the left must struggle to build upon the best, most generous, and justice-serving "residual" elements in our traditions, rather than only deploying in exclusivist and elitist fashion politically and/or culturally "advanced" positions.[57] Parochialism is no less a problem for the vanguard and the avant-garde than for populist communitarians. And a left that wants to be truly counterhegemonic cannot afford to do without any of these strands.

This left-conservative "new populism" needs to be set within and against other populist strands (which do not necessarily use the label), including the (conflicted) grass-roots and electoral components of the Rainbow Coalition, various American "green" political groups modeled on Germany's *die Grünen*, and the antinuclear, peace, solidarity, and ecofeminist direct action movements. All of these groups themselves contain strong internal tensions between culturally traditional and culturally experimental factions, but generate political agendas that agree in opposing a whole panoply of contemporary injustices.

The strongest counterhegemonic project is most likely to emerge from a strategically mobilized play between traditional ways threatened by (post)modernization and new possibilities opened by capitalism's most recent sundering of its own ideological structures. Against new versions of an abstract socialist "labor metaphysic" or an equally abstract "citizen metaphysic" or an equally abstract "formalist metaphysic," the left needs

strategically and ironically to play tradition and (post)modernity, rooted
community realisms and floating transcultural postmodernisms against
each other. Irony here is about the willingness to faithfully hold in theory
and practice to "contradictions that do not resolve into larger wholes,
even dialectically, about the tension of holding incompatible things together because both or all are necessary and true."[58] And politics here is
about knowing those points where the immediate, purist pursuit of one's
full cultural-political agenda undermines the very means of achieving any
significant part of that agenda.

Within this really ironic or ironically realist politics, leftist cultural intellectuals play an important role in mediating various levels of the cultural apparatus, helping build counterhegemonic public spheres in and
beyond the academy to strengthen and expand movement cultures as
semi-autonomous (con)texts of articulation and action against the
material/symbolic conditions that generate hegemonic realisms and
postmodernisms alike.[59] There is room in this process for critical
(re)articulations of texts ranging from the most classical to the most
avant-garde, the most elite to the most popular;[60] or, more to the point,
there is room for the kind of reading strategies that erase these distinctions as class-based categories, extending the democratic appropriation
of high culture and intensifying the radicalization of popular culture.[61]
Particularly important to these efforts is support for mediating cultural
institutions like the Alliance for Cultural Democracy, the Feminist Press,
and dozens of similar efforts that link academics with community-based
cultural-political activists.

In the course of his tour de force reading of postmodernist architecture
as embodied (entombed?) in the Bonaventure Hotel in Los Angeles, Fredric Jameson speaks of a "false populism" resident in the eclecticism of
the postmodern aesthetic. This is an important point about the way in
which certain elite elements of the postmodern avant-garde offer their
audience a sense of superiority even as they offer nothing but empty pastiches of the presumed emptiness of most "popular culture." This is one
of the ways that "high culture" does not erase its difference from the
"popular" but maintains a class-based difference that mirrors "popular
culture" at a self-consciously different level of a postmodernist cultural
dominant.

But against this "false populism" and against the towering and disorienting image of the hotel itself, one can set a truly populist image that
is in fact a part of this same landscape. Looked at from a slightly lower

angle of vision than offered anywhere in Jameson's analysis, one can see a mural in the line of sight of the surrounding neighborhood's view of the hotel. The mural is the work of Chicana artist Judy Baca, who, using multiracial crews of male and female youth, has covered Los Angeles with literally miles of mural conveying the history and political struggles of the diverse ethnic populations of the city. The mural is one of many acts through which the local neighborhoods reclaim turf taken by the aesthetico-capitalist bandits who built the Bonaventure. The Bonaventure is indeed locked into its glossy postmodern self-reflections, but what is reflected there when one looks more closely is a city and a nation riddled with sources of contradiction, resistance, and transformation. While conservative postmodernism continues to write its paeans to the surfaceness of surfaces, postmodern subjects continue spraying very different messages on the surfaces of our cities: these graffiti writers too are forming the conditions of our postmodernity through messages of resistance and through the struggles for justice from which they arise.

Notes

CHAPTER 1. LITERARY POLITICS AND THE
POETICS OF SOCIAL MOVEMENTS

1. Theorist Barbara Johnson, for example, wrote recently that "the day of
Theory (in its monolithic, hegemonic form) may be passing." But note the qual-
ifiers. Johnson goes on to suggest that the very success of "Theory" has resulted
in its breakup, and she makes it clear that the real theoretical work is just beginning. Jonathan Arac and Barbara Johnson, eds., *The Consequences of Theory*,
vii–viii.

2. This restlessness has been emerging for some time. As a few varied, early
examples among influential critics who continue to take theory seriously, I would
cite Edward Said's essay "Opponents, Audiences, Constituencies, and Community"; Terry Eagleton's piece "The Idealism of American Criticism"; Frank Lentricchia's *Criticism and Social Change*, which "fraternally" criticizes the above-
mentioned critics; Russell Reising, *The Unusable Past*, esp. chap. 5; Barbara
Christian, "The Race for Theory"; the introduction by editors Judith Newton
and Deborah Rosenfelt to *Feminist Criticism and Social Change;* Jim Merod,
The Political Responsibility of the Critic; and Barbara Johnson's move from *The
Critical Difference* to *A World of Difference*. Gayatri Chakravorty Spivak's similar move from the word to the world in the title and later essays of *In Other
Worlds: Essays in Cultural Politics* also seems to mark a desire for greater world-
liness. Less formal evidence for this restlessness is gleaned from listening to colleagues and surveying current work in progress.

3. For a marvelously rich parody of this process vis-à-vis literary theory, see
Bernard Sharratt's unclassifiable novel/theoretical tract, *Reading Relations:
Structures of Literary Production—A Dialectical Text/Book*.

4. E. D. Hirsch, *The Aims of Interpretation*, 135; Tzvetan Todorov, "The Notion of Literature"; Terry Eagleton, *Literary Theory: An Introduction*, chap. 1;

and Rita Felski, *Beyond Feminist Aesthetics: Feminist Literature and Social Change.*

5. The following works provide useful (and varied) examples of work in the field of radical rhetorical studies beginning from a primarily literary standpoint: Judith Newton and Deborah Rosenfelt, eds., *Feminist Criticism and Social Change;* Henry Louis Gates, Jr., *The Signifying Monkey: A Theory of Afro-American Literary Theory* and *Figures in Black: Words, Signs, and the 'Racial' Self;* Houston A. Baker, Jr., *Blues, Ideology and Afro-American Literature: A Vernacular Theory;* Hazel Carby, *Reconstructing Womanhood: The Emergence of the Afro-American Woman Novelist;* Eagleton, *Literary Theory;* Lentricchia, *Criticism and Social Change;* Edward Said, *The World, the Text, and the Critic;* Robert Scholes, *Textual Power: Literary Theory and the Teaching of English;* Steven Mailloux, *Rhetorical Power;* and Spivak, *In Other Worlds.* Recent work on textuality and power in ethnographic writing can be found in James Clifford and George Marcus, eds., *Writing Culture: The Poetics and Politics of Ethnography;* George Marcus and Michael Fisher, *Anthropology as Cultural Critique;* and James Clifford, *The Predicament of Culture: Twentieth Century Ethnography, Literature and Art.* On rhetorical criticism and historiography, see Hayden White, *Metahistory, Tropics of Discourse,* and *The Content of the Form;* and Dominick LaCapra, *Rethinking Intellectual History, History and Criticism,* and *Soundings in Cultural Criticism.* On rhetorical criticism in political theory, see John S. Nelson, "Political Theory as Political Rhetoric." On the role of textual criticism in the more general field of "cultural studies," see Richard Johnson, "What Is Cultural Studies Anyway?"

6. "Literariness" is, in fact, just a code name for the dominant current of modernist aesthetics.

7. Eagleton, *Literary Theory,* 8.

8. On the emergence of the concept "literature" in English history, see Raymond Williams, *Marxism and Literature,* 45–54.

9. Fredric Jameson, *The Political Unconscious: Narrative as a Socially Symbolic Act.*

10. For an insightful critique of these theoretical tendencies, see Mary Louise Pratt, "Interpretive Strategies/Strategic Interpretations: On Anglo-American Reader-Response Criticism."

11. Gregory S. Jay, "American Literature and the New Historicism," 3.

12. Two recent, suggestive American examples of this style of historical rhetorical criticism are Cathy Davidson, *Revolution and the Word: The Rise of the Novel in America,* and Michael Denning, *Mechanic Accents: Dime Novels and Working Class Culture in America.* For a general argument about the need to reconstruct particular historical "reading formations" (communities of/as readers), see Tony Bennett, "Texts in History."

13. Even Stanley Fish's ostensibly absurdist claim, for example, that an "Eskimo interpretation" (following a comment of Norman Holland) of Faulkner's "A Rose for Emily" cannot be ruled out, is based on the elaboration of an as yet unknown critical criteria established intersubjectively in a given cultural/critical matrix, and Fish's own attempts to contain his notion of "interpretive communities" to academia are culturally and politically determined (note, for example,

Fish and Holland's ethnocentricity in choosing "Eskimo" as exotically absurd). See Fish, *Is There a Text in This Class?*

14. The very old notion of the political as a realm of contingency and judgment is argued clearly and strongly in contemporary terms by Hannah Arendt in *The Human Condition;* by John Schaar in *Legitimacy and the Modern State;* by William Connolly in *The Terms of Political Discourse;* and by Benjamin Barber in *Strong Democracy;* and explored philosophically by Ronald Beiner in *Political Judgement.* Beiner also explores the specifically rhetorical nature of politics, arguing for the Aristotelian notion of *phronesis* as the communal basis for rhetorical practice. The contemporary theorist who has given the most sustained and systematic attention to questions about the discursive context of political action is no doubt Jürgen Habermas. Although I am critical of many of Habermas's positions and think that he has moved too far away from questions about the material preconditions for discursive equality, his suggestive work, too easily dismissed by postmodern theorists, informs my assumptions here. For the fullest statements of his position, see *A Theory of Communicative Action*, part 1, *Reason and the Rationalization of Society* and part 2, *Lifeworld and System.* For a lucid use and critique of Habermas from a feminist perspective, see Nancy Fraser, *Unruly Practices.*

15. Newton and Rosenfelt, eds., *Feminist Criticism and Social Change*, xxix.

16. For three interesting, rather different works, each of which entails a serious encounter between radical humanist critical theory and postmodern/poststructuralist theory, see Peter Dews, *Logics of Disintegration;* Christopher Norris, *What's Wrong with Postmodernism?;* and John McGowan, *Postmodernism and Its Critics.*

17. For tentative efforts in this direction, see Ernesto Laclau and Chantal Mouffe, *Hegemony and Socialist Strategy;* and Mouffe, "Radical Democracy: Modern or Postmodern." Two severe, related deficiencies mar these important works. First, in concentrating on the philosophical level of the radical democratic tradition they efface the political struggles that made those articulations possible (thus also sounding at times as though they had invented a radical democratic position that in fact has a long, rich history). Second, they use a reductive notion of "discourse" that largely ignores the material, institutional, and cultural processes by which discourses are created and stabilized. They thus reinscribe the textualist illusion that virtually any discourse can be "articulated" with or "disarticulated" from any other by formal fiat rather than through struggle with and over specific, layered, often entrenched, local traditions, conditions, and practices.

18. The term "new social movements" was coined in Europe to describe a host of movements (feminist, "green," antinuclear, squatter/urban, etc.) that arose there in the seventies. In the United States a similar wave of movements looks less "new," and I use the term to include much of the social movement activity here in the fifties and sixties as well. The literature on these movements is vast and uneven. For a general historical and critical overview, see Carl Boggs, *Social Movements and Political Power;* for the most sophisticated theory of the emergence and nature of the new movements, see Alberto Melucci, *Nomads of the Present;* for general theory and strategy to link these movements, compare

Toni Negri and Felix Guattari, *Communists Like Us* with Laclau and Mouffe, *Hegemony and Socialist Strategy;* among numerous studies combining empirical case studies and theory/strategy questions, see Barbara Epstein, *Political Protest and Cultural Revolution*, Noël Sturgeon, "Direct Theory and Political Action," and Margit Mayer, ed., *New Social Movements in Western Europe and the United States;* for the American radical democratic left tradition as it anticipates (and in some ways critiques) new social movement theory and practice, see Richard Flacks, *Making History: The American Left and the American Mind*. Both new social movement theory and Flacks's work suffer from lack of a feminist theoretical component.

19. Melucci, "The Symbolic Challenge of Contemporary Movements," 815.

20. The relation of radical democracy to Marxism is a vexed one for me, since my work is deeply informed by and sympathetic to, but also highly critical of, some Marxist traditions. To the extent that Marxism remains the most appropriate name for radical, anticapitalist political economic thought, then radical democratic social movements need to be Marxist. But to the extent that various Marxist political positions continue to privilege class at the expense of race, gender, and other "contradictions," and to the extent that various Marxisms continue to either accept existing democratic forms (as do some social democrats) or claim that they are bourgeois and superfluous (as do some Communists), Marxism remains an impediment to radical thought and practice. Historically much of Marxism has been at once too conservative as a practice (one too willing to conserve various forms of hierarchy) and too radical as a rhetoric (exaggerating the possibility of revolutionary breaks with the past). In any event, since most Americans have still not been given a full understanding of various Marxisms, there should be no question of pursuing some post-Marxist radicalism in this country, but rather every attempt should be made to translate the best insights of the Marxist tradition more fully into an American idiom. For an argument about "democracy" as the key notion in the "tradition of the left" in the United States, see Flacks, *Making History*. For something of a counterargument about the centrality of Marxist movements and ideas, see Paul Buhle, *Marxism in the USA*. For a cogent plea for the ongoing need for a full encounter with Marxism in America, see Michael Denning, "'The Special American Conditions': Marxism and American Studies."

21. William Cain and Frank Lentricchia have recently made similar calls for connecting radical thought and practice to traditional forms. See their respective contributions in Gerald Graff and Reginald Gibbons, eds., *Criticism in the University*.

22. The notion of an alternative public sphere centered in oppositional social movements (with regard to a "feminist public sphere") is elaborated in Felski, *Beyond Feminist Aesthetics*, esp. 164–74, and in Nancy Fraser, "Rethinking the Public Sphere" and *Unruly Practices*. Both Fraser and Felski draw on Jürgen Habermas's discussion of the "bourgeois public sphere" in his "The Public Sphere: An Encyclopaedia Article," and in his larger work, *The Structural Transformation of the Public Sphere*. Habermas refines his use of the term in his more recent *Lifeworld and System* (Part 2 of *A Theory of Communicative Action*).

23. Michael Ryan, "Postmodern Politics," 574.

24. Janice Radway, "Identifying Ideological Seams: Mass Culture, Analytical Method, and Political Practice."

25. One lucid, influential statement of this critique of "realism" is that of Colin MacCabe, "Realism and Cinema: Notes on Brechtian Theses."

26. Pierre Bourdieu, "The Aristocracy of Culture," *Media, Culture, and Society.*

27. One critic who has always tried to articulate this need for articulation is Stuart Hall. For his recent thoughts on this topic, see the interview "On Postmodernism and Articulation."

28. See, for example, the essays by Craig Owens, Rosalind Krauss, and Kenneth Frampton in Hal Foster, ed., *The Anti-Aesthetic: Essays on Postmodern Culture.* Fredric Jameson has also come to acknowledge this, positing what he calls "homeopathic" postmodernism as a strategy for using the logic of postmodernism against itself; see his interview in Andrew Ross, ed., *Universal Abandon? The Politics of Postmodernism.* Linda Hutcheon develops something similar in her notion of "historiographic metafiction," though it is not always clear whether she sees this as a subcategory of the postmodern or as *the* postmodern form of historical or historiographic literary consciousness. In any event my concept of postmodernist realism is critical of the notion that the paradoxes posed by postmodernism free us from certain doxical, political choices, and the related notion that paradoxicality is itself politically liberatory. See Hutcheon, *A Poetics of Postmodernism.*

29. For an interesting example of how such an analysis might proceed vis-à-vis one postmodern critic, see Jennifer Wicke's discussion of Baudrillard's repression of the material production processes that make possible the apparently free-floating "hyperreality" he claims has made questions of material production obsolete. Wicke, "Postmodernism: The Perfume of Information."

30. I do not mean this to suggest that genres are ever escaped by this crossing process. Derrida's comment sums up my sense of how one might think about "postmodernist realism" as a genre: "Every text participates in one or several genres, there is no genreless text; there is always a genre and genres, yet participation never amounts to belonging," "La Loi du Genre/The Law of Genre," 212. I also share the observation of Tzvetan Todorov that a genre only lives by being transgressed. Thus there is never a transcendence of genre, at best only its affirmation through denial. See Todorov, "The Origin of Genres."

31. Spivak, *In Other Worlds*, 95.

CHAPTER 2. AESTHETICS AND THE OVERPRIVILEGED

1. A major exception to this is William Stott's reading of *Praise* in *Documentary Expression and Thirties America.* He sees the text as both an aesthetic and a documentary work that explodes the latter genre. In addition to Stott's perceptive reading of *Praise*, to which I am indebted throughout this chapter despite certain disagreements, the following works inform my analysis: Peter Ohlin, *Agee;* Kenneth Seib, *James Agee: Promise and Fulfillment;* Alfred Barson, *A Way of Seeing;* David Madden, ed., *Remembering James Agee;* Victor Kramer, *James Agee;* Genevieve Moreau, *The Restless Journey of James Agee;* Laurence Ber-

green, *James Agee: A Life;* Ronald Weber, *The Literature of Fact: Literary Non-fiction in American Writing;* Ross Spears and Jude Cassidy, eds., *Agee: His Life Remembered;* and John Hersey, "Introduction: Agee."

2. For a discussion of some of the issues raised here, see Jonathan Arac's introduction to *Postmodernism and Politics,* and James Clifford's introduction to Clifford and George Marcus, eds., *Writing Culture: The Poetics and Politics of Ethnography.*

3. I think the closest parallel to what Agee was trying to achieve lies not among any American contemporaries but rather in that of a German contemporary whom I do not think he could have known, Walter Benjamin. Agee's peculiar blend of theological and political concerns, as well as his interest in rhetorical violence, in photography and film, and his appreciation/use of the Dada/surrealist moment, among other things, suggests an affinity with Benjamin. Benjamin's essay "The Author as Producer" also contains a critique of documentary realism (in prose and photography) akin to that of Agee and Evans.

4. On the question of the common aesthetic-political roots and development of the word "representation," see Hanna Pitkin, *The Concept of Representation.*

5. James Agee and Walker Evans, *Let Us Now Praise Famous Men,* l–li. All subsequent citations to this work will be given in parentheses within my text.

6. James Agee, *Collected Short Prose of James Agee,* 134.

7. James Agee, *Letters of James Agee to Father Flye,* 102.

8. See Stott, *Documentary Expression,* for an excellent account of the centrality and meaning of various documentary projects during the Depression decade and *Praise*'s relation to those projects. One book, Erskine Caldwell and Margaret Bourke-White's *You Have Seen Their Faces,* a photo-prose best-seller about sharecroppers, may in particular have served as a negative example for Evans and Agee. See their scathing send-up of Bourke-White in the appendix to *Praise.*

9. For an attack on "well-thought-out" radical efforts that parallels this attack on liberal *Fortune* readers, see, for example, *Praise,* 215.

10. See Stott, *Documentary Expression,* chap. 15.

11. One could fault Agee here for thereby condescending to his audience, and his text is not without its own sentimentalizing of the tenants, though this is clearly counterbalanced by a profound respect largely lacking in other accounts. In hurling these insults at his readers he sought to separate the serious from the casual reader, or better, to turn casual readers into serious ones. And I suspect he intended to give his privileged readers a small taste of the daily indignities suffered by the families of which he is writing. But I am not at all sure this justifies the tactic, and Evans, by contrast, was able to maintain a consistent respect for his audience, not hectoring or shouting at them but continually inviting them to change their way of seeing.

12. Agee's care in trying even on the level of detail to give a sense of his text as but part of ongoing existence is suggested by the phrase "daily living" in place of the more common "daily life." This is one of many places in the text that, borrowing perhaps from Gertrude Stein, use gerunds to give a more dynamic sense of movement and process. He does not wish to capture some reified "life" but to give a sense of ongoing "living."

13. See Stott, *Documentary Expression,* 264, 301.

14. The most astute work on this boundary question remains that of Mikhail Bakhtin. See especially the essay collection *The Dialogic Imagination* and *Marxism and the Philosophy of Language*. Barbara Herrnstein Smith also takes up these issues in her work *On the Margins of Discourse*.

15. For a general discussion of these issues, see Raymond Williams, *Marxism and Literature*, 145–50. On the early use of the term "novel" in English, see Lennard Davis, "A Social History of Fact and Fiction: Authorial Disavowal in the Early English Novel."

16. This is, of course, not an absolute position. Certainly many people have had their perceptions of their everyday lives profoundly changed by works labeled "fiction." Nevertheless, Agee's main point is well taken—the tendency to seal off art from life is deep, and diminishes both art and life.

17. On the notion of "framing" as the prime means for separating what she calls "natural" from "fictive" discourse, see Smith, *On the Margins*.

18. Erskine Caldwell, quoted in Stott, *Documentary Expression*, 219.

19. The text's characterization of the relation of photos and words shows interesting similarities to claims made by Roland Barthes in his text "on" Japan. Compare Agee's remark that "the photographs are not illustrative. They, and the text, are coequal, mutually independent, and fully collaborative," with Barthes's claim: "The text does not 'gloss' the images, which do not 'illustrate' the text. For me, each has been no more than the onset of a kind of visual uncertainty, analogous perhaps to that *loss of meaning* zen calls a *satori*," in *Empire of Signs*, xi. The comparison between the two texts goes deeper than this, though I have no space to pursue it here, except to remark that each could be characterized as a kind of "defamiliarizing" ethnography, with Agee and Evans making their subject fully as "exotic" as Barthes's Orient.

20. These passages have been objected to by some critics as inconsistent with the general tenor of the text. I think there is some justice in this claim, but it should be noted that these "representative" bits of landlord speech (and similar bits from the families) float free in the text as if attaching them to individuals would violate some compositional-ethical principle.

21. Indeed, much of the text can be seen as a kind of phenomenological treatment of its subject, closer to the existential, perceptual phenomenology of Maurice Merleau-Ponty than to the line of eidetic phenomenology descending through Edmund Husserl to Alfred Schutz, but with a touch of each. For a phenomenologist's appreciation of *Let Us Now Praise Famous Men* as phenomenology, see Maurice Natanson, "Rhetoric and Counter-Espionage."

22. I suspect Agee modeled this scene, not wholly successfully, on the liturgical shaving scene in James Joyce's *Ulysses*. Indeed, the influence of Joyce is apparent throughout the text, from the use of such words as "deeplighted" to the aesthetic passion for documentation itself, which, as G. B. Shaw once remarked, is brought to a new level of intensity in *Ulysses*.

23. Agee sees himself as raging against "every deadly habit in the use of the senses and of language" including "every 'artistic' habit of distortion in the evaluation of experience" (241).

24. Agee directly comments that his text should most resemble a "set of tones rather less like those of narrative than of music," and in a note adds that its forms

may also resemble those of film (244). But these suggestions must be played against the numerous implicit references to drama—a list of dramatis personae at the beginning, sections entitled "Curtain Speech" and "Intermission," and so on—that occur throughout. Similarly, the section given subtitles from parts of the Catholic Mass, "Recessional," "Introit," etc., are Agee's way of again crossing discursive boundaries, trying both to suffuse the religious into the profane and to show the aesthetic dimension of spiritual experience.

25. Agee uses dialogue in the text, but rather sparingly. His explanation for this is typical of the politics of the text—he fears that the use of dialect will serve only to amuse his privileged readers and detract from the dignity of the speakers (328). This resistance to dialogue and scene construction is discussed perceptively by Ronald Weber, *The Literature of Fact*, 63.

26. Agee was very fond of the word "silence"; it occurs frequently in the text and is used in a variety of ways (sometimes, for example, it is an index to the unspeakable, at other times it is part of an effort to induce a contemplative mood, to so slow down the process of perception that it becomes palpable, more fully conscious). Open spaces in many of Evans's photos seem to function analogously as a kind of silence. For an interesting essay on the subject, though one I disagree with in many respects, see James A. Ward, "James Agee's Aesthetics of Silence."

27. Agee actually wrote a longer version of the "Work" chapter, one that more fully and with intentional monotony enacts the daily labors of the tenants. But this portion was edited out, apparently by the publisher for reasons of cost. See Victor Kramer, "The Complete 'Work' Chapter for James Agee's *Let Us Now Praise Famous Men*." The article includes the omitted portion.

28. As should be clear by now, I do not see Evans as the naive realist representer of the underprivileged that he is sometimes portrayed to be. A similarly narrow reading of him as modernist technician seems closer to the truth but, in the context of *Praise* at least, is not wholly apt. Thus when Sherry Levine brilliantly appropriates Evans's photographs as "her own" by simply rephotographing them in her series of photos entitled *After Walker Evans*, I read this gesture less as an attack on Evans than as an attack on what the critical establishment has made of his work, as well as part of a more general critique of patriarchal dominance in photography and criticism. My own appropriation here is perhaps less blatant, but no more innocent.

29. This was not an absolute aesthetic principle with Evans, nor was his avoidance of candid shots of the tenants (which in other work he often made quite spectacular use of), but rather seems to have grown out of a more or less implicit understanding he had with Agee that for this project a scrupulous attempt to avoid overt manipulation of context would be part of their self-discipline, their attempt to show the impossibility of unmediated, nonmanipulative representation. For a general discussion of Evans's work and his evolving aesthetic position in relation to other photographers, to the modernist and documentary traditions, and to the Farm Security Administration photo project, see Alan Trachtenberg, *Reading American Photographs*, and Maren Stange, *"Symbols of Ideal Life": Social Documentary Photography in America, 1890–1950*, esp. 114–17, 129. For analyses of the politics of photographic documentation, see Abigail Solomon-Godeau, *Photography at the Dock*, esp. part 3; Victor Bur-

gin, ed., *Thinking Photography;* and Martha Rosler, "In, around, and after-thoughts (on documentary photography)." Rosler's incisive critique also includes remarks on questionable recent journalistic attempts to "expose" Agee and Evans as victimizers that actually reinscribe the tenants as victims, esp. 68–69, 77. For an important analysis of the women photographers involved in the FSA and other New Deal projects, see Andrea Fisher, *Let Us Now Praise Famous Women.*

30. In a footnote (and one would need to add the self-polemical, or self-dialogical, footnote as another element of the text's polyphony), Agee adds that now (as the book is going to press a year after the initial writing) he thinks the "sin" is in ever questioning the rightness of seeing and telling of the beauty.

31. For a brilliant analysis of aesthetic privilege and underprivilege as it shapes class and other social structures, see Pierre Bourdieu, *Distinction: A Social Critique of Judgement and Taste.*

32. Throughout this section I am drawing on what one might call the "morte d'auteur" school of literary criticism, the most succinct statements of which occur in Michel Foucault, "What Is an Author?" and Roland Barthes, "Death of the Author."

33. This scene is also notable for the way in which Agee parodies his own style and most cherished beliefs. For example, he writes: "There is nothing that exists, or in imagination, that is not much more than beautiful, and a lot I care about that" (384).

34. I do not wish to be misunderstood here as romanticizing "face-to-faceness" per se. As symbolic interactionists like Erving Goffman have shown, such encounters are highly structured, highly mediated. If you like, think of face-to-face as a metaphor for a political relationship in which reciprocity becomes possible.

35. Two projects returning to the scene of Agee and Evans's crimes give us information about how the tenants received the text, and how their lives developed. See Dale Maharidge and Michael Williamson, *And Their Children After Them: The Legacy of "Let Us Now Praise Famous Men": James Agee, Walker Evans, and the Rise and Fall of Cotton in the South,* and "Let Us Now Praise Famous Men—Revisited." Responses from the tenants and their offspring have ranged from outrage that they never got any royalties from the book (neither did Agee during his lifetime, but his executors or Evans could have remedied this after the book's late-blooming success), to sleepiness while reading, to Allie Mae Burroughs's [Annie Mae Gudger] comment: "What they wrote in the book was true." "Praise—Revisited," 14–15. See also comments from some of the tenants in Spears and Cassidy, eds., *Agee.*

36. The distinction I employ here between "book" and "text" is as a variation on the distinction between "work" and "text" made by Barthes, Julia Kristeva, and others, a distinction between a putatively self-sufficient artifact and one caught in a web of intertextual and extratextual relations. See Barthes, "From Work to Text."

37. See Robert Coles, "James Agee's 'Famous Men' Seen Again," and Hersey, "Introduction: Agee," xxxvi–xxxviii. Agee and Evans at first wanted to live with at least one black tenant family, but they found that racism had created an unbridgeable gulf, a gulf symbolized in *Praise* by Agee's encounter with a young

African-American couple clearly frightened to be talking to a white man (this is one of several scenes in the text that contradict the claim made by some critics that Agee glosses over Southern racism in general and the racism of white tenants in particular). The lack in *Praise* of a full treatment of African-American tenants is more than compensated for by the superb (auto)biography of one black " 'cropper," Nate Shaw [Ned Cobb], as told in Theodore Rosengarten's *All God's Dangers*. (Rosengarten, incidentally, went to Ned Cobb's house with a well-thumbed copy of *Praise* under his arm.) Cobb/Shaw's story includes other dimensions left out of *Praise* as well, particularly such elements of the "sonata's" second movement as the struggles of the Alabama Sharecroppers Union, formed by the Communist party but acting sometimes also in alliance with New Dealers. For a superb analysis of these efforts, see Robin D. G. Kelly, *Hammer and Hoe: Alabama Communists During the Great Depression*.

38. In typical Agee fashion it also suggests a self-ironic allusion to the drowsy state of the reader who has endured his massive, passionate extravagance for hundreds of pages. As Paula Rabinowitz has argued, there is also a cozily homoerotic element in this scene, one that I think suggests male-bonded homo-*text*uality that is one clear limit to the book. See Rabinowitz, "Voyeurism and Class Consciousness."

CHAPTER 3. INVISIBLE MOVEMENTS, BLACK POWERS

1. Cited in Kerry McSweeney, *Invisible Man: Race and Identity*, xiv.

2. Critic Harold Bloom has gone so far as to "prophesy that *Invisible Man* will be judged, some day, as the principal work of American fiction between Faulkner's major phase and Pynchon's *Gravity's Rainbow*." Harold Bloom, ed., *Ralph Ellison*, 1.

3. Early negative reviews from critics in the orbit of American communism included an anonymous attack in the *Daily Worker* and John Killen's scathing review in the journal *Freedom*. Irving Howe's review "Black Boys and Native Sons" appreciated the novel's aesthetic richness, but accused it of being insufficiently in alliance with black protest. Ellison replied to Howe in an essay entitled "The World and the Jug" (reprinted in *Shadow and Act*), defending his aesthetic and racial integrity. Attacks on Ellison by promoters of a "Black Aesthetic" in the 1960s are epitomized by Addison Gayle's remarks in his *Black Aesthetic*, 392, and in *The Way of the New World*, xxii, xxiii, 257. These views began to change with the publication of "black aesthetic" critic Larry Neal's brilliant, positive reading of *Invisible Man*, "Ellison's Zoot Suit." For a history of recent black criticism that contextualizes changing attitudes toward Ellison's work, see Houston A. Baker, Jr., "Discovering America: Generational Shifts, Afro-American Literary Criticism, and the Study of Expressive Culture," in his *Blues, Ideology, and Afro-American Literature: A Vernacular Theory*, 64–112. For a general summary of the critical reception of *Invisible Man*, see Ernest Kaiser, "A Critical Look at Ellison's Fiction," and McSweeney, *Invisible Man*, 15–26.

4. Much of the most interesting new criticism on *Invisible Man* can be found in three recent anthologies: Kimberly Benston, ed., *Speaking for You: The Vision of Ralph Ellison*, especially the essays by Hortense Spillers, Claudia Tate, Hous-

ton Baker, Michel Fabre, and Charles Davis; Harold Bloom, ed., *Ralph Ellison*, especially essays by Robert B. Stepto, Susan L. Blake, Charles Davis, and Berndt Ostendorf; and Robert G. O'Meally, ed., *New Essays on Invisible Man*. See also the brilliant chapter on Ellison in Keith E. Byerman, *Fingering the Jagged Grain: Tradition and Form in Recent Black Fiction*, and the equally brilliant treatment of Ellison by Henry Louis Gates, Jr., in "The Blackness of Blackness: A Critique of the Sign and the Signifying Monkey," and in revised form in Gates, *The Signifying Monkey: A Theory of Afro-American Literary Criticism*, 217–38 (note the greater respect accorded Ellison at the conclusion of this version). Two book-length studies of Ellison's work have also influenced me: Robert G. O'Meally, *The Craft of Ralph Ellison*, and Alan Nadel, *Invisible Criticism: Ralph Ellison and the American Canon*. Two earlier anthologies that suggest the nature, range, and limits of previous Ellison criticism are John Hersey, ed., *Ralph Ellison: A Collection of Critical Essays*, and John M. Reilly, ed., *Twentieth Century Interpretations of Invisible Man*.

5. Ralph Ellison, *Shadow and Act*, 38, 84, and 167–83.

6. The term "double-consciousness" derives, of course, from W. E. B. Du Bois. A number of critics have played with versions of the idea of double-voicedness, and double vision, in black writing. My own seriously playful concept is informed by these others, but is not identical with any of them.

7. See especially Nadel's *Invisible Criticism*, the most detailed study of allusion in Ellison's work. Gates, in *The Signifying Monkey*, offers a general theory of black literary intertextuality that reads *Invisible Man* as "signifyin(g)" on Richard Wright in particular, as well as such Euro-American figures as Melville, Eliot, Twain, Crane, and Emerson. See esp. xxvii, 105–7, and 218.

8. Reprinted in *Shadow and Act*, 24–44.

9. Ellison quoted in Benston, *Speaking for You*, 4.

10. See, for example, Mary Helen Washington's remarks comparing the critical reception given *Invisible Man* and Gwendolyn Brooks' *Maud Martha*, published only one year after Ellison's book, in her essay "'The Darkened Eye Restored': Towards a New Literary History of Black Women," esp. 31–33, 41n.

11. Ellison makes all this explicit in a direct response to black aestheticians: "The 'Black Aesthetic' crowd buys this idea of total cultural separation between blacks and whites, suggesting that we've been left out of the mainstream. But when we examine American music and literature in terms of its themes, symbolism, rhythms, tonalities, idioms and images it is obvious that those rejected 'Negroes' have been a vital part of the mainstream from the beginning." Quoted in W. Lawrence Hogue, *Discourse and the Other: The Production of the Afro-American Text*, 61.

12. Ralph Ellison, *Invisible Man*, 196–97. All subsequent citations of *Invisible Man* will be given in parentheses within my text.

13. On the social construction of "whiteness," see Ruth Frankenberg, *White Women, Race Matters*.

14. Neal, "Ellison's Zoot Suit," 115.

15. Berndt Ostendorf, "Anthropology, Modernism, and Jazz."

16. In "Change the Joke and Slip the Yoke," for example, Ellison speaks of

folklore as valuable to those "who are able to translate [folkloric] meanings into wider, more precise vocabularies," *Shadow and Act*, 73.

17. The folkloric component of *Invisible Man* has been explored richly by a number of critics. See the essays by Neal and Ostendorf cited above, as well as the following: Susan L. Blake, "Ritual and Rationalization: Black Folklore in the Works of Ralph Ellison"; Robert O'Meally, "Riffs and Rituals: Folklore in the Work of Ralph Ellison"; George Kent, "Ralph Ellison and the Afro-American Folk and Cultural Tradition." Albert Murray's classic, *The Omni-Americans*, also contains some astute observations on the blues dimension of *Invisible Man*, and Baker discusses Ellison's ambivalent attitude toward folklore in his *Blues, Ideology, and Afro-American Literature*, 172–76.

18. See Thomas Schaub, *American Fiction in the Cold War*, esp. 91–115.

19. Ralph Ellison, "Remembering Richard Wright," 194, 196.

20. Cedric J. Robinson, in his monumental study, *Black Marxism*, 416–40, has argued that Richard Wright's novels were in fact more important works of Marxist theory than anything produced by white or black American Communist party theorists during this period.

21. Ellison quoted in Michel Fabre, "From *Native Son* to *Invisible Man*: Some Notes on Ralph Ellison's Evolution in the 1950s," 212.

22. See Fabre's essay cited above, and in addition to Ellison's own remarks in "Remembering Richard Wright," see Joseph T. Skerrett, Jr., "The Wright Interpretation: Ralph Ellison and the Anxiety of Influence."

23. Quoted in Hogue, *Discourse and the Other*, 45.

24. See Hogue, *Discourse and the Other*, esp. 44–47.

25. This is the claim put forth by H. Bruce Franklin in his ground-breaking work, *The Victim as Criminal and Artist*, and since elaborated by numerous African-American scholars.

26. Henry Louis Gates, Jr., explores the complexities of the search for the authentic black self via autobiography in *Figures in Black: Words, Signs, and the 'Racial' Self*. Compare Gates with Robert Stepto, *From Behind the Veil*.

27. For Ellison's comments on this process, see his essay "The World and the Jug," in *Shadow and Act*, esp. 115–16.

28. See Valerie Smith, "Ellison's Invisible Autobiographer," in *Self-Discovery and Authority*, for a somewhat parallel reading.

29. These ideas are explored intricately in Kimberly Benston, "I yam what I yam: The Topos of (Un)Naming in Afro-American Literature."

30. Among the most important rereadings of, or signifyings upon, the Trueblood episode occur in Toni Morrison's novel *The Bluest Eye* and Alice Walker's *The Color Purple*. Michael Awkward addresses Morrison's revision in *Inspiriting Influences: Tradition, Revision, and Afro-American Women's Novels*, 81–87, partly in response to Houston Baker's influential essay, "To Move Without Moving: Creativity and Commerce in Ralph Ellison's Trueblood Episode." Awkward begins to reveal the sexist dimension of Baker's reading, but he does not fully bring forth the womanist power of Morrison's rereading and he lets Baker off the hook too easily.

31. It also represents an example of how hegemonic assumptions about "the" tradition of "American" literature have been narrowly European in their field of reference—the same people who think it "natural" to know a Greek god when

one pops up in Emerson think it merely exotic or obscure when a voodoo god turns up in Zora Neale Hurston or Ishmael Reed. The work of Houston Baker and Henry Louis Gates, building on the work of Hurston, Ellison, and others, is reconstructing a specifically, but not essentially, black literary tradition rooted in the particulars of African-American vernacular (from Latin, *verna*, a home-born slave) culture as it has been shaped by and has shaped "the" "Western" tradition.

32. Indeed, in his hostile early review, John Killens accused the novel of being nothing but a string of stereotypes and degraded images; see excerpts from Killens's review in Neal, "Ellison's Zoot Suit," 109. Killens's reaction is ironically similar to the reaction of some black males to the allegedly degraded images of black men in recent fiction by black women.

33. Byerman, *Fingering the Jagged Grain*, 11–40.

34. Anne Moody, *Coming of Age in Mississippi*, 307. On the dialectics of dreaming, see also *Invisible Man*, 14.

35. Ellison himself compares his writing to jazz on a number of occasions, as have a number of his critics. John Callahan has recently developed this jazz analogy with particular regard to invisible man's speeches; see the chapter on Ellison, "Frequences of Eloquence: The Performance and Composition of *Invisible Man*," in Callahan, *In the African-American Grain*. I am indebted throughout this section to Callahan's gloss of Ellison's notion of "eloquence" as the connection of word to audience, and to the notion that a composition becomes eloquent only in the performance, one dependent upon an audience, though as should be clear I find this connection more problematic and the audience's role more active than does Callahan.

36. Mark Naison, *Communists in Harlem During the Depression*. On communism and black America, see also Harold Cruse, *Crisis of the Negro Intellectual*, and Richard Wright's contribution to Richard Crossman, ed., *The God that Failed*.

37. Benston, "From *Native Son* to *Invisible Man*," in Benston, ed., *Speaking for You*, 212.

38. For a provocative attempt to theorize constructions of "race" in recent U.S. history, see Michael Omi and Howard Winant, *Racial Formation in the United States: From the 1960s to the 1980s*.

CHAPTER 4. DISRUPTING THE THEATER OF WAR

1. Two brilliant recent examples stressing the complicity of novelistic discourses in the creation of the liberal, bourgeois subject are Nancy Armstrong, *Desire and Domestic Fiction: A Political History of the Novel*, and D. A. Miller, *The Novel and the Police*. The social and psychological dimensions of novel reading are explored in terms of their resistance to collective action in Lennard Davis, *Resisting Novels: Ideology and Fiction*.

2. On one level I am suggesting that *Armies of the Night* and the march on the Pentagon were symptomatic, perhaps peculiarly American versions of an epistemological and political crisis that elsewhere is articulated primarily at the level of theory in Marxist, poststructuralist, and hermeneutic circles in the last few decades. The text's "solution" to this particular legitimation crisis, imper-

fectly articulated, and existing mainly at the formal level, points toward a radically democratic, participatory hermeneutics that would reshape every level of the social formation, from philosophy to science to art.

3. Norman Mailer, *The Armies of the Night: History as a Novel, The Novel as History*, 49. All subsequent citations to *Armies* will appear in parentheses within my text.

4. A few works of Mailer criticism do get beyond this polarized realist/postmodernist dichotomy. For my purposes I found the following useful: Richard Poirier, *Norman Mailer;* Tony Tanner, *City of Words: American Fiction, 1950–1970;* and Warner Berthoff, *Fictions and Events.* Four general works on contemporary American nonfiction prose have also illuminated my reading of Mailer: John Hollowell, *Fact and Fiction: The New Journalism and the Nonfiction Novel;* Ronald Weber, *The Literature of Fact: Literary Nonfiction in American Writing;* John Hellman, *Fables of Fact: The New Journalism as New Fiction;* and Chris Anderson, *Style as Argument: Contemporary American Nonfiction.*

5. Mailer uses the slippery term "New Left" rather loosely to indicate mostly the white, student component of the sixties movement or movements, thus distinguishing it from the Civil Rights/Black Power movement(s) that profoundly shaped the New Left, and from the women's, gay, and other movements that grew partly out of and in critique of the New Left. I'll follow Mailer's usage here.

6. Dave Dellinger, *More Power Than We Know: The People's Movement Toward Democracy*, 112. I have altered the tenses for the sake of suspense. Mailer gives a briefer version of Dellinger's plan in *Armies* (252) and the context of coalition building in which the plan evolved (246–52).

7. I use the term "spectacle" here as it is used by situationist theorist Guy Debord. See Debord, *The Society of the Spectacle.* The archetypal modern spectacle is perhaps the Nazi rally as captured by Leni Riefenstahl's film *Triumph of the Will.* The key quality of spectacles is that they seek to be unambiguous, to eliminate "theorizing" (in both its classical and modern senses) in the spectator. Events, by contrast, are always ambiguous, always dependent on active interpretation by participants or participating viewers. A political undoing of the spectacular is thus largely an education in the rhetoric of viewing. The task is to see, beneath the spectacular surface, the contradictions, the multiple, double visions or dialogical voices that the spectacle's dazzle tries to hide. There is thus no rigid line to be drawn between event and spectacle—events (like the Pentagon march) are constantly being turned into spectacles by the media, while the left must seek to turn spectacles into events through collective reinterpretations (through, for example, the "people's inaugural" or through creation of armies of the night to challenge the spectacle of war). But the success of these efforts depends on the elaboration of some kind of formal but open-ended, collective hermeneutic that is only beginning to be theorized.

8. The passage, for example, suggests parallels with phenomenological hermeneutics. Mailer even at one point, somewhat facetiously, refers to his effort to be "scrupulously phenomenological," and his use of noun capitalization in this passage and throughout may be mimicking German convention. In any event, Mailer's methodical claims are similar to the most basic claims of those working

in the hermeneutical tradition and parallel Anglo-Saxon interpretive schools such as ethnomethodology (which is developing about the time Mailer is writing his text). He is claiming to be providing a record of his "prejudices" and to be leading us through a kind of hermeneutic circle. I'll not push the parallel very far, since as Mailer would be the first to admit, he is far from being a systematic philosopher, but *Armies* does exhibit some of the virtues and some of the limitations of phenomenological hermeneutics as practiced by Hans-Georg Gadamer, Paul Ricoeur, and other lesser figures, and it is precisely the fact that he seems to have come to his position independently of these schools that makes the parallel interesting. Mailer's text seems in particular to embody some of the theses on text and action suggested by Ricoeur in his essay "The Model of the Text: Meaningful Action Considered as a Text." Of particular relevance to Mailer's text is Ricoeur's claim that a written text develops a degree of autonomy from its author that is quite similar to the autonomy of an action vis-à-vis its "author(s)" and that subsequent interpreters of social action face a task similar to that of the textual critic. I'll return to these questions at the conclusion of this chapter.

9. Mailer in fact composed Book 1 first, published it separately in a special issue of *Esquire* magazine, then later decided to add Book 2.

10. Berthoff, *Fictions and Events*, 303–7.

11. The precedent for this device might well be *The Education of Henry Adams*, another generically curious text in which personality and history interweave in ways similar to the play of person and event in *Armies*.

12. Note that the subtitle inverts the manifest descriptions of the text I gave above. In this same passage Mailer playfully remarks that "it is obvious the first book is a history in the guise or dress or manifest of a novel, and the second a real or true novel—no less!—presented in the style of a history" (284). Whatever else this notion is, it is not "obvious." But it embodies the text's doubling back on itself that I noted above. Given the generic or formal confusion built into the text, it is not surprising that critics have had some difficulty knowing just what to make of *Armies of the Night*. But surely the problem can't be solved by simply chopping out either its novelistic or its historical elements.

13. The most developed of these readings is that of Kenneth Seib, "Mailer's March: The Epic Structure of *The Armies of the Night*." But Seib like other critics fails to explain these epic elements as much more than adornment.

14. See Alasdair MacIntyre, *After Virtue*.

15. See, for example, Jürgen Habermas, *Knowledge and Human Interests*.

16. For speculations on the political economic transition to late capitalism as the motor of the sixties, see Fredric Jameson, "Periodizing the Sixties."

17. Todd Gitlin has explored various aspects of the media/movement relationship in more detail in *The Whole World Is Watching: The Media in the Making and Unmaking of the New Left*.

18. Susan Sontag develops this theme lucidly in her book *On Photography*.

19. Abbie Hoffman in his intermittently reliable autobiographical account of the sixties, *Soon to Be a Major Motion Picture*, argues that beginning with the Pentagon march the New Left had a strategy of providing room for both "straight," traditional and "hip," countercultural forms of protest, each of which had an important role to play and neither of which was sufficient by itself. But

the problem is not so easily resolved. As Jean Baudrillard and others have shown, both reason and irrationalism, the claim to realism and the explosions of surrealism, can now be made to serve domination. The disruptions are folded back into the totality through the media. See Baudrillard, "Requiem for the Media." This belief in the subversiveness of spontaneity is a central thesis in Henri Lefebvre's important book on May '68, *The Explosion*. But Lefebvre underestimates (as Baudrillard overestimates) the capacity of established governments to use disruption to solidify their position, and neither adequately theorizes the dialectic between spontaneity and organization, community and instrumental action.

20. Again, this is the most persuasive aspect of Baudrillard's "Requiem for the Media."

21. See Hoffman, *Soon to Be a Major Motion Picture*.

22. The term "participatory journalism" is used to describe Mailer's work in Morris Dickstein, *Gates of Eden: American Culture in the 1960s*.

23. See, for example, the discussion of existentialism as an influence on New Left and Civil Rights movement thought in Sara Evans, *Personal Politics*, as well as in James Miller, *"Democracy Is in the Streets": From Port Huron to the Siege of Chicago*.

24. Jameson, "Periodizing the Sixties." I find Jameson's particular economic analysis of this break reductive because I see an unevenly developed series of breaks rather than a single cataclysmic one, but I find his linking of the sixties to a postmodern economic-cultural crisis more persuasive.

25. Publication in the summer of 1967 of Regis Debray's *Revolution in the Revolution?* with its theorization of Castro and Che Guevara's guerrilla warfare played into the emerging revolutionary fantasies of some New Leftists, and may have been a source for Mailer's speculations on the New Left aesthetic.

26. The particular books I have in mind include Tom Hayden, *Reunion: A Memoir;* Todd Gitlin, *The Sixties: Years of Hope, Days of Rage;* and Miller, *"Democracy Is in the Streets."* Each book has considerable virtues, despite the limitations I note below. Both Hayden and Gitlin are vivid stylists who illuminate important aspects of the sixties, and Miller's different style of book is a very valuable intellectual history of the early New Left (though its dismissal of the Civil Rights movement as a source of democratic theorizing is terribly wrongheaded, if not implicitly racist). Each also contributes significantly to undoing both the egregious right-wing attacks on the sixties that flourished during the Reagan years, and the equally egregious sixties nostalgism promulgated by the mass media.

27. Ronald Grele, "A Second Reading of Experience: Memoirs of the 1960s," 161.

28. The existing histories of the New Left are also skewed by the fact that they tend to concentrate on a few leaders and on the national office of SDS, when in fact the Movement in general as well as SDS itself was very decentralized; the picture from the provinces no doubt looks quite different from the picture given of the national level. For evidence of the continuing activism of New Leftists, see Doug McAdam, *Freedom Summer*.

29. See Wini Breines, *Community and Organization in the New Left, 1962–1968: The Great Refusal*, and "Who's New Left?" Insightful readings of the New

Left can also be found in Stewart Burns, *Social Movements of the 1960s: Searching for Democracy*, and Gregory Calvert, *Democracy from the Heart*.

30. Breines, "Who's New Left?," 542.

31. Breines, "Who's New Left?," 544.

CHAPTER 5. DRAMATIC ECOFEMINISM

1. For a study of the culture and politics of the Livermore Action Group, see Barbara Epstein, *Political Protest and Cultural Revolution*.

2. Women's actions at the Pentagon go back at least to Women Strike for Peace actions of the 1950s as well as to actions during the early days of Second Wave feminism in the late sixties and early seventies.

3. A number of artful demonstrations in the early 1980s by groups like Ad-hoc Artists for November 12th, Artists' Call Against US Intervention in Central America, and Art Against Apartheid, for instance, acknowledge the WPA as an inspiration. Developing criticism of demonstration art can be found in a series of articles and reports in the journal *Upfront*, published in New York by the Political Art Documentation/Distribution (PADD) project, a key resource group for the theory and practice of political art that has, unfortunately, recently disbanded. Looking backward, the WPA could also be seen as in some degree reviving the feminist "pageant" of the suffrage era, or such other large-scale theatrical presentations as the Paterson textile strike reenactment directed by John Reed or Marcus Garvey's one-thousand-person "Ethiopia." For the early history of progressive/left demonstration theater in the United States, see Susan Davis, *Parades and Power*. For more recent European and American inter-play between theater and the demonstration form, see Joel Schechter, *Durov's Pig: Clowns, Politics and Theatre*.

4. Ecofeminism is an extremely complex and diverse international phenomenon that has been treated rather reductively by many on the Left who have tended to single out easy targets and the most dubious positions among its adherents. Identified too easily with "cultural feminism," the term is used in self-description by some materialist and poststructuralist feminists as well, and is thus providing one site for transcending such labels. For some sense of the variety and scope of ecofeminist positions, see Donna Haraway, "Overhauling the Meaning Machines"; Vandana Shiva, *Staying Alive: Women, Ecology, and Survival in India*; Wilmette Brown, *Roots: Ghetto Ecology*; Zoë Sofia, "Exterminating Fetuses: Abortion, Disarmament and the Sexo-semiotics of Extraterrestrialism"; Ynestra King, *What Is Ecofeminism?* and *Ecofeminism: The Reenchantment of Nature*; Irene Diamond and Gloria Feman Orenstein, eds., *Reweaving the World: The Emergence of Ecofeminism*; Judith Plant, ed., *Healing the Wounds: The Promise of Ecofeminism*; Karen Warren, "Feminism and Ecology: Making Connections"; and articles collected in the special issue of *Hypatia* on "Ecological Feminism" (Spring 1991).

5. See Sara Evans, *Personal Politics*.

6. I say this to write against a prevalent form of token gesturing wherein feminism is incorporated by male leftists without appreciably changing their priorities. For a witty analysis of this dynamic vis-à-vis male critics using feminist lit-

erary theories and methods, see Elaine Showalter, "Critical Cross-Dressing: Male Feminists and the Woman of the Year." One male critic, Terry Eagleton, has responded to Showalter; Showalter's article, Eagleton's response, and Showalter's reaction to his response are all printed in Alice Jardine and Paul Smith, eds., *Men in Feminism*. For a critical extension of Showalter's argument, see Tania Modleski, "Feminism and the Power of Interpretation."

7. Ynestra King, "All is Connectedness: Scenes from the Women's Pentagon Action, USA," 40.

8. For an important reconceptualization of women's experience as ongoing semiotic process, see Teresa de Lauretis, *Alice Doesn't: Feminism, Semiotics, Cinema*, esp. chap. 6.

9. For samples of this large body of literature, see Gloria Anzaldúa, ed., *Making Face, Making Soul: Haciendo Caras;* Chela Sandoval, "Women Respond to Racism: A Report on the National Women's Studies Association Conference"; Gloria Hull, Patricia Bell Scott, and Barbara Smith, eds., *All the Women Are White, All the Blacks Are Men, But Some of Us Are Brave: Black Women's Studies;* Cherríe Moraga and Gloria Anzaldúa, eds., *This Bridge Called My Back: Writings of Radical Women of Color;* Barbara Smith, ed., *Home Girls: A Black Feminist Anthology;* two books by bell hooks, *Ain't I a Woman: Black Women and Feminism* and *Feminist Theory: From Margin to Center;* Bonnie Thorton Dill, "Race, Class, and Gender: Prospects and All-Inclusive Sisterhood." Two more recent books have taken up the question of essentialism in feminism more generally (including its possible reinscription in some of the texts cited above): Diana Fuss, *Essentially Speaking: Feminism, Nature, and Difference*, and Elizabeth Spelman, *Inessential Woman: Problems of Exclusion in Feminist Thought*. Among a number of interesting attempts to mediate the essentialist/constructionist debate, see Linda Alcoff, "Cultural Feminism versus Post-structuralism: The Identity Crisis in Feminist Theory"; Steven Epstein, "Gay Politics/Ethnic Identity: The Limits of Constructionism"; and the special issue of *Differences*, "The Essential Difference: Another Look at Essentialism."

10. Donna Warnock, "Mobilizing Emotion: Organizing the Women's Pentagon Action: An Interview with Donna Warnock." Rhoda Linton and Michele Whitham, "With Mourning, Rage, Empowerment, and Defiance: The 1981 Women's Pentagon Action."

11. It is therefore quite appropriate that this chapter itself is very much indebted to a more than usually dialogic process. Much of its argument has emerged from verbal and written dialogue with friends and political coworkers, particularly Noël Sturgeon and Don Beggs. Sturgeon's important work on the antinuclear direct action movement deeply informs my analysis here, most formally through her "Direct Theory and Political Action: The American Nonviolent Direct Action Movement," and her paper "Poststructuralist Feminism, Ecofeminism, and Radical Feminism Revisited." I have drawn directly and indirectly on conversations with Beggs and from his unpublished manuscript, "Being Enthusiastic Reactions to and Impressionistic Speculations on Barbara Epstein's 'The Culture of Direct Action.'" I would also like to thank Ruth Roach Pierson for comments on an early draft of this chapter.

12. Discussions of the future usefulness of consciousness-raising partly in-

volve historical arguments as to what "cr" originally was, arguments that range from the psychologistic (relating cr to encounter or T-groups) to revolutionist (relating cr to Maoist criticism/self-criticism cadre sessions). For an analysis of the ways in which consciousness-raising has been written and rewritten from various interested feminist political standpoints, see Katie King, "The Situation of Lesbianism as Feminism's Magical Sign: Contests for Meaning and the U.S. Women's Movement, 1968–1972." On the nature and history of cr, see also Pamela Allen, *Free Space: A Perspective on the Small Group in the Women's Movement;* Nancy McWilliams, "Contemporary Feminism, Consciousness-raising, and Changing Views of the Political"; and Sandra Bartky, *Femininity and Domination: Studies in the Phenomenology of Gender,* chap. 1.

13. I am not suggesting that cr should be seen as the only feminist method. Patricia Yaeger has suggested that it might be considered one among at least seven major modes of feminist theoretical practice. See Yaeger, *Honey-Mad Women: Emancipatory Strategies in Women's Writing.* Catherine MacKinnon makes one of the strongest claims for the centrality of cr in her influential, controversial essay, "Feminism, Marxism, Method and the State."

14. For a more detailed discussion of feminism, "consensus process," and their interrelations, see Sturgeon, "Direct Theory and Political Action."

15. Tracie Dejanikus and Stella Dawson, "Women's Pentagon Action," 285. Ynestra King also stresses that this desire to cross political boundaries was part of the Action from the beginning. See King, "All is Connectedness."

16. Such a perspective can be seen as, in effect, a translation of the caucus system (by which subgroups—women, blacks, gays, gay black men, etc.—within movement organizations maintain their necessary separate collective identities) into an active public force for re-thinking the interconnections between crucial issues, rather than repeating one's particular grievance in isolation.

17. Warnock, "Mobilizing Emotion," 37.

18. The text of the "Unity Statement" can be found in Lynne Jones, ed., *Keeping the Peace: A Women's Peace Handbook,* 42–43.

19. Dejanikus and Dawson, "Women's Pentagon Action," 286.

20. Warnock, "Mobilizing Emotion," 40.

21. For an analysis of the inadequacy of such terms in defining the feminisms active in the antinuclear direct action and ecofeminist movements, see Sturgeon, "Poststructuralist Feminism."

22. Linton and Whitham, "With Mourning," 16.

23. Linton and Whitham, "With Mourning," 20. I too am not trying to put down large-scale demonstrations, which have their own, empowering, and political-instrumental dimensions; I too am only trying to show ways that the Pentagon Actions were significantly and usefully different.

24. This was true as well in Brecht's theater where acting was not meant to be convincing or realistic but rather awkwardly formulaic, for which reason Brecht preferred amateur actors.

25. King, "All is Connectedness," 42.

26. Micaela di Leonardo, "Morals, Mothers, and Militarism: Antimilitarism and Feminist Theory." This essay offers an excellent introduction to a range of theoretical and strategic questions regarding relationships between feminism and

militarism. For a broader, more biting critique of "cultural feminism," see Alice Echols, "The New Feminism of Yin and Yang."

27. Di Leonardo, "Morals, Mothers," 602.

28. See, for example, Dejanikus and Dawson, "Women's Pentagon Action."

29. See, for example, Ellen Willis, *Village Voice*, June 23, 1980, and July 16–22, 1980. Ynestra King replied to this and similar critiques by arguing that it perpetuates a false dichotomy between cultural and socialist feminism, with both sides guilty of a species of essentialism. I share King's assumption that the WPA was aimed at breaking down such debilitating binary oppositions and the related binary of nature/culture. See King, "Feminism and the Revolt of Nature," *Heresies* 13 (Fall 1982), reprinted in her collection, *What Is Ecofeminism?*

30. I am referring here to Scott's exemplary essay, "Gender: A Useful Category of Historical Analysis." Carol Cohn's important essay, "Sex and Death in the Rational World of Defense Intellectuals," is one rich example of such an analysis. Two uneven but provocative books by Cynthia Enloe, *Does Khaki Become You? The Militarization of Women's Lives* and *Bananas, Beaches, and Bases: Making Feminist Sense of International Politics*, provide useful introductions to the feminist analysis of militarism. See also Sara Ruddick, *Maternal Thinking*, who resolves the "moral mother" problematic by analyzing "mothering" as a social role, not a biological state, one thus even available to males.

31. Warnock, "Mobilizing Emotion," 40.

32. For an interesting meditation on women and public festivity, see Mary Russo, "Female Grotesques: Carnival and Theory."

33. Linton and Whitham, "With Mourning," 22.

34. King, "All is Connectedness," 46.

35. Linton and Whitham, "With Mourning," 24.

36. On this question, see Staughton Lynd, "The Prospects of the New Left."

37. See King, "All is Connectedness," 54–63, for a discussion of the jail experience.

38. Warnock, "Mobilizing Emotion," 46.

39. Russo, "Female Grotesques," 213. In her introduction to *Making a Spectacle*, Lynda Hart points out that feminist theater and feminist theatrical criticism have been under a deeper taboo than fiction and poetry, for example, and are emerging more slowly out of their patriarchal constraints. All the more reason to view the WPA as an importantly transgressive moment. For a generally excellent introduction to major issues in feminist spectatorship, see Jill Dolan, *The Feminist Spectator as Critic*. Dolan, however, perpetuates an exaggerated dichotomy between "cultural" and "materialist" feminisms that the WPA can be read as undermining. See also the essays in Hart, *Making a Spectacle*, and Sue-Ellen Coe, ed., *Performing Feminisms*.

40. See Alison Young, *Femininity in Dissent*.

41. King, "All is Connectedness," 46.

42. King, "All is Connectedness," 46.

43. See Sturgeon, "Direct Theory," for a discussion of the complex genesis of consensus process.

44. Key early statements of Habermas's position include "On Systematically

Distorted Communication," "Towards a Theory of Communicative Competence," and *Communication and the Evolution of Society*. For his more recent thoughts on these questions, see *A Theory of Communicative Action*, volumes 1 and 2.

45. More generously, one could simply claim that Habermas is writing on a different (traditionally philosophical) plane. But even as I would defend the need for specialist languages to carry out some theoretical operations that is no excuse for failing to acknowledge parallel arguments on other planes of discourse.

46. Beggs, "Being Enthusiastic."

47. Beggs, "Being Enthusiastic."

48. See Linton and Whitham, "With Mourning." I would add that specific cultural biases within the practice of consensus need to be examined for their marginalizing potential.

49. I say "relatively undistorted" as a cautionary note. Habermas employed the notions of "ideal speech situation" and "undistorted communication" primarily as heuristics, but some of his readers have been less careful; there is a danger not only in theory but in movement practice of believing that such communication has been achieved. It seems to me far more prudent to think of such communication as an always deferred goal, rather than an achievable possibility.

50. Noël Sturgeon, "Collective Theorizing in the U.S. Direct Action Movement: Oppositional Structures and Practices."

51. For a sampling of Brecht's ideas in English, see *Brecht on Theatre*. For an exploration of Brechtian ideas similar in some ways to those I explore here, see Darko Suvin, "Brecht's *Caucasian Chalk Circle* and Marxist Figuralism: Open Dramaturgy as Open History." A more or less direct Brechtian influence on the Action comes through Brecht student Peter Schumann's "Bread and Puppet Theater," which provided not only the huge papier-mâché puppets used in the Pentagon "play" but also general inspiration through the troupe's various large-scale "Domestic Resurrection" circuses. For pictures and analysis of some of the theater's recent work, see Schumann, *Bread and Puppet: Stories of Struggle and Faith from Central America*.

For an overview of feminist performance pieces, see Moira Roth, ed., *The Amazing Decade: Women and Performance Art in America, 1970–1980*, as well as Dolan, *The Feminist Spectator*. Of particular relevance, as its title suggests, is the feminist performance piece by Leslie Labowitz and Suzanne Lacy entitled "In Mourning and Rage" performed on the streets of Los Angeles in 1978 as a protest against media sensationalizing of the "Hillside strangler."

52. I am being reductively unfair to Artaud here, using him as an emblem of what his work degenerated into in the hands of less imaginative people. For Artaud's own explanations of his theatrical ideas, see *The Theater and Its Double* and *Selected Writings of Antonin Artaud*.

53. Dolan, *The Feminist Spectator*, 84.

54. On this issue of the New Left's use of and abuse by the media, see Todd Gitlin, *The Whole World Is Watching*.

55. For a lucid discussion of feminist strategies for influencing media representations that is relevant to other social movements as well, see Leslie Labowitz and Suzanne Lacy, "Feminist Media Strategies for Political Performance."

CHAPTER 6. TOWARD SOME POSTMODERNIST POPULISMS

1. Frank Lentricchia, *Criticism and Social Change*, 9–10.

2. What you mean, "we"? The vaguely collective "we" I use here is a rightly suspect term. I am trying throughout this chapter to acknowledge on the one hand that "I" am implicated in the critical moves I critique, and to acknowledge that the alternative positions I describe are also collectively generated ones. With these notions in mind I have mostly avoided naming names of the guilty but have tried through my footnotes to suggest some of the myriad sources for the emerging alternatives I outline.

3. Nancy Fraser suggests something of what this might look like in her book, *Unruly Practices*. Fraser wends skillfully between the disabling particularities of Foucault, Derrida, and Rorty on the one hand, and the reductive universality of Habermas on the other. She accomplishes this by foregrounding specific feminist questions that highlight possibilities and limits in each philosophical stance.

4. See, for example, Gayatri Chakravorty Spivak, "Can the Subaltern Speak?" and Jim Merod, *The Political Responsibility of the Critic*. For a contesting view, see Paul Bové, *Intellectuals in Power: A Genealogy of Critical Humanism*. See also the essays in Bruce Robbins, ed., *Intellectuals: Aesthetics, Politics, Academics*.

5. These questions are discussed cogently in a number of the essays in Andrew Ross, ed., *Universal Abandon? The Politics of Postmodernism*.

6. Janice Radway, "Identifying Ideological Seams: Mass Culture, Analytical Method, and Political Practice"; Edward Said, "Opponents, Audiences, Constituencies, and Community" and *The World, the Text, the Critic*; Cornel West, interview with Anders Stephanson.

7. Catherine Gallagher convincingly makes this point about the rise of the "new historicism" with its attempt to synthesize poststructuralism, feminism, and neo-Marxism, each of which are energized by questions emerging from sixties movements. See Gallagher, "Marxism and the New Historicism."

8. See Noël Sturgeon, "Collective Theorizing."

9. In a telling example of theorized confusion or confused theorizing, Jean Baudrillard declared confidently just before the very real carnage began that the war would not be fought because in hyperreal postmodernity the literalization of war is no longer necessary. A post-mortem assessment of the "text" of 100,000 or so Iraqi bodies would seem to refute this particular post-modern hypothesis.

10. Jean-François Lyotard perhaps best epitomizes this problematic position.

11. For a sense of the complexities involved in this critique, see Spivak, "Can the Subaltern Speak?"; and the essays collected in Abdul JanMohamed and David Lloyd, eds., *The Nature and Context of Minority Discourse*, especially the articles by Caren Kaplan, R. Radhakrishnan, José Rabasa, and Lata Mani. All postmodern theory cannot be reduced to an effect of that vast decolonization (of nations, minds, bodies, genders, races, sexualities) we too neatly call "the sixties," but much of it is literally unthinkable without the world-historical movements of that era, beginning with the anticolonial struggles of the fifties and continuing today (Derrida may owe as much intellectually to the Algerian

independence movement as to Heidegger or Nietzsche, and Foucault, despite occasional denials, clearly was shaped by those events coded "Mai '68").

12. West, interview, 273.

13. Diana Fuss, *Essentially Speaking: Feminism, Nature, and Difference*, xi–xii.

14. For a critique of the tendency of constructionist and materialist feminists, for example, to identify activists as the "quintessentialists," see Noël Sturgeon, "Poststructuralist Feminism, Ecofeminism, and Radical Feminism Revisited."

15. Chela Sandoval, "Women Respond to Racism: A Report on the National Women's Studies Association Conference." More recently, Sandoval develops this idea in "U.S. Third World Feminism." Sandoval's published and unpublished work has influenced numerous feminist theorists, including Donna Haraway, Teresa de Lauretis, and Gloria Anzaldúa. For a more general discussion and critique of recent theoretical (de)constructions of the "subject," see Paul Smith, *Discerning the Subject.*

16. Ernesto Laclau and Chantal Mouffe, *Hegemony and Socialist Strategy: Toward a Radical Democratic Politics.* For an attack on Laclau and Mouffe, see Norman Geras, "Post-Marxism?" and for Laclau and Mouffe's reply, see "Post-Marxism without Apologies." For more balanced critiques, see Stuart Hall's interview in *Journal of Communication Inquiry;* and Stanley Aronowitz, "Theory and Socialist Strategy."

17. Fredric Jameson, "Postmodernism, or The Cultural Logic of Late Capitalism," 55.

18. Quoted in Jameson, "Postmodernism," 66.

19. Jameson, "Postmodernism," 81.

20. More recently, Jameson seems to have come to this conclusion himself, and he now speaks of fissures within the postmodern and the possibility of "homeopathically" turning postmodernism against itself. See, for example, his interview with Anders Stephanson. His book-length expansion of his argument, however, does not depart significantly from his basic position. See *Postmodernism, or The Cultural Logic of Late Capitalism.*

21. David Harvey, *The Condition of Postmodernity.* Harvey offers a rich account of the various attempts to define a postmodern economic condition, as well as a summary of various arguments about postmodernist aesthetics. Like Jameson he flirts dangerously with a simple base-superstructure model, and like Jameson he pays only largely cursory attention to factors other than class (while nodding toward feminist and other movements, he uses as examples a number of aesthetic texts where questions of gender are clearly central yet says nothing about those dimensions). For an overview of debates about post-Fordism or economic New Times, see the special issue of *Socialist Review* on "Post-Fordism."

22. Hall, "On Postmodernism and Articulation," 46.

23. The subtitle of this section is borrowed from Ron Silliman's *What*, 43. Fred Pfeil, "Makin' Flippy-Floppy: Postmodernism and the Baby-Boom PMC."

24. Pfeil, "Flippy-Floppy," 264.

25. Pfeil, "Flippy-Floppy," 272.

26. On Germany, for example, see Claus Offe, "New Social Movements: Challenging the Boundaries of Institutional Politics." On France, see Alain Touraine, *Post-Industrial Society*.

27. Pfeil, "Flippy-Floppy," 278, 282–83.

28. For a compelling critique in the sixties of middle-class guilt in the New Left and a call for a "new working class" theory, see Greg Calvert, "In White America."

29. On this, see Offe, "New Social Movements."

30. Pfeil, "Flippy-Floppy," 292.

31. In his own book, *Recodings: Art, Spectacle, Cultural Politics*, and in his introduction to *The Anti-Aesthetic: Essays on Postmodern Culture*, Hal Foster distinguishes between what he calls oppositional and reactionary postmodernisms. In the former volume, see especially, "For a Concept of the Political in Contemporary Art." In the latter volume, see, in addition to Foster's introduction, articles on various media by Frampton (architecture), Krauss (sculpture), and Ulmer (criticism).

32. Craig Owens, "The Discourse of Others: Feminism and Postmodernism."

33. This situation is changing as marked by the publication of such anthologies of feminist writing on postmodernism as Linda J. Nicholson, ed., *Feminism/Postmodernism*.

34. Meaghan Morris, *The Pirate's Fiancee: Feminism, Reading, Postmodernism*, 1–23. Morris includes here a bibliography of work on postmodernism by women that is generally ignored in genealogies of postmodern thought.

35. The most recent version of this much-anthologized essay occurs as "A Cyborg Manifesto" in Haraway's *Simians, Cyborgs, and Women*.

36. See, for example, Jose David Saldívar's argument on behalf of "local knowledges" against "postmodern culture collecting" with regard to Chicano/a writings: "The Limits of Cultural Studies." For a brilliant characterization of the complex cultural flows of the postmodern world system, see Arjun Appadurai, "Disjuncture and Difference in the Global Cultural Economy."

37. For a thoughtfully nuanced use of Gilles Deleuze and Felix Guattari's concepts, see Caren Kaplan, "Deterritorializations: The Rewriting of Home and Exile in Western Feminist Discourse."

38. Toni Cade Bambara, *The Salt Eaters;* Cherríe Moraga, *Loving in the War Years: lo que nunca paso por sus labios;* Gloria Anzaldúa, *Borderlands/La Frontera*. For an introduction to Baca's work, see her interview, "Our People Are the Internal Exiles."

39. A recent example of recuperative highbrow encodings of the popular can be found in the Museum of Modern Art's exhibit, "High and Low: Modern Art and Popular Culture," which, contrary to much of its publicity, shows only a one-way movement of the low up into the high; nothing suggesting the collapse of art into the popular is present.

40. Andreas Huyssen, *After the Great Divide*.

41. For an illuminating reading of the politics of "pop" and "kitsch," see Andrew Ross, *No Respect: Intellectuals and Popular Culture*.

42. John Fiske, *Understanding Popular Culture*, 161.

43. On the complexities of these issues, see Foster, *Recodings*, esp. part 2.

44. The most useful history of the avant-garde remains that of Peter Bürger, *Theory of the Avant-Garde*.

45. On Gran Fury and AIDS activist art generally, see Douglas Crimp and Adam Rolston, *AIDS Demo Graphics*.

46. The parts of popular culture that most need examination are the various modes by which the kind of rebellious energy Fiske correctly identifies is turned harmless, is directed away from key nodes of power/knowledge. For an argument on behalf of populist aesthetic radicalism, see Laura Kipnis, "'Refunctioning' Reconsidered: Towards a Left Popular Culture."

47. In his book *No Respect*, Ross details a variety of key moments during the last half century in which aesthetico-political elitism has led left intellectuals to a disdain for popular culture that has played into the hands of the right.

48. Richard Flacks, *Making History: The American Left and the American Mind*.

49. On the most successful moment of American populism in the latter half of the nineteenth century, see Lawrence Goodwyn, *Democratic Promise*, reprinted in condensed form as *The Populist Moment*.

50. For a cogent analysis of various kinds of "populisms," see Ernesto Laclau, *Politics and Ideology in Marxist Theory: Capitalism-Fascism-Populism*.

51. See, for example, Harry Boyte, *The Backyard Revolution: Understanding the New Citizen Movement* and *Community Is Possible: Repairing America's Roots;* Boyte, Heather Booth, and Steve Max, eds., *Citizen Action and the New Populism;* and Carl Boggs, *Social Movements and Political Power*, esp. 129–69.

52. Harry Boyte and Sara Evans, "Strategies in Search of America: Cultural Radicalism, Populism, and Democratic Culture," 84.

53. Harvey, *Condition of Postmodernity*, 303.

54. But for fair-minded, thoughtful attempts to put the "new populism" in dialogue with other radical positions, see David Plotke, "Democracy, Modernization, *democracy*," and Boggs, *Social Movements and Political Power*, 129–69. For debates between traditional Marxian left, populist, and postmodern articulations of socialism/radical democracy, see the articles collected as "Is that all there is? Reappraising Social Movements," a special issue of the *Socialist Review*.

55. For an analysis of the global dimension of urban politics, see Margit Mayer, "Politics in the Post-Fordist City."

56. See Fraser, *Unruly Practices*, for an excellent discussion of the contradictory, positive/negative effects of the welfare bureaucracy on women in the United States. Similarly, we need a notion of "repressive decentralization" to describe one characteristic of the current era of transnational capitalism.

57. See Boyte and Evans, "Strategies in Search of America."

58. Haraway, "A Cyborg Manifesto."

59. Boyte and Evans explore a version of this notion in their book, *Free Spaces*. Again I think they often fail to confront the particular postmodern conditions that must be dealt with if this "free space" strategy is to avoid reappro-

priation, and don't sufficiently explore the postmodern argument that we are always partly inside that which we claim to critique (i.e., no space is really free), but the book is helpful, especially as it surveys historical examples of such free spaces in/as movements.

60. For one model of how this range looks in practice, and for an argument for strengthening this practice vis-à-vis a "feminist public sphere," see Rita Felski, *Beyond Feminist Aesthetics: Feminist Literature and Social Change*.

61. See Foster, "Readings in Cultural Resistance," in *Recodings*, for thoughts on some of the possibilities and difficulties of accomplishing such reaccentings.

Works Cited

Agee, James. *Collected Short Prose of James Agee*. Boston: Houghton Mifflin, 1986.

———. *Letters of James Agee to Father Flye*. New York: Bantam, 1962.

Agee, James, and Walker Evans. *Let Us Now Praise Famous Men*. 1941. New York: Houghton Mifflin, 1988.

Alcoff, Linda. "Cultural Feminism versus Post-structuralism: The Identity Crisis in Feminist Theory." *Signs* 13 (Spring 1988): 405–36.

Allen, Pamela. *Free Space: A Perspective on the Small Group in the Women's Movement*. New York: Times Change Press, 1970.

Anderson, Chris. *Style as Argument: Contemporary American Nonfiction*. Carbondale: Southern Illinois University Press, 1987.

Anzaldúa, Gloria. *Borderlands/La Frontera: The New Mestiza*. San Francisco: Aunt Lutte Foundation Press, 1987.

———, ed. *Making Face, Making Soul: Haciendo Caras*. San Francisco: Aunt Lutte Foundation Press, 1990.

Appadurai, Arjun. "Disjuncture and Difference in the Global Cultural Economy." *Public Culture* 2.2 (Spring 1990): 1–24.

Arac, Jonathan, ed. *Postmodernism and Politics*. Minneapolis: University of Minnesota Press, 1987.

Arac, Jonathan, and Barbara Johnson, eds. *The Consequences of Theory*. Baltimore: Johns Hopkins University Press, 1991.

Arendt, Hannah. *The Human Condition*. Chicago: University of Chicago Press, 1958.

Armstrong, Nancy. *Desire and Domestic Fiction: A Political History of the Novel*. New York: Oxford University Press, 1987.

Aronowitz, Stanley. "Remaking the American Left, Part 2." *Socialist Review* 13.1 (1983): 7–42.

————. "Theory and Socialist Strategy." *Social Text* 16 (1986–87): 1–16.

Artaud, Antonin. *Selected Writings of Antonin Artaud*. Ed. Susan Sontag, trans. Helen Weaver. New York: Farrar, Straus and Giroux, 1976.

————. *The Theater and Its Double*. Trans. Mary Caroline Richards. New York: Grove Press, 1958.

Awkward, Michael. *Inspiriting Influences: Tradition, Revision, and Afro-American Women's Novels*. Chicago: University of Chicago Press, 1989.

Baca, Judy. "Our People Are the Internal Exiles." Interview in Kahn and Neumaier, eds., *Cultures in Contention*.

Baker, Houston A., Jr. *Blues, Ideology and Afro-American Literature: A Vernacular Theory*. Chicago: University of Chicago Press, 1984.

————. "To Move Without Moving: Creativity and Commerce in Ralph Ellison's Trueblood Episode." *PMLA* 98 (1983): 828–45.

Bakhtin, Mikhail. *The Dialogic Imagination*. Ed. and trans. Michael Holquist and Caryl Emerson. Austin: University of Texas Press, 1981.

———— [Voloshinov]. *Marxism and the Philosophy of Language*. Trans. L. Matejka and R. Titunik. New York: Seminar Press, 1973.

Bambara, Toni Cade. *The Salt Eaters*. New York: Vintage, 1980.

Barber, Benjamin. *Strong Democracy*. Berkeley: University of California Press, 1984.

Barson, Alfred. *A Way of Seeing*. Amherst: University of Massachusetts Press, 1972.

Barthes, Roland. "Death of the Author." In *Image-Music-Text*. Trans. Stephen Heath. New York: Hill and Wang, 1977.

————. *Empire of Signs*. Trans. Richard Howard. New York: Hill and Wang, 1982.

————. "From Work to Text." In *Image-Music-Text*.

Bartky, Sandra. *Femininity and Domination: Studies in the Phenomenology of Gender*. New York: Routledge, 1990.

Baudrillard, Jean. "Requiem for the Media." In *For a Critique of the Political Economy of the Sign*. Trans. Charles Levin. St. Louis: Telos Press, 1981.

Beggs, Donald. "Being Enthusiastic Reactions to and Impressionistic Speculations on Barbara Epstein's 'The Culture of Direct Action.'" Unpublished essay, 1986.

Beiner, Ronald. *Political Judgement*. Chicago: University of Chicago Press, 1983.

Benjamin, Walter. "The Author As Producer." In Peter Demetz, ed., *Reflections—Walter Benjamin: Essays, Aphorisms, Autobiographical Writing*. Trans. Edmund Jephcott. New York: Harcourt Brace Jovanovich, 1978.

Bennett, Tony. "Texts in History." In Derek Attridge et al., eds., *Poststructuralism and the Question of History*. London: Cambridge University Press, 1987.

Benston, Kimberly. "I yam what I yam: The Topós of (Un)Naming in Afro-American Literature." In Henry Louis Gates, Jr., ed., *Black Literature and Literary Theory*. London: Methuen, 1984.

————, ed. *Speaking for You: The Vision of Ralph Ellison*. Washington, DC: Howard University Press, 1987.

Bergreen, Laurence. *James Agee: A Life*. New York: Penguin, 1984.

Berthoff, Warner. *Fictions and Events*. New York: E. P. Dutton, 1971.

Blake, Susan L. "Ritual and Rationalization: Black Folklore in the Works of Ralph Ellison." In Bloom, ed., *Ralph Ellison*.

Bloom, Harold, ed. *Ralph Ellison*. New York: Chelsea House, 1986.

Boggs, Carl. *Social Movements and Political Power*. Philadelphia: Temple University Press, 1986.

Bourdieu, Pierre. "The Aristocracy of Culture." *Media, Culture and Society* 2.3 (1980): 225–54.

———. *Distinction: A Social Critique of Judgement and Taste*. Trans. Richard Nice. Cambridge: Harvard University Press, 1984.

Bové, Paul. *Intellectuals in Power: A Genealogy of Critical Humanism*. New York: Columbia University Press, 1986.

Boyte, Harry. *The Backyard Revolution: Understanding the New Citizen Movement*. Philadelphia: Temple University Press, 1980.

———. *Community Is Possible: Repairing America's Roots*. New York: Harper and Row, 1984.

Boyte, Harry, and Sara Evans. *Free Spaces*. New York: Harper and Row, 1986.

———. "Strategies in Search of America: Cultural Radicalism, Populism, and Democratic Culture." *Socialist Review* 14.3–4 (1984): 73–100.

Boyte, Harry, Heather Booth, and Steven Max, eds. *Citizen Action and the New Populism*. Philadelphia: Temple University Press, 1986.

Brecht, Bertolt. *Brecht on Theatre*. Ed. and trans. John Willet. New York: Hill and Wang, 1964.

Breines, Wini. *Community and Organization in the New Left, 1962–1968: The Great Refusal*. New York: Praeger, 1982.

———. "Who's New Left?" *Journal of American History* 75.2 (1988): 528–45.

Brown, Wilmette. *Roots: Ghetto Ecology*. London: Housewives in Dialogue, 1986.

Buhle, Paul. *Marxism in the USA*. London: Verso, 1987.

Bürger, Peter. *Theory of the Avant-Garde*. Trans. Michael Shaw. Minneapolis: University of Minnesota Press, 1984.

Burgin, Victor, ed. *Thinking Photography*. Atlantic Highlands, NJ: Humanities Press, 1982.

Burns, Stewart. *Social Movements of the 1960s: Searching for Democracy*. Boston: Twayne, 1990.

Byerman, Keith E. *Fingering the Jagged Grain: Tradition and Form in Recent Black Fiction*. Athens: University of Georgia Press, 1985.

Callahan, John. *In the African-American Grain*. Urbana: University of Illinois Press, 1988.

Calvert, Gregory. *Democracy from the Heart*. Eugene, Ore.: Communitas Press, 1991.

———. "In White America." In Massimo Teodori, ed., *The New Left: A Documentary History*. New York: Bobbs-Merrill, 1969.

Christian, Barbara. "The Race for Theory." *Feminist Studies* 14.1 (1988): 67–80.

Clifford, James. *The Predicament of Culture: Twentieth Century Ethnography, Literature and Art*. Cambridge: Harvard University Press, 1988.

Clifford, James, and George Marcus, eds. *Writing Culture: The Poetics and Politics of Ethnography.* Berkeley: University of California Press, 1986.

Coe, Sue-Ellen, ed. *Performing Feminisms: Feminist Critical Theory for the Theatre.* Baltimore: Johns Hopkins University Press, 1990.

Cohn, Carol. "Sex and Death in the Rational World of Defense Intellectuals." In Diana E. H. Russell, ed., *Exposing Nuclear Phallacies.* New York: Pergamon, 1989.

Coles, Robert. "James Agee's 'Famous Men' Seen Again." *Harvard Advocate* 105.4 (1972): 42–46.

Connolly, William. *The Terms of Political Discourse.* Princeton: Princeton University Press, 1983.

Crimp, Douglas, and Adam Rolston. *AIDS Demo Graphics.* Seattle: Bay Press, 1990.

Crossman, Richard, ed. *The God That Failed.* New York: Bantam, 1952.

Cruse, Harold. *Crisis of the Negro Intellectual.* New York: Morrow, 1967.

Davidson, Cathy. *Revolution and the Word: The Rise of the Novel in America.* New York: Oxford University Press, 1986.

Davis, Lennard. *Resisting Novels: Ideology and Fiction.* New York: Methuen, 1987.

———. "A Social History of Fact and Fiction: Authorial Disavowal in the Early English Novel." In Edward Said, ed., *Literature and Society.* Baltimore: Johns Hopkins University Press, 1980.

Davis, Susan. *Parades and Power.* Berkeley: University of California Press, 1986.

Debord, Guy. *The Society of the Spectacle.* Detroit: Black and Red Press, 1977.

Debray, Regis. *Revolution in the Revolution?* Trans. Bobbye Ortiz. New York: Monthly Review Press, 1967.

Dejanikus, Tracie, and Stella Dawson. "Women's Pentagon Action." In Frederique Delacoste and Felice Newman, eds., *Fight Back! Feminist Resistance to Male Violence.* Minneapolis: Cleis Press, 1981.

de Lauretis, Teresa. *Alice Doesn't: Feminism, Semiotics, Cinema.* Bloomington: Indiana University Press, 1984.

Dellinger, Dave. *More Power Than We Know: The People's Movement Toward Democracy.* Garden City: Anchor/Doubleday, 1975.

Denning, Michael. *Mechanic Accents: Dime Novels and Working Class Culture in America.* London: Verso, 1987.

———. "'The Special American Conditions': Marxism and American Studies." *American Quarterly* 38.3 (1986): 356–80.

Derrida, Jacques. "La Loi du Genre/The Law of Genre." *Glyph* 7 (1980): 176–232.

Dews, Peter. *Logics of Disintegration.* London: Verso, 1987.

Diamond, Irene, and Gloria Feman Orenstein, eds. *Reweaving the World: The Emergence of Ecofeminism.* San Francisco: Sierra Club Books, 1990.

Dickstein, Morris. *Gates of Eden: American Culture in the 1960s.* New York: Basic Books, 1977.

di Leonardo, Micaela. "Morals, Mothers, and Militarism: Antimilitarism and Feminist Theory." *Feminist Studies* 11.3 (1985): 599–617.

Dolan, Jill. *The Feminist Spectator as Critic.* Ann Arbor: UMI Research Press, 1988.

Eagleton, Terry. "The Idealism of American Criticism." In *Against the Grain: Selected Essays*. London: Verso, 1986.

———. *Literary Theory: An Introduction*. Minneapolis: University of Minnesota Press, 1983.

Echols, Alice. "The New Feminism of Yin and Yang." In Ann Snitow et al., eds., *Powers of Desire*. New York: Monthly Review Press, 1983.

Ecological Feminism. Special issue of *Hypatia* (Spring 1991).

Ellison, Ralph. *Invisible Man*. New York: Vintage, 1972 [1952].

———. "Remembering Richard Wright." In Benston, ed., *Speaking for You*.

———. *Shadow and Act*. New York: Vintage, 1972 [1964].

Enloe, Cynthia. *Bananas, Beaches, and Bases: Making Feminist Sense of International Politics*. Berkeley: University of California Press, 1989.

———. *Does Khaki Become You? The Militarization of Women's Lives*. Boston: South End Press, 1983.

Epstein, Barbara. *Political Protest and Cultural Revolution: Nonviolent Direct Action in the 1970s and 1980s*. Berkeley: University of California Press, 1991.

Epstein, Steven. "Gay Politics/Ethnic Identity: The Limits of Constructionism." *Socialist Review* 17.3–4 (May/Aug. 1987): 9–54.

The Essential Difference: Another Look at Essentialism. Special issue of *Differences* 1.2 (Summer 1989).

Evans, Sara. *Personal Politics*. New York: Vintage, 1979.

Fabre, Michel. "From *Native Son* to *Invisible Man*: Some Notes on Ralph Ellison's Evolution in the 1950's." In Benston, ed., *Speaking for You*.

Felski, Rita. *Beyond Feminist Aesthetics: Feminist Literature and Social Change*. Cambridge: Harvard University Press, 1989.

Fish, Stanley. *Is There a Text in This Class?* Cambridge: Harvard University Press, 1980.

Fisher, Andrea. *Let Us Now Praise Famous Women*. New York: Pandora Press, 1987.

Fiske, John. *Television Culture*. London: Routledge, 1987.

———. *Understanding Popular Culture*. Boston: Unwin Hyman, 1989.

Flacks, Richard. *Making History: The American Left and the American Mind*. New York: Columbia University Press, 1989.

Foster, Hal, ed. *The Anti-Aesthetic: Essays on Postmodern Culture*. Port Townsend, WA: Bay Press, 1983.

———. *Recodings: Art, Spectacle, Cultural Politics*. Seattle: Bay Press, 1985.

Foucault, Michel. "What Is an Author?" In *Language, Counter-Memory, and Practice: Selected Interviews and Essays*. Ed. Donald F. Bouchard, trans. Bouchard and Sherry Simon. Ithaca: Cornell University Press, 1977.

Frankenberg, Ruth. *White Women, Race Matters*. Berkeley: University of California Press (forthcoming).

Franklin, H. Bruce. *The Victim as Criminal and Artist*. New York: Oxford University Press, 1978.

Fraser, Nancy. "Rethinking the Public Sphere." Working Paper No. 10. Milwaukee: Center for Twentieth Century Studies, 1990–91.

———. *Unruly Practices*. Minneapolis: University of Minnesota Press, 1989.

Fuss, Diana. *Essentially Speaking: Feminism, Nature, and Difference*. London: Routledge, 1989.

Gallagher, Catherine. "Marxism and the New Historicism." In H. Aram Veeser, ed., *The New Historicism*. London: Routledge, 1989.

Gates, Henry Louis, Jr. "The Blackness of Blackness: A Critique of the Sign and the Signifying Monkey." In Gates, ed., *Black Literature and Literary Theory*. London: Methuen, 1984.

————. *Figures in Black: Words, Signs, and the 'Racial' Self*. New York: Oxford University Press, 1987.

————. *The Signifying Monkey: A Theory of Afro-American Literary Criticism*. New York: Oxford University Press, 1989.

Gayle, Addison. *Black Aesthetic*. Garden City: Doubleday Anchor, 1972.

————. *The Way of the New World*. Garden City: Doubleday Anchor, 1976.

Geras, Norman. "Post-Marxism?" *New Left Review* 163 (May-June 1987): 40–82.

Gitlin, Todd. *The Sixties: Years of Hope, Days of Rage*. New York: Bantam, 1987.

————. *The Whole World Is Watching: The Media in the Making and Unmaking of the New Left*. Berkeley: University of California Press, 1980.

Goodwyn, Lawrence. *Democratic Promise*. New York: Oxford University Press, 1977.

————. *The Populist Moment*. New York: Oxford University Press, 1978.

Graff, Gerald, and Reginald Gibbons, eds. *Criticism in the University*. Evanston: Northwestern University Press, 1985.

Grele, Ronald. "A Second Reading of Experience: Memoirs of the 1960s." *Radical History Review* 44 (1989): 159–66.

Habermas, Jürgen. *Communication and the Evolution of Society*. Trans. Thomas McCarthy. London: Heinemann, 1979.

————. *Knowledge and Human Interests*. Trans. Jeremy Shapiro. London: Heinemann, 1971.

————. "On Systematically Distorted Communication." *Inquiry* 13 (1970): 205–18.

————. "The Public Sphere: An Encyclopaedia Article." *New German Critique* 1.3 (1974): 49–55.

————. *The Structural Transformation of the Public Sphere*. Trans. Thomas Burger. Cambridge: Massachusetts Institute of Technology Press, 1989.

————. *A Theory of Communicative Action*. Part 1, *Reason and the Rationalization of the Life World*. Trans. Thomas McCarthy. Boston: Beacon Press, 1981.

————. *A Theory of Communicative Action*. Part 2, *Lifeworld and System*. Trans. Thomas McCarthy. Boston: Beacon, 1987.

————. "Towards a Theory of Communicative Competence." *Inquiry* 13 (1970): 360–75.

Hall, Stuart. "On Postmodernism and Articulation: An Interview." *Journal of Communication Inquiry* 10.2 (1986): 45–60.

Haraway, Donna. "A Cyborg Manifesto." In *Simians, Cyborgs, and Women*. London: Routledge, 1989.

————. "Overhauling the Meaning Machines: An Interview with Donna Haraway." *Socialist Review* 21.2 (1991): 65–84.

Hart, Lynda, ed. *Making a Spectacle: Feminist Essays on Contemporary Women's Theatre*. Ann Arbor: University of Michigan Press, 1989.

Harvey, David. *The Condition of Postmodernity*. London: Basil Blackwell, 1989.

Hayden, Tom. *Reunion: A Memoir*. New York: Random House, 1988.

Heidegger, Martin. "The Origin of the Work of Art." Trans. Albert Hofstadter. In David Krell, ed., *Heidegger: Basic Writings*. New York: Harper and Row, 1977.

Hellman, John. *Fables of Fact: The New Journalism as New Fiction*. Urbana: University of Illinois Press, 1981.

Hersey, John. "Introduction: Agee." *Let Us Now Praise Famous Men*. Boston: Houghton-Mifflin, 1988.

———, ed. *Ralph Ellison: A Collection of Critical Essays*. Englewood Cliffs: Prentice-Hall, 1974.

Hirsch, E. D. *The Aims of Interpretation*. Chicago: University of Chicago Press, 1976.

Hoffman, Abbie. *Soon to Be a Major Motion Picture*. New York: Berkeley Books, 1982.

Hogue, W. Lawrence. *Discourse and the Other: The Production of the Afro-American Text*. Durham, NC: Duke University Press, 1986.

Hollowell, John. *Fact and Fiction: The New Journalism and the Non-fiction Novel*. Chapel Hill: University of North Carolina Press, 1977.

hooks, bell. *Ain't I a Woman: Black Women and Feminism*. Boston: South End Press, 1981.

———. *Feminist Theory: From Margin to Center*. Boston: South End Press, 1984.

Hull, Gloria, Patricia Bell Scott, and Barbara Smith, eds. *All the Women Are White, All the Blacks Are Men, But Some of Us Are Brave: Black Women's Studies*. Old Westbury, CT: Feminist Press, 1982.

Hutcheon, Linda. *A Poetics of Postmodernism*. London: Routledge, 1988.

Huyssen, Andreas. *After the Great Divide*. Bloomington: Indiana University Press, 1986.

Is That All There Is? Reappraising Social Movements. Special issue of *Socialist Review* 20.1 (1990): 35–150.

Jameson, Fredric. Interviewed by Anders Stephanson. In Ross, ed., *Universal Abandon?*

———. "Periodizing the Sixties." In Sohnya Sayers et al., eds., *The Sixties Without Apology*. Minneapolis: University of Minnesota Press, 1984.

———. *The Political Unconscious: Narrative as a Socially Symbolic Act*. Ithaca: Cornell University Press, 1981.

———. *Postmodernism, or The Cultural Logic of Late Capitalism*. Durham, NC: Duke University Press, 1991.

———. "Postmodernism, Or, The Cultural Logic of Late Capitalism." *New Left Review* 146 (1984): 53–94.

JanMohamed, Abdul, and David Lloyd, eds. *The Nature and Context of Minority Discourse*. New York: Oxford University Press, 1990.

Jardine, Alice, and Paul Smith, eds. *Men in Feminism*. New York: Methuen, 1987.

Jay, Gregory. "American Literature and the New Historicism." Working Paper No. 10. Milwaukee: Center for Twentieth Century Studies, 1988.

Johnson, Barbara. *The Critical Difference*. Baltimore: Johns Hopkins University Press, 1980.

———. *A World of Difference*. Baltimore: Johns Hopkins University Press, 1987.

Johnson, Richard. "What Is Cultural Studies Anyway?" *Social Text* 6.1 (1986–87): 38–80.

Jones, Lynne, ed. *Keeping the Peace: A Women's Peace Handbook*. London: Women's Press, 1983.

Kahn, Douglas, and Dianne Neumaier, eds. *Cultures in Contention*. Seattle: Real Comet Press, 1985.

Kaiser, Ernest. "A Critical Look at Ellison's Fiction." *Black World* 20.2 (1970): 53–59, 81–97.

Kaplan, Caren. "Deterritorializations: The Rewriting of Home and Exile in Western Feminist Discourse." In JanMohamed and Lloyd, eds., *Nature and Context of Minority Discourse*.

Kelly, Robin D. G. *Hammer and Hoe: Alabama Communists During the Great Depression*. Chapel Hill: University of North Carolina Press, 1990.

Kent, George. "Ralph Ellison and the Afro-American Folk and Cultural Tradition." In Benston, ed., *Speaking for You*.

King, Katie. "The Situation of Lesbianism as Feminism's Magical Sign: Contests for Meaning and the U.S. Women's Movement, 1968–1972." *Communication* 9 (1986): 65–91.

King, Ynestra. "All is Connectedness: Scenes from the Women's Pentagon Action, USA." In Jones, ed., *Keeping the Peace*.

———. *Ecofeminism: The Reenchantment of Nature*. Boston: Beacon Press, forthcoming.

———. *What Is Ecofeminism?* New York: Ecofeminist Resources, 1990.

Kipnis, Laura. "'Refunctioning' Reconsidered: Towards a Left Popular Culture." In Colin MacCabe, ed., *High Theory/Low Culture*. New York: St. Martin's Press, 1986.

Kramer, Victor. "The Complete 'Work' Chapter for James Agee's *Let Us Now Praise Famous Men*." *Texas Quarterly* 15.2 (1972): 27–48.

———. *James Agee*. Boston: Twayne, 1975.

Labowitz, Leslie, and Suzanne Lacy. "Feminist Strategies for Political Performance." In Kahn and Neumaier, eds., *Cultures in Contention*.

LaCapra, Dominick. *History and Criticism*. Ithaca: Cornell University Press, 1985.

———. *Rethinking Intellectual History*. Ithaca: Cornell University Press, 1983.

———. *Soundings in Cultural Criticism*. Ithaca: Cornell University Press, 1990.

Laclau, Ernesto. *Politics and Ideology in Marxist Theory: Capitalism-Fascism-Populism*. London: Verso, 1979.

———. "Post-Marxism Without Apologies." *New Left Review* 166 (1987): 79–106.

Laclau, Ernesto, and Chantal Mouffe. *Hegemony and Socialist Strategy*. Trans. Winston Moore and Paul Cammack. London: Verso, 1985.

Lefebvre, Henri. *The Explosion*. New York: Monthly Review Press, 1969.

Lentricchia, Frank. *Criticism and Social Change*. Chicago: University of Chicago Press, 1983.

"Let Us Now Praise Famous Men—Revisited." *The American Experience*, no. 109. WGBH Educational Foundation, transcript, original PBS broadcast November 29, 1988.

Linton, Rhoda, and Michele Whitham. "With Mourning, Rage, Empowerment, and Defiance: The 1981 Women's Pentagon Action." *Socialist Review* 12.3–4 (1982): 11–36.

Lynd, Staughton. "The Prospects of the New Left." In J. Laslett and S. Lipset, eds., *Failure of a Dream?* Garden City: Anchor Press/Doubleday, 1974.

MacCabe, Colin. "Realism and Cinema: Notes on Some Brechtian Theses." *Screen* 15.2 (1974): 7–27.

MacIntyre, Alasdair. *After Virtue*. Notre Dame, IN: Notre Dame University Press, 1981.

MacKinnon, Catharine. "Feminism, Marxism, Method and the State." In Nannerl Keohane et al., eds., *Feminist Theory: A Critique of Ideology*. Chicago: University of Chicago Press, 1982.

Madden, David, ed. *Remembering James Agee*. Baton Rouge: University of Louisiana Press, 1974.

Maharidge, Dale, and Michael Williamson. *And Their Children After Them: The Legacy of "Let Us Now Praise Famous Men": James Agee, Walker Evans, and the Rise and Fall of Cotton in the South*. New York: Pantheon, 1989.

Mailer, Norman. *The Armies of the Night: History as a Novel, The Novel as History*. New York: New American Library, Signet Paperback, 1968.

Mailloux, Steven. *Rhetorical Power*. Ithaca: Cornell University Press, 1989.

Marcus, George, and Michael Fisher. *Anthropology as Cultural Critique*. Chicago: University of Chicago Press, 1986.

Mayer, Margit, ed. *New Social Movements in Western Europe and the United States*. New York: Unwin Hyman, forthcoming.

———. "Politics in the Post-Fordist City." *Socialist Review* 21.1 (1991): 105–24.

McAdam, Doug. *Freedom Summer*. London: Oxford University Press, 1989.

McGowan, John. *Postmodernism and Its Critics*. Ithaca: Cornell University Press, 1991.

McSweeney, Kerry. *Invisible Man: Race and Identity*. Boston: Twayne, 1988.

McWilliams, Nancy. "Contemporary Feminism, Consciousness-raising, and Changing Views of the Political." In Jane Jaquette, ed., *Women and Politics*. New York: John Wiley and Sons, 1974.

Melucci, Alberto. *Nomads of the Present*. Philadelphia: Temple University Press, 1989.

———. "The Symbolic Challenge of Contemporary Movements." *Social Research* 52.4 (1985): 789–816.

Merod, Jim. *The Political Responsibility of the Critic*. Ithaca: Cornell University Press, 1987.

Miller, D. A. *The Novel and the Police*. Berkeley: University of California Press, 1987.

Miller, James. *"Democracy Is in the Streets": From Port Huron to the Siege of Chicago*. New York: Simon and Schuster, 1987.

Modleski, Tania. "Feminism and the Power of Interpretation." In Teresa de Lauretis, ed., *Feminist Studies/Critical Studies*. Bloomington: Indiana University Press, 1986.

Moody, Anne. *Coming of Age in Mississippi*. New York: Dial Press, 1968.

Moraga, Cherríe. *Loving in the War Years: lo que nunca paso por sus labios*. Boston: South End Press, 1983.

Moraga, Cherríe, and Gloria Anzaldúa, eds. *This Bridge Called My Back: Writings of Radical Women of Color*. Watertown, MA: Persephone Press, 1981.

Moreau, Genevieve. *The Restless Journey of James Agee*. New York: William Morrow, 1977.

Morris, Meaghan. *The Pirate's Fiancee: Feminism, Reading, Postmodernism*. London: Verso, 1988.

Mouffe, Chantal. "Radical Democracy: Modern or Postmodern." In Ross, ed., *Universal Abandon?*

Murray, Albert. *The Omni-Americans*. New York: Outerbridge and Dienstfrey, 1970.

Nadel, Alan. *Invisible Criticism: Ralph Ellison and the American Canon*. Iowa City: University of Iowa Press, 1988.

Naison, Mark. *Communists in Harlem During the Depression*. Urbana: University of Illinois Press, 1983.

Natanson, Maurice. "Rhetoric and Counter-Espionage." *Journal of Existential Psychology* 1.2 (1966): 188–94.

Neal, Larry. "Ellison's Zoot Suit." In Benston, ed., *Speaking for You*.

Negri, Toni, and Felix Guattari. *Communists Like Us*. Trans. Michael Ryan. New York: Semiotext(e), 1988.

Nelson, John S. "Political Theory as Political Rhetoric." In John S. Nelson, ed., *What Should Political Theory Be Now?* Albany: State University of New York Press, 1983.

Newton, Judith, and Deborah Rosenfelt, eds. *Feminist Criticism and Social Change*. London: Methuen, 1985.

Nicholson, Linda J., ed. *Feminism/Postmodernism*. New York: Routledge, 1989.

Norris, Christopher. *What's Wrong with Postmodernism?* Baltimore: Johns Hopkins University Press, 1990.

Offe, Claus. "New Social Movements: Challenging the Boundaries of Institutional Politics." *Social Research* 52.4 (1985): 817–68.

Ohlin, Peter. *Agee*. New York: Ivan Oblensky, 1966.

O'Meally, Robert G., ed. *The Craft of Ralph Ellison*. Cambridge: Harvard University Press, 1980.

———. *New Essays on Invisible Man*. London: Cambridge University Press, 1989.

———. "Riffs and Rituals: Folklore in the Work of Ralph Ellison." In Dexter Fisher and Robert B. Stepto, eds., *Afro-American Literature: The Reconstruction of Instruction*. New York: Modern Language Association, 1979.

Omi, Michael, and Howard Winant. *Racial Formation in the United States: From the 1960s to the 1980s.* New York: Routledge, 1986.

Ostendorf, Berndt. "Anthropology, Modernism, and Jazz." In Bloom, ed., *Ralph Ellison.*

Owens, Craig. "The Discourse of Others: Feminism and Postmodernism." In Foster, ed., *The Anti-Aesthetic.*

Pfeil, Fred. "Makin' Flippy-Floppy: Postmodernism and the Baby-Boom PMC." In Mike Davis, Fred Pfeil, and Michael Sprinker, eds., *The Year Left: An American Socialist Yearbook.* London: Verso, 1985.

Pitkin, Hanna. *The Concept of Representation.* Berkeley: University of California Press, 1967.

Plant, Judith, ed. *Healing the Wounds: The Promise of Ecofeminism.* Santa Cruz: New Society, 1989.

Plotke, David. "Democracy, Modernization, *democracy*." *Socialist Review* 14.2 (1984): 29–53.

Poirier, Richard. *Norman Mailer.* New York: Viking, 1972.

Post-Fordism. Special issue of *Socialist Review* 21.1 (1991): 53–153.

Pratt, Mary Louise. "Interpretive Strategies/Strategic Interpretations: On Anglo-American Reader-Response Criticism." In Arac, ed., *Postmodernism and Politics.*

Rabinowitz, Paula. "Voyeurism and Class Consciousness." *Cultural Critique* 21 (1992): 133–70.

Radway, Janice. "Identifying Ideological Seams: Mass Culture, Analytical Method, and Political Practice." *Communication* 9 (1986): 93–123.

Reilly, John M., ed. *Twentieth Century Interpretations of Invisible Man.* Englewood Cliffs: Prentice-Hall, 1970.

Reising, Russell. *The Unusable Past.* London: Methuen, 1986.

Ricoeur, Paul. "The Model of the Text: Meaningful Action Considered as a Text." *New Literary History* 5 (1973): 91–117.

Robbins, Bruce, ed. *Intellectuals: Aesthetics, Politics, Academics.* Minneapolis: University of Minnesota, Social Text, 1990.

Robinson, Cedric J. *Black Marxism.* London: Zed Press, 1983.

Rosler, Martha. "In, around, and afterthoughts (on documentary photography)." In *3 Works.* Halifax, Nova Scotia: The Press of Halifax Nova Scotia College of Art and Design, 1981.

Ross, Andrew. *No Respect: Intellectuals and Popular Culture.* London: Routledge, 1989.

———, ed. *Universal Abandon?: The Politics of Postmodernism.* Minneapolis: University of Minnesota, Social Text, 1990.

Roth, Moira, ed. *The Amazing Decade: Women and Performance Art in America, 1970–1980.* Los Angeles: Astro Artz, 1983.

Ruddick, Sara. *Maternal Thinking: Towards a Politics of Peace.* New York: Ballantine, 1989.

Russo, Mary. "Female Grotesques: Carnival and Theory." In Teresa de Lauretis, ed., *Feminist Studies/Critical Studies.* Bloomington: Indiana University Press, 1986.

Ryan, Michael. "Postmodern Politics." *Theory, Culture and Society* 5 (1988): 559–76.

Said, Edward. "Opponents, Audiences, Constituencies, and Community." In W. J. T. Mitchell, ed., *The Politics of Interpretation*. Chicago: University of Chicago Press, 1983.

———. *The World, the Text, and the Critic*. Cambridge: Harvard University Press, 1983.

Saldívar, José David. "The Limits of Cultural Studies." *American Literary History* 2.2 (Summer 1990): 251–66.

Sandoval, Chela. "U.S. Third World Feminism: The Theory and Method of Oppositional Consciousness in the Postmodern World." *Genders* 10 (Spring 1991): 1–24.

———. "Women Respond to Racism: A Report on the National Women's Studies Association Conference." Oakland, CA: Center for Third World Organizing, [1982]. Reprinted in Anzaldúa, ed., *Making Face, Making Soul: Haciendo Caras*.

Schaar, John H. *Legitimacy and the Modern State*. New Brunswick, NJ: Transaction, 1981.

Schaub, Thomas. *American Fiction in the Cold War*. Madison: University of Wisconsin Press, 1991.

Schechter, Joel. *Durov's Pig: Clowns, Politics and Theatre*. New York: Theatre Communications Group, 1985.

Scholes, Robert. *Textual Power: Literary Theory and the Teaching of English*. New Haven: Yale University Press, 1985.

Schumann, Peter. *Bread and Puppet: Stories of Struggle and Faith from Central America*. Compiled by Susan Green. Burlington, VT: Green Valley Film and Art, 1985.

Scott, Joan. "Gender: A Useful Category of Historical Analysis." In Weed, ed., *Coming to Terms*.

Seib, Kenneth. *James Agee: Promise and Fulfillment*. Pittsburgh, PA: University of Pittsburgh Press, 1969.

———. "Mailer's March: The Epic Structure of *The Armies of the Night*." *Essays in Literature* 1.1 (1974): 89–94.

Sharratt, Bernard. *Reading Relations: Structures of Literary Production—A Dialectical Text/Book*. Atlantic Highlands, NJ: Humanities Press, 1982.

Shaw, Nate. *All God's Dangers*. Ed. Theodore Rosengarten. New York: Avon, 1974.

Shiva, Vandana. *Staying Alive: Women, Ecology and Survival in India*. London: Zed Books, 1988.

Showalter, Elaine. "Critical Cross-Dressing: Male Feminists and The Woman of the Year." *Raritan* 3.2 (1983): 130–49. Reprinted in Jardine and Smith, eds., *Men in Feminism*.

Silliman, Ron. *What*. Great Barrington, MA: The Figures, 1988.

Skerrett, Joseph T., Jr. "The Wright Interpretation: Ralph Ellison and the Anxiety of Influence." In Benston, ed., *Speaking for You*.

Smith, Barbara, ed. *Home Girls: A Black Feminist Anthology*. New York: Kitchen Table Press, 1983.

Smith, Barbara Herrnstein. *On the Margins of Discourse*. Chicago: University of Chicago Press, 1978.

Smith, Paul. *Discerning the Subject*. Minneapolis: University of Minnesota Press, 1988.

Smith, Valerie. *Self-Discovery and Authority in Afro-American Narrative*. Cambridge: Harvard University Press, 1987.

Social Movements. Special issue of *Social Research* 52.4 (1985).

Sofia [Sofoulis], Zoë. "Exterminating Fetuses: Abortion, Disarmament and Sexosemiotics of Extraterrestrialism." *Diacritics* 14.2 (Summer 1984): 47–59.

Solomon-Godeau, Abigail. *Photography at the Dock*. Minneapolis: University of Minnesota Press, 1991.

Sontag, Susan. *On Photography*. New York: Farrar, Straus, and Giroux, 1980.

Spears, Ross, and Jude Cassidy, eds. *Agee: His Life Remembered*. From the film script with additional narrative by John Coles. New York: Holt, Rinehart and Winston, 1985.

Spelman, Elizabeth. *Inessential Woman: Problems of Exclusion in Feminist Thought*. Boston: Beacon Press, 1988.

Spivak, Gayatri Chakravorty. "Can the Subaltern Speak?" In Cary Nelson and Lawrence Grossberg, eds., *Marxism and the Interpretation of Culture*. Urbana: University of Illinois Press, 1988.

———. *In Other Worlds: Essays in Cultural Politics*. London: Methuen, 1987.

Stange, Maren. *"Symbols of Ideal Life": Social Documentary Photography in America, 1890–1950*. New York: Cambridge University Press, 1988.

Stepto, Robert. *From Behind the Veil*. Urbana: University of Illinois Press, 1979.

Stott, William. *Documentary Expression and Thirties America*. Oxford: Oxford University Press, 1973.

Sturgeon, Noël. "Collective Theorizing in the U.S. Direct Action Movement: Oppositional Structures and Practices." In Margit Mayer, ed., *New Social Movements*.

———. "Direct Theory and Political Action: The American Nonviolent Direct Action Movement." Ph.D. diss., History of Consciousness, University of California, Santa Cruz, 1991.

———. "Poststructuralist Feminism, Ecofeminism, and Radical Feminism Revisited." Paper presented at the meeting of the National Women's Studies Association, June 1989.

Suvin, Darko. "Brecht's *Caucasian Chalk Circle* and Marxist Figuralism: Open Dramaturgy as Open History." In Norman Rudich, ed., *Weapons of Criticism*. Palo Alto: Ramparts Press, 1976.

Tanner, Tony. *City of Words: American Fiction, 1950–1970*. New York: Harper and Row, 1971.

Todorov, Tzvetan. "The Notion of Literature." *New Literary History* 5.1 (1973): 5–16.

———. "The Origin of Genres." *New Literary History* 8.1 (1976): 159–70.

Touraine, Alain. *Post-Industrial Society*. Trans. Leonard F. X. Mayhew. New York: Random House, 1971.

———. *The Voice and the Eye*. Trans. Alan Duff. New York: Cambridge University Press, 1981.

Trachtenberg, Alan. *Reading American Photographs*. New York: Hill and Wang, 1989.

Trinh, Minh-ha T. *Woman, Native, Other: Writing Postcoloniality and Feminism*. Bloomington: Indiana University Press, 1989.

Ward, James A. "James Agee's Aesthetics of Silence." *Tulane Studies in English* 23 (1978): 193–206.

Warnock, Donna. "Mobilizing Emotion: Organizing the Women's Pentagon Action: An Interview with Donna Warnock." *Socialist Review* 12.3–4 (1982): 37–49.

Warren, Karen. "Feminism and Ecology: Making Connections." *Environmental Ethics* (Spring 1987): 3–20.

Washington, Mary Helen. " 'The Darkened Eye Restored': Towards a New Literary History of Black Women." In Henry Louis Gates, Jr., ed., *Reading Black, Reading Feminist*. New York: Meridian, Penguin, 1990.

Weber, Ronald. *The Literature of Fact: Literary Nonfiction in American Writing*. Athens: Ohio University Press, 1980.

Weed, Elizabeth, ed. *Coming to Terms: Feminism, Theory, Politics*. London: Routledge, 1989.

West, Cornel. Interviewed by Anders Stephanson. In Ross, ed., *Universal Abandon?*

White, Hayden. *The Content of the Form*. Baltimore: Johns Hopkins University Press, 1987.

———. *Metahistory*. Baltimore: Johns Hopkins University Press, 1973.

———. *Tropics of Discourse*. Baltimore: Johns Hopkins University Press, 1978.

Wicke, Jennifer. "Postmodernism: The Perfume of Information." *Yale Journal of Criticism* 1.2 (Winter 1987): 146–60.

Williams, Raymond. *Marxism and Literature*. New York: Oxford University Press, 1977.

Yaeger, Patricia. *Honey-Mad Women: Emancipatory Strategies in Women's Writing*. New York: Columbia University Press, 1988.

Young, Alison. *Femininity in Dissent*. New York: Routledge, 1990.

Zavarzadeh, Mas'ud. *The Mythopoeic Reality: The Postwar American Nonfiction Novel*. Urbana: University of Illinois Press, 1976.

Index

Adorno, Theodor, 56
Aesthetics: in *Armies of the Night*, 108–9, 114–16, 188n.25; and ideology, 5–7; in *Invisible Man*, 58–60; in *Let Us Now Praise Famous Men*, 31, 45–47; and reading formations, 6
Affinity groups, in Women's Pentagon Action(s), 135, 138
Agee, James: as character in *Let Us Now Praise Famous Men*, 52, 53–54; and Evans, as collaborators, 180–81n.29; relationship with tenant families, 31, 46–47, 51–52, 54; style contrasted to Evans, 32. See also *Let Us Now Praise Famous Men*
AIDS activism, 162, 163
Anzaldúa, Gloria: *Borderlands/La Frontera*, 161
Armies of the Night (Mailer): and American rites of passage, 111–12; counterculture analyzed in, 105–7; as critique of mass media, 90, 93, 94, 101–3; and *Education of Henry Adams*, 89, 95, 103–4, 187n.11; and epic tradition, 98–100, 112; as event, 90, 111–12, 113; as historiography, 90, 92–99, 109–10, 112, 113, 187n.12; as journalism, 88, 90, 101; and legitimation crisis, 185–86n.2; Lowell as character in, 104–5; and New Left aesthetic, 92, 108–9, 114–16, 188n.25; as novel, 89–90, 92–99, 109–10, 113, 187n.12; Old Left critiqued in, 115, 116; as phenomenology, 186–87n.8; postmodernist read-

ings of, 88–89; as postmodernist realism, 88; publishing history of, 187n.9; and realism, 102, 112; realist readings of, 88–89; and spectacle, 92, 186n.7; strategy of, 89–94; and surrealism, 102–3, 187–88n.19. *See also* Mailer, Norman
Artaud, Antonin, dramatic theory of, 139, 193n.52
Articulation, 7, 20, 175n.17, 177n.27
Avant-garde: cooptation by mass media, 19–20, 162–65; limitations of, 147, 163, 166, 169; as model for poststructuralist criticism, 3; modernist left version of, 162; and political strategies, 147; versus popular culture, 162–65

Baca, Judith, murals of, 161, 171
Baker, Ella, 79, 86
Bambara, Toni Cade: *The Salt Eaters*, 161
Baudrillard, Jean, 158, 162, 164, 177n.29, 187–88n.19, 194n.9
Beggs, Donald, 136
Benjamin, Walter, 22, 100, 178n.3
Berthoff, Warner, 95
Birmingham Center for Contemporary Cultural Studies, 8, 156
Black Aesthetic, and *Invisible Man*, 59, 64, 82–83, 183n.11
Black nationalism, and *Invisible Man*, 64–67
Black Power movement, and *Invisible Man*, 60, 64, 66, 80

Compositor:	Wilsted & Taylor
Printer:	Bookcrafters
Binder:	Bookcrafters
Text:	10/13 Sabon
Display:	Sabon